THE CALLS OF ISLAM

D0940043

PUBLIC CULTURES OF THE MIDDLE EAST AND NORTH AFRICA

Paul A. Silverstein, Susan Slyomovics, and Ted Swedenburg, *editors*

# THE CALLS OF ISLAM

*Sufis, Islamists, and Mass Mediation in Urban Morocco*

Emilio Spadola

Indiana University Press

Bloomington and Indianapolis

This book is a publication of

Indiana University Press
Office of Scholarly Publishing
Herman B Wells Library 350
1320 East 10th Street
Bloomington, Indiana 47405 USA

iupress.indiana.edu

*Telephone*    800–842–6796
*Fax*          812–855–7931

© 2014 by Emilio Spadola

All rights reserved

No part of this book may be reproduced or utilized in any form or
by any means, electronic or mechanical, including photocopying
and recording, or by any information storage and retrieval system,
without permission in writing from the publisher. The Association
of American University Presses' Resolution on Permissions constitutes the only exception to this prohibition.

♾ The paper used in this publication meets the minimum require-
ments of the American National Standard for Information Sciences—Permanence of Paper for Printed Library Materials, ANSI
Z39.48–1992.

Manufactured in the United States of America

Cataloging-in-Publication Data is available
from the Library of Congress.

ISBN 978-0-253-01136-7 (cloth)
ISBN 978-0-253-01137-4 (paperback)
ISBN 978-0-253-01145-9 (e-book)

1 2 3 4 5 19 18 17 16 15 14

# Contents

# Acknowledgments

IT IS THE gift of cultural anthropology to demand a researcher's commitment of body, heart, and mind. I am grateful to the many institutions and individuals in Morocco and the United States who supported my research and this book. Moroccan acquaintances, colleagues, and dear friends in Rabat and Fez set the gold standard for hospitality and collaboration. I am especially grateful to the extended family of Hajja Fatima and Hajj Abdelqader in Fez medina with whom I lived, and to their loving children (among them Sanae, Mounia, and Fatiha) and grandchildren who welcomed me in and sheltered and fed me, from my first fieldwork stint to my last. Sanae's help in establishing contacts in and beyond the medina significantly advanced my research with women trance specialists and participants and, later, with participants in the Green March. Sanae and her family's generosity extended far beyond this, however, to moments of flexibility and forgiveness of which I'm sure I remain ignorant. We are family. Also in Fez, I met my brother and friend, Mohammed, and his loving family. In calling me to Islam with nothing less than his ordinary example, and in renaming me Ibrahim, Mohammed offered me gifts beyond any return. As a modest substitute, I offer my love of Fez and a promise, *insha' Allah*, to return as often as I can.

The research for this book relied on numerous interlocuters in Fez as well as Rabat, across different ritual spaces, traditions, and social positions. I thank those who welcomed me despite my habit of crossing these boundaries: the experts who took time and care to teach me the details, context, and significance of the practices, and the clients, participants, and outright critics who shared their own experiences and observations of religious and daily life in Fez. I especially thank Madame Houria al-Wazzani and Dr. Antoine Fleury, who introduced me to the work of Mohamed Hassan al-Wazzani and kindly included me in several family celebrations. I also thank Aisha, author of "Hajjayat Dada Gnawiyya" in Chapter 6, both for permission to reproduce and translate her work and for sharing her private experiences with the unseen that inform her public activism.

In Rabat, I enjoyed the institutional support of the Société Nationale de Radiodiffusion et Télévision, the Centre Cinématographique Marocain, the Ministry of Communication, the Bibliothèque Nationale, the Moroccan American Center for Educational and Cultural Exchange (MACECE), and the Center for Cross Cultural Learning (CCCL). I am grateful to the directors and staff who permitted my entry and facilitated my research at each place, especially Mr. Daoud Casewit at MACECE and Dr. Abdelhay Moudden at CCCL. Abdelhay's work as scholar and novelist, our far-ranging discussions, and his generous friendship prompted my interest in "the People" and the Green March as central figures and events of Moroccan modernity. At the Centre Jacques Berque in Rabat, I have recently enjoyed discussions of Sufism and politics with Aziz

Hlaoua, Nazarena Lanza, Cédric Baylocq, and Marouane Laouina. My friend and colleague, Yelins Mahttat, also CCCL, improved my translation of "Hajjayat Dada." Others in Rabat, including Ann Hawley, John Swepston, Mohammed Zahir, Abdellah and Halim Ait Ougharram, and the Ait Ougharram family, provided friendship, insight, humor, and often a place to stay as well.

This book was conceived of in New York City in conversation with members of Columbia University's Department of Anthropology. Brink Messick patiently taught me the crafts of research design and grant writing, shared his love of Morocco, and provided gentle guidance both during fieldwork and after. Elaine Combs-Schilling's helpful criticisms of my thinking and moral support always came when most needed. I benefitted greatly from the advice and teaching of John Pemberton, Val Daniel, Marilyn Ivy, Lawrence Rosen, Kathy Ewing, and Vincent Crapanzano. Kathy and Vincent deserve special thanks for their contributions to an earlier draft of the book. Crossing and joining paths with fellow anthropology students Amira Mittermaier, Todd Ochoa, Deirdre de la Cruz, Juan Obarrio, Yukiko Koga, and Jenny Sime always improved my work and spirits. Above all at Columbia, I owe a debt of gratitude to Roz Morris, whom I affectionately call my "(tor)mentor." While Roz's contributions to anthropologies of media and religion are well known, these are equaled by her generous interventions as a teacher, reader, and colleague. Her capacities to listen and respond to ideas (and to elicit more rigorous engagement with them) have set the standard for me as a scholar.

While preparing the book manuscript at Colgate University, I enjoyed the intellectual camaraderie and thorough guidance of my fine anthropology and sociology colleagues, among them Nancy Ries, Mary Moran, and Paul Lopes. Bruce Rutherford, Georgia Frank, and Barbara Regenspan lent editorial wisdom, and good cheer. My spring 2013 anthropology of media students deserve special praise for reading and responding to the book still in manuscript form.

Many other colleagues and friends in numerous fields have shaped this book directly and indirectly. In religion and media, I thank Charles Hirschkind, Brian Larkin, Rafael Sanchez, Lisa Mitchell, Jenny Sime, Martin Zillinger, Maria José (Zé) de Abréu, and Yasmin Moll. Martin has provided excellent forums for exchanging and developing our overlapping research in Morocco. Zé read two chapters in late stages of preparation and provided spot-on comments. Yasmin very generously lent me the epigraph ("Religion is communication") gathered from her own research amongst "New Callers" in Egypt; her work is extending the calls of Islam in yet-to-be-imagined directions. Exchanges with scholars of Morocco (and much else) Brian Karl, Nadia Guessous, Brendan Hart, and Hisham Aidi stimulated and guided the thinking in this book as well. Hisham kindly read the manuscript and pointed me to key references. Susan Slyomovics, Paul Silverstein, Ted Swedenburg, and Rebecca Tolen provided editing guidance and encouragement at Indiana University Press, as did Tim Roberts. To Bruce Grant, my dear friend and mentor since Swarthmore College, I offer my endless gratitude. Bruce carefully read the full book manuscript and improved it with impeccable editorial counsel and encouragement.

Any remaining errors in this work derive not from the fine guidance of my intellectual comrades, but from my—I hope rare—failures to heed it.

After all else, I am grateful to my beloved Alex Spadola. Her tenderness, humor, and love infused my daily work of writing. To Alex, and to our marvelous boys, Bruno and Orlando, I happily dedicate this book.

Financial support for this book came from Colgate University's Research Council, the Social Science Research Council, the US Department of Education Fulbright-Hays Program, and the Woodrow Wilson Foundation, through the Charlotte W. Newcombe Fellowship for Religion and Ethics. I gratefully acknowledge permission to include texts previously published elsewhere. Sections of Chapter 2 first appeared in *Contemporary Islam* (2008) 2, available at http://www.springer.com/. A version of Chapter 3 was first published in *Anthropology of the Middle East and North Africa: Into the New Millennium*, ed. Sherine Hafez and Susan Slyomovics (Bloomington: Indiana University Press). Excerpts of Chapter 4 were originally published in the *Journal of North African Studies* (2009) 14:2, available at www.tandfonline.com.

# Note on Transliteration

TRANSLITERATION SYSTEMS ATTEMPT, and repeatedly fail, to assimilate different written languages. Transcribing Moroccan dialectal Arabic (*darija*), standard Arabic, and French provides multiple such opportunities. In aiming for imperfect assimilation, I use two diacritical marks for darija and standard Arabic, ʿ for ʿayn, and ʾ for hamza. I quote different French and English versions of Arabic terms as they appear in original sources (Aïssaoua, Aïssâoua, and ʿIsawa; Sidi Mohammed and Muhammad V). Other names of known figures and place names appear as they are commonly recognized in English (the prophet Muhammad, the city of Fez).

# THE CALLS OF ISLAM

# Introduction

It is not an exaggeration to say that the future of modern society and the stability of its inner life depend in large part on the maintenance of an equilibrium between the strength of the techniques of communication and the capacity of the individual's own reaction.
—Pope Pius XII, quoted in Marshall McLuhan, *Understanding Media*


Religion is communication [*al-Din 'ilam*].
—Television producers for Amr Khalid, one of Egypt's "New Callers"


OVER THE PAST decade in Fez, Morocco, and throughout the Muslim ecumene, young Islamist activists have produced and distributed videos of spirit exorcisms as part of an ongoing revivalist call to Islam. The videos are formulaic but nonetheless dramatic; a well-known video circulated by an Islamist association in the old city of Fez shows two leaders of the group performing an "Islamic exorcism" to cure a young Muslim man who feels "strange, like someone's always with me." "Pass me the microphone," one exorcist commands the other, "and I'll recite on him.'" Qur'anic verse pours forth in crystalline voice. The possessed man's shoulders heave and shudder, his mouth gapes and drools. Then Aisha, a legendary jinn in Moroccan popular Sufism, begins to speak from his cavernous mouth, identifying herself as a 350–year-old Jew. The audience gasps. The exorcists pass the microphone several times, their echoing Qur'anic recitation eliciting defiant screams and then pathetic whimpers as they extract her conversion. She converts and flees as the patient jolts awake, disoriented and sweating before the camera.

Rituals of "Islamic exorcisms" or "legitimate curing" (*al-ruqya al-shar'iyya*) and their video dissemination are recent developments, though not ones unique to Morocco. One finds them on YouTube, posted by "Islamic curers" (*raqiyyin*) in the postcolonial Maghrib and West Africa, Egypt, and South Asia. Across these different settings they demonstrate power and authority: to denounce and expel local, often Sufi, customs, and above all to call (*yad'u*; *da'wa*) their audiences to "legitimate" (*shar'i*) practice. That is to say, they arise where Muslim rituals give visceral presence to competing sources of spiritual power—competing calls of

Islam. If Sufism's foreign powers (its ostensibly archaic, Jewish authorities) *possess* Moroccans, the video messages of "legitimate curing" are a cultural exorcism, summoning up pure Muslim subjects and publics in their very response to the technologized call.

This book examines competing calls to Islam in underclass and struggling middle-class neighborhoods of the classical Muslim city of Fez, Morocco. Focusing on popular Sufi rituals of saint veneration and jinn curing, the book examines the modernization and, more specifically, the technologization of Islam's authoritative calls: how old practices and practitioners of Sufi trance and exorcism and new stagings of Islamic exorcism and national Sufi culture summon urban Moroccans into mass-mediated politics, power, and social order. These processes are grounded in the recent history of the Moroccan king Mohammed VI's rule: in militant Islamic terrorist attacks of May 16, 2003, and the 2011 Arab uprisings; and conversely, in an elite revival of distinctly "Moroccan" Sufism and growing state surveillance and control of Muslim practices and media. The technologization of Muslim practices, and marginal Sufism in particular, is more deeply grounded, however, in Moroccan society and politics of the twentieth century. As in other colonial and postcolonial Muslim societies, twentieth-century Moroccan Muslims witnessed technological transitions from oral, scribal, and other corporeal ritual forms of spiritual mediation to mass-market and mass-mediated stagings. In this same era Muslims witnessed a broad discrediting of once-given Sufi rituals and beliefs, and of the explicitly hierarchical and particularistic ties of person and community these reproduced, in favor of new and unprecedented mass imaginings of a national Moroccan community on a global stage.

The revivalist exorcism of Aisha, technologically reproduced and reproducible, illustrates the place of the call in this modern history of religious and political deracination and reenracination. It signals Muslims' ongoing efforts to reestablish personal ties, status, and authority through practical acts and ritual stagings appropriate to the larger-scale and anonymous media networks of national and global Islam. Just as crucial, it suggests that the call and its mass mediation are themselves Moroccan Muslims' concerns—that local discourses and acts of religious selfhood and social life are explicitly bound up with changing discourses and acts of media. As Muslims of different genders, classes, and power have witnessed and continue to navigate the changing "scale or pace or pattern" that new technologies bring to social life (McLuhan 2001, 8), new mass-mediated religious figures and rituals attempt explicitly to call them to communal belonging. How have new and competing calls of Islam—staged and received in ritually and technologically reproducible media—overturned or amplified old logics and locations of personhood and power in urban Morocco? How have practices and discourses of mass-mediation *as* call come to establish the conditions for piety and society in twentieth and twenty-first century Muslim modernities?

## Modern Muslim Politics of the Call

The discourse of the call is in fact central to numerous contemporary Islamic reviv-alist movements in postcolonial and postconflict nation-states. Different reformist movements, including both Islamist and more recent Sufi-based efforts, articulate goals specific to their particular local and national contexts. Yet, these differences notwithstanding, revivalists nearly everywhere frame their task as *daʿwa*—literally, a call, summons, or invitation. Islamic daʿwa efforts include popular mobilization or recruitment for political parties, protest, or armed resistance (Edwards 1993; Wick-ham 2002; J. Anderson 2005; Eickelman and Piscatori 2004).[1] But they also include and define modern Muslim politics in the broadest sense of symbolic practice, persua-sion, and transformation beyond the state or formal politics: Islamic feminists carry out public outreach through mosque lessons (Mahmood 2005) and perform charity and community building during Ramadan and other religious holidays (Deeb 2006). Muslim revivalists focus on dissuading Muslims from other ostensibly impious rituals (Masquelier 2001, 2009; Deeb 2006; Boddy 1989; Bernal 1994), disseminating sermons in cassettes and loudspeakers, and in digital and online media (Larkin 2008, 2012; Hirschkind 2006, 2012). Still other callers combine efforts for the public good with explicit self-promotion and enrichment (Masquelier 2009; Soares 2004, 2007).

The communicative nature of "the call" seems obvious in these public forms of practice. Yet Muslims' current emphasis on this discourse and practice is also histori-cally specific. Why, across very different locales, do current Islamic movements take the explicit form *of a call at all?*

Some recent scholarship on the call has emphasized the politics of Muslim bodies, and more specifically of self-fashioning, including veiling and prayer and the cultiva-tion of pious affect. For Mahmood (2005), the call is understood through a distinctly Islamic politics of embodiment—a historically embedded visceral politics (denied or elided in typical liberal politics) through which the multiplication of individual practices of worship (*ʿibada*) will generate a pious society. Yet, as much as the call concerns individual practice, it also concerns the ostensibly exterior environment to which Muslim bodies are deemed receptive. Indeed, Muslim discourses of the call assume the capacity of exterior forces and messages, good or ill, to breach individual bodies; pious selfhood and social order are explicitly framed as problems and prom-ises of communication and its media, whether ritual or technological or both. In Bei-rut, the changing norms of public Shiʿi mourning anticipate greater public visibility for the rites (Deeb 2006). In Cairo Islamic callers imagine a continuous and uniform soundscape of receptive bodies connected by the flow of technologized voice (Hirsch-kind 2006). Put otherwise, enacting a call to Islam explicitly foregrounds the *force* of communication, and in so doing defines Muslim subjects and societies as commu-nications' material effects.[2] To call is to assume a capacity of rituals (and attendant media) to communicate, and to expect that Muslim bodies will transmit their force, necessitating at once an inoculation against impious calls and cultivating their receptivity to, and full absorption into, salutary social relations.[3]

This communicative imaginary portends both crisis and promise: crises of social transformation, promises of passage from impious mediating structures—state secularism, capitalist decadence, Sufi heterodoxies—to new. Thus, in the past century explicit calls to reform have provoked Muslims' attention as colonial and market incursions and attendant technological transformations have destabilized and discredited established social, political, economic, and religious structures and norms (Siegel 2000b). The calls of Islam arise in social and historical interstices. As new social and political conditions reinvent and restage old mediating practices, absent figures emerge on the horizon as the subjects and the society Muslim callers wish to summon forth.[4] The calls of Islam are situated thus in urban Morocco, as they have been for the past century in the Muslim world, as Muslims inhabit emergent mediating social and technological structures and grasp new and old subjects and social relations as the practical effects of their call.

## The Medium of the Call/The Call of the Medium

To view Muslim subjects and societies as effects of the call (as contemporary callers do) is to accept a more capacious view of media and mediation (as media scholars do), where media include technological, social, and ritual structures of communicative possibility, and mediation refers to the repeated processes and practical acts of communication.[5] In this view, the calls of Islam implicate the material structures and media infrastructures that "determine our situation" (Kittler 1999, xxxix; cf. Larkin 2008); but they also implicate the social and political hierarchies in which these are embedded, and the repeated practices by which people come to inhabit and identify with them. It is the mark of our mass-mediated era—in which Muslims, as cited in the epigraph, may equate "religion" with "communication"—that practices and promises of the call readily overlap with an equally expansive media theory of social and subjective life.

### Calls of Islam: Episodes of Reform

This is not at all to suggest that the call is strictly modern. Sources of Islamic discursive tradition repeatedly invoke the Divine call and define piety as responsibility to it. The current revivalist emphasis on da'wa is only the latest articulation of this theme. The story of the Qur'an is the story of God's call reaching humankind through the angel Jibril and then through the Prophet Muhammad. According to the prophetic biographies, Muhammad received the first revelation in a time and place of seclusion. The experience was overwhelming and terrifying; a voice commanded Muhammad to "recite."[6] The origin of this command was unclear to Muhammad. It would only later be recognized by a local Meccan Christian as the call of the One God who called Abrahim, Moses, David, and Jesus, among others. That is to say, God's call to

Muhammad, or rather through Muhammad to humankind, was not new but rather a re-call to the original monotheism of Abraham.

The Qur'an (the primary source of Islam's discursive tradition) repeatedly emphasizes God's basic call, or da'wa, to humankind as the founding possibility of a truly just and pious community (*umma*) and of truly pious believers or Muslims. In this context the term evokes God's call as *command*, the only proper response to which is service and "obedience"—'*ibada*, commonly translated as "ritual" or "worship"—to God alone (Zahniser 2002, 557). That is, the Qur'anic text makes clear that individual Muslims (male and female) will be judged by virtue of their heeding the call. Piety emerges from, in Talal Asad's terms, "apt performance," and apt performance is structured as a response to God's command; piety and servitude to God consists in literal response-ability to His call (Asad 1993, 62).

God's call was not the only call, however, to which Meccans could respond. Indeed, the discursive tradition posits multiple calls—competing sources of command, invitation, and incitation—to which humans will be subjected, with "unbelievers . . . 'drawn to the caller [*da'i*] irresistibly'" (Qur'an 54:6–8; Zahniser 2002, 558). The call is, in this sense, the test, and responding to differing calls and responding differently (sincerely, attentively) elicits the very division between communities of faith and unfaith. For the early community, the strength and continuity of God's da'wa was paramount, as illustrated by the institutional repetition of that call in the call to prayer (*adhan*) to summon the faithful, and in the Prophet's choice of Bilal ibn Rabah as the first *muezzin*, for his powerful voice. The Qur'anic call, of course, did not stay with Muhammad's initial community of believers, but expanded well beyond the confines of Arabia. In time, the limits of the call's audibility—and the listeners' responsivity—would be one measure of inclusion or exclusion from a particular Muslim community, and the Muslim umma as a whole.[7]

Marshall Hodgson has characterized Islam's expansion as the mediation of the original call, or the "cultural dialectic" of Islam: on the one hand, God's call outlined in the Qur'anic revelation; on the other, humankind's response to that call (Hodgson 1974). Hodgson argued that if the original call remained the same, sovereign and singular, the "venture" of Islam comprised its fragmentation, mediation, and repetition through reinterpretation. It involved global institution-building, in schools of law, philosophy and letters, Sufi orders, and institutions of governance. For Hodgson, there is one Islam and multiple Muslim, or "Islamicate," societies. Put otherwise, the Muslim world's multiple institutions and traditions, its *material* forms or intermediaries, have constituted not one, but many *calls* of Islam. Whether in the Book or in books, in ritual, scribal or oral transmissions, in the bodies of saints and scholars and Sufis, or in physical edifices of mosques, saints' tombs, or Sufi *zawiyas* (meeting houses), authority accrues to those who repeat the call—whose mediation is *authorized*.

The power of the call in Islam is thus inseparable from the authority of its mediations and from the political and social positions of *particular* media and repetitions.

Where doctrinal and sociopolitical differences emerge within Muslim societies, as they do presently, the status of mediators of the call—material, technological, and human structures and repeated stagings—is a central and explicit issue.[8]

### *The Call in Anthropology: Subjects of the Structure; Repetition and Difference*

In fact, the possibility of mediation—repeatability—is not merely one quality of Islam's calls, but rather the necessary condition for their origination and dissemination. If Muslim authority and community has rested partly on institutions' control over such repeatability, sociocultural perspectives likewise foreground the power of mediating structures (of language, ritual, the state) and their repeated performances to summon subjects within a coherent social order. In Louis Althusser's theory of "interpellation" of individuals as subjects, the "ideological state apparatus" constitutes subjects through repeated acts of address from afar: "the practical telecommunication of hailings" (1994, 131). Such stagings of the call are formalized—"an everyday practice subject to a precise ritual" (1994, 139n17)—and potentially dramatic. In Althusser's central example, a policeman addresses a pedestrian from afar, "Hey, you there!" The pedestrian recognizes him- or herself as the object of address (within range of the naked ear) and, in responding, accedes to the subject position so assigned (1994, 131).

The state's summons is comparable to the call of the church, Althusser suggests, in that hailing compels subjects to respond by invoking or wielding an inaccessible source—"Unique, Absolute *Other Subject*, i.e., God" (Althusser 1994, 133). That power seems to reside somewhere behind the policeman's summons, as somewhere behind the church sermon. For Althusser, hailing seems to work, succeeding "nine times out of ten" in inducing auto-recognition in the accused (1994, 131). As with Foucault's explorations of the history of sexuality's "incitement to discourse" or modern clinics' and prisons' provocative disciplinary gaze, Althusser defines the "subject" as one who seems "freely" to obey the obligatory call (Foucault 1978, 1979).

Althusser's image of interpellation emphasizes an invisible, even absent power—which the conscientious pedestrian acknowledges and obeys. However, the suggestion that hailing works at all (and more or less perfectly) requires further explanation. In Althusser's "theoretical theatre" there is little competition for the state; even the church's summons remains within its purview (1994, 131). More fundamentally, the call seems to work because it is *recognized as such*, by virtue of repetitions ostensibly free of error. If interpellation is a "way of *staging the call*" (Butler 1997a, 107, original emphasis), for Althusser it is "subject to a precise ritual" (1994, 131). Ritual in the simplest sense—any ritual—requires formal repeatability; every particular performance, in order to be recognized as such, rests on a "performative structure" of codified signs, an archive of gestures—which is to say, a medium (Derrida 1988; Butler 1997b, 5). One learns to recognize the police uniform, the gestures, the tone of address, and with these, the power of the state.

The medium is thus a structure that makes a particular act of the call—its staging, recognition, and reception—possible. That medium may be a "social structure" or a history of ritual practices known and codified in oral and corporeal traditions; it may be a technological infrastructure built with mechanical or electronic storage and recall. What constitutes the medium is repetition, or more precisely, repeatability. The fact of repeatability as an open possibility, however, also makes the call vulnerable to *mis*communication. For Althusser, this repeatability remains within the control of the state. Indeed, the "precision" and success with which Althusser invests the state's ritualized summons suggests a certain divine perfection. (As Judith Butler observes, Althusser "assimilates social interpellation to the divine performative" [1997a, 110].) Althusser's essay does not pursue the failed calls, nor those pedestrians who properly ignore the call given that it addresses another (see Larkin 2012). Rather, even as Althusser identifies the medium of the call—the state apparatus, the ritual structure— he elides its disruptive or transformative potential, assuming its more or less perfect repetition. The pedestrian seems not to notice the police at all; the latter is a perfect medium, "lending his voice" to the state (see Siegel 2000a).

To acknowledge the mediating structure is to acknowledge something in excess of the origin of the call and its recipient—the possibility of repetition—that remains potentially beyond the control of either. Whether from the state, God, or another spiritual figure, the call is never simply dyadic—never a self and other facing one another, no matter how asymmetrical or veiled. Every call is collective, not only because it anticipates an audience to be addressed, but because of the network or structure— a third-person plural—to which each repetition, indeed, the call's very repeatability, owes its possibility.[9] Contemporary Muslim discourses and practices of the call foreground both individual and collective piety and impiety, both order and disorder, as effects of mediation; put otherwise, the Muslim politics of the call concerns the kinds of subject and society particular media and processes of mediation summon forth. Indeed, in this social and historical moment, it is not the medium of the call that matters, but the medium *that* calls—the call of the medium.

## Morocco, Sufism, and Mass Mediation: Itinerary of Chapters

Ubiquitous twentieth- and twenty-first-century Muslim discourses and practices of the call highlight both the proliferating global technological media and the modern experiences and frames of political and social collectivity and order—imperialism and nationhood, in particular—that these made possible. In urban Morocco, as much as anywhere, the calls of Islam have been bound up with the coercive powers of the state and with the nation as the most readily imaginable and viable form of political community (B. Anderson 2006). As across the Muslim world, Morocco's colonization provoked competing views of Sufism based emphatically on their social and religious effects within these new political frameworks. Colonial-era technological mediations and transformations of popular Sufi rituals were central both to the state's efforts to summon and control a distinctly national religious identity and field, and also to disputes regarding their ostensibly salutary or deleterious effects on the nation and its subjects. These competing views continue into the postcolonial present.[10] Broadly speaking, for contemporary Moroccan advocates and authorities of popular Sufism, local ritual practices, strengthened by state support and by technological mediation, repeatedly summon devotees and the broader society to pious order. Conversely, for opponents of popular Sufi authority, pervasive and repeated ritual practices summon urban Moroccans away from the pious personal and social responsibilities that contemporary political conditions and crises now demand of ordinary Muslims.

These competing views and practices within the urban space of Fez medina provide a critical context for Islamists' calls, in the medium of the exorcism videos with which I opened this discussion. On the one hand the exorcism concerns merely one body, but its explicit publicity calls to a broader public assumed to recognize Aisha and, moreover, to venerate her in rituals of pilgrimage, sacrifice, and trance. It is this ritual structure, with real social connections—enhanced and amplified by state sponsorship and broadcast—that calls in Aisha's voice: the call of the cultural network that she names and to which other Moroccans habitually respond. Put otherwise, Islamic exorcists in Morocco view their middle- and underclass audiences as embodied subjects *entranced* by the nation's Sufi call. To exorcise Aisha via the call to Islam is to demonstrate one's power over that other (Sufi) call, that is, to expel the social structure and network in which she is recognized and authorized. The call to which one responds defines the piety and quality of the subject within a Moroccan context—entranced, in the case of those who receive Aisha's ritualized call; strong, healthy, and pious, in the case of the exorcists' call. The framing of exorcism as a call situates Sufism, Islamism, and power within the deeper history and broader present of Muslim politics.

The following chapters trace the discourse, rituals, and technologies linking popular Sufism to personal piety and social and political order in Fez, and Morocco more broadly, from the colonial past to the postcolonial present. They examine particular rituals, including saint veneration and royal audiences, jinn trance and talismanic writing, and Sufi festivals and Islamic exorcism, as well as their different advocates and critics and their social and political significance. The focus on popular Sufism takes shape in part through an emphasis on the power of Sufi sainthood in Morocco, but also on jinns (Ar. *jinn*; Mor. Ar. *jnun*, sing. *jinn*)—invisible spirits, from which is derived the Western image of genies—and rituals of their summoning and exorcism. The first chapter proposes why, beyond the well-studied institutions of saint veneration, jinns warrant particular attention in Moroccan modernity. As ambivalent figures of both danger and power, difference and disruption, jinns and jinn rites are conventionally tied to the danger and difference of socially marginal Muslims (N. Khan 2006; Spadola 2004). The calls of popular Sufism have, in large measure, staged a socioreligious power to call forth and control local differences between elite and underclass. The call aims to control people, but also to control the *medium that calls*—ritual repeatability itself—as a hierarchical but also potentially disruptive force. At present (and especially after militant Islamist terrorist attacks in Casablanca in 2003), I suggest technological mediations of jinn rites intersect with concerns over differences within national order and piety. On the one hand, newly technologized Sufi trance rites promise to summon underclass and "detached" middle-class Moroccans to a unified national difference qua "Moroccan Islam" (Cohen 2003); on the other, interconnected mediated space raises anxieties of uncontrolled difference. This is most evident in national discourses about uncontrolled and thus socially destructive jinn rituals, and in new norms of ritual trance that emphasize self-consciousness, cultural performance and public propriety.

Chapters 2 and 3 provide historical background for understanding the specifically national—mass-mediated—politics of these popular Sufi calls and the subjects and society they summon forth. Chapter 2 focuses on the emergence of Moroccan nationalism that combined efforts both to eradicate underclass Sufi trance and to stage a novel call to national belonging grounded in veneration of the Sufi monarch. While outlining the emergence of a dominant Sufi national culture, it also tells a general story of Islamic modernist thought common across the Muslim world: on the one hand, discrediting or destroying the established intermediary structures summoning Muslims; on the other, reframing social order and subjective piety in terms of a population's responsibility to a uniformly broadcast, national call. Chapter 3 examines the more immediate historical expectations and conditions of religious uniformity in which current ritual calls and countercalls in urban Morocco are voiced, namely, the centralized call of the monarchy bound to the state control of broadcast media. In particular, the chapter looks at the watershed events and aftermath of the 1975 Green March in which King Hassan II summoned hundreds of thousands of largely underclass Moroccans to march unarmed into then Spanish-occupied Western Sahara. In effectively claiming the calls of Islam as its own, the monarchy established the political norm of religious and national unity within which current urban Moroccans practice.

The following two chapters return to the ethnographic present in Fez medina and focus on everyday Sufi practices of the call among underclass and middle-class men and women in urban Morocco. The first looks at petty Qur'anic scholars, or *fuqaha'* (Ar. sing. *faqih*; Mor. coll. *fqih*) who use curative talismanic writing to summon and control jinns, both for curing purposes as well as occult production of wealth. The second looks at curative trance rites of the Gnawa, a marginal Sufi order comprising the descendants of slaves, who summon and venerate a pantheon of "*mluk al-jinn*," the "possessors," or "owners," among the jinns, including Aisha, to whom Islamic exorcists introduced us. The two chapters are linked narratively, following the efforts of a thirty-year-old woman, Zuhur, possessed by Aisha, first to find a talismanic cure for her affliction and then to submit to the jinn and become (as Aisha demands) her medium—a seer. The chapters are also linked thematically, as struggling middle-class Muslims like Zuhur seek to achieve socioeconomic stability and status by way of the nationalized

Sufi hierarchies outlined in the two prior chapters. Experts in both rites seek to summon and placate jinns and appropriate them as signs of authority, that is, to foster hierarchy on the basis of calling and controlling difference; those who succeed draw on a substantial informal economy of curing rites. At the same time, however, these rituals clash with and violate reformist norms of public piety and social unity, of piety as reception of an undifferentiated, broadcast call. Practitioners of these calls know this and remain caught between middle-class aspirations and pious norms and harder economic realities.

The next two chapters examine elite Sufi revivalist efforts and contrasting Islamist calls through their distinct treatments of jinns, differing bodily ethics, and different political and social status in Fez. These practices, however, are also thematically, structurally, and historically linked in their assimilation of mass-mediated social consciousness: despite practical differences, Sufi elites and Islamic exorcists separately (but similarly) emphasize conscious responsibility to their mass-mediated calls as the conditions for a coherent and unified Moroccan subjectivity and society. At the same time, they demonstrate the different sources of authority (Sufi or Islamist) on which middle-class Moroccans may draw. Chapter 6 in particular examines elite Moroccans' celebration of popular Sufism and spirit veneration in Fez, grounded in both state-sponsored festivals and in the global market for Sufi trance music and performance. Here I suggest the state's support of trance hierarchy is clearest, as are novel demands for a conscious practice of trance. The chapter draws particular attention to a political activist and actress in Fez ("Aisha") who publicly stages Gnawa trance rites in festivals and on state radio as a conscious "call" to cultural renewal and national unity. Indeed, Aisha is not alone; many middle- and upper-class Moroccans are now "discovering" their own affinity to Gnawa trance in its public, "festivalized" form. The stark differences, however, between conventional forms of spirit mediumship or reception and its mass-mediated ritual forms illustrate the pious (and largely middle-class) norms attending the technologized call: pious Muslims are to be conscious recipients and transmitters of the sacred call and its differentiating force originating, in this case, with the nation-state.

Returning to "Islamic exorcism" and its practitioners' call to Islam in Fez, the final ethnographic chapter examines the nature of the Islamist call as itself an exorcism of difference and of the uncontrolled communication that technological media have made possible in Morocco. What for many scholars of political Islam seems incomprehensible—*Islamists* performing *jinn exorcisms*?—makes sense within the modern history of the call. It is a reformist gesture to generate responsible, pious, and self-present subjects and society, and a discrediting or destruction of those other performative structures of the sacred—the Sufi hierarchy—that have literally entranced Moroccan Muslims. For Islamic exorcists, or *raqiyyin,* the critical forces to expel are talismanic writing and trance rites—precisely those communicative practices that give body to jinns in secret, but which, in aggregate, produce mass (national) social and cultural effects.

The call and exorcism are thus inextricable: in one sense for *raqiyyin*, exorcism is specifically a practice of the call, a way to summon Muslims to proper practice. But more important, the call is itself an act of exorcism: Islamic exorcism aims to eradicate the intermediaries and differences between people to form an ostensibly unified social body. In one sense these are Sufi structures to which, in private and public technologized forms, Moroccans have continued to respond; by contrast, these ritual media, seen from Islamists' mass political perspective, are the endemic communicative media that separate and unfairly stratify an otherwise unified mass society. The technologized call makes sense only for such a mass community—as an attempt to master the very distances and differences that technological media have generated at the moment they promise to overcome them.

The book's final chapter examines broader themes of technologized calls in current Moroccan politics, namely, the pro-democracy calls following the Tunisian and Egyptian revolutions in 2011. Young digital activists in urban Morocco, like similar groups across the Middle East and North Africa, are explicitly drawing on technologies and discourses of the call, including the unity of "the People"; yet political observers and my local interlocutors in Fez and other cities attest to the movement's fragmentary and ambivalent results. On the one hand, the monarchy has largely succeeded in co-opting reform and violently repressing activism; on the other, activists have failed to summon an effective response or critical mass among middle-class and underclass urban Moroccans, who view the movement largely as antinational. How might these results speak to the history of the call in Morocco, and its relationship to Sufi logics and practices?

More generally speaking, how might we rethink the force and effect of technological media, religion, and politics through the call and its differentiating effects? How might we think of communication as a force of difference and division rather than of commonality and community? Media studies in the past two decades have relied on public-sphere theories to emphasize the rationality of newly "democratized" media, as well as the (largely middle-class) sense of transparent and shared communication and consensus. The popular Sufi practices of calling traced here signal the differentiating force of calls and the conflicts, rather than consensus, arising from their stagings. The present postrevolutionary fragmentations of Middle Eastern and North African nations thus at once belie the theory and demand new conceptual and ethnographic labor to grasp their intensity and anguish. The Epilogue urges scholars of the region, Islam, and media studies more broadly to consider how these might overlap. How might the logic of the call help us to understand the differences unleashed, rather than resolved, in current social and religious movements?

# 1 Competing Calls in Urban Morocco

They see you, he [Shaytan] and his tribe, from where you do not see them.
—Qur'an 7:27

MUCH COLONIAL AND postcolonial scholarship on Islam in Morocco emphasizes "Moroccan Islam," a national veneration of Sufi authorities and pious exemplars (Geertz 1968; Michaux-Bellaire 1926; Eickelman 1976). Historically, Sufi "saints" or "friends of God" (*awliya'*, sing. *wali*; in colonial literature, *marabouts*) have ranged from urban and rural bearers of divine blessing (*baraka*), juridical science (*'ilm*), or mystical knowledge (*ma'rifa*) to holy warriors and wise fools. But from the late fifteenth century to present, the dominant political culture now figured as "Moroccan" has been a "sharifian" tradition of Sufism, in which sacred inviolability and sovereignty are attributed to the prophet Mohammed's descendants, *shurafa'* (sing. *sharif*) (Cornell 1998; Kugle 2006).[1] In this tradition, the city of Fez marks the axis mundi. Established in the late eighth and early ninth centuries and by shurafa' Idris I and his son Idris II, Fez remained a regional economic, religious, and political capital of Muslim dynasties in North Africa and al-Andalus for the next millennium. The fifteenth-century discovery of Idriss II's tomb, in particular, marked the regional rise of sharifian dominance in the Muslim world's "Far West" (*al-Maghrib al-aqsa*) (Kugle 2006, 85–89). From the subsequent sharifian revolution in 1465, to the sharifian Sa'dian dynasty's control of Fez in 1549, and through the twenty-first century 'Alawite monarchy, shurafa' have formed every ruling dynasty of what is now modern-day Morocco.

From precolonial sultanate to postcolonial monarchy, Morocco's dominant sharifian Sufi hierarchies in Fez and other urban centers (such as Meknes, Salé, Tetouan, Marrakech, and Madagh) have supported the ruling regime and infused the social order and religious life in explicit and subtle ways. Hundreds of saints' shrines and Sufi *zawiyas*, or meeting houses, dot Fez. Fas al-Bali, the "old city" or "medina"—distinct from Fas al-Jadid (Fez Jadid, or New Fez, c. 1300s) and from the twentieth-century French Ville Nouvelle and twenty-first-century urban sprawl—is occasionally described as a single *zawiya* (Skali 2007). More broadly, different sharifian lineages have developed Sufi "orders" (*turuq*; sing. *tariqa*) of devoted adepts and peripheral followers, with different ritual practices appealing to different socioeconomic strata. In private homes and public meetings, elite and middle-class Sufi orders follow weekly and annual meditative *dhikr* rites (remembrance of God) of textual recitation and particular prayers (*wird*), which induce mild ecstasy and a sense of closeness (*qurba*) to God. In annual public rituals around saints' tombs, adepts and followers of underclass orders, protected by the blessing (*baraka*) of the saint, perform spectacular jinn trances and (less common) acts of self-mortification—self-cutting, swallowing glass and boiling water, and devouring raw and bloody meat (Crapanzano 1973, 1977, 1980; Zillinger 2010). In private homes, men and women of these same groups perform more frequent curing rites for themselves and clients, summoning tutelary jinns to appease them with trance, tribute, and sacrifice.

Observers of "Moroccan Islam," not surprisingly, have discerned in these ritual differences and social distinctions the durable structures and processes—that is to say, the media—of political hierarchy (Combs-Schilling 1989; Geertz 1968; Hammoudi 1997; Maarouf 2007; Tozy 1999). Social distinctions have not merely found ritual expression; rather, political cultural elites and subordinates have reproduced social difference by way of ritual expression and its multiple media. Thus, historically, as sharifian lineages retained power through material signs of recognition (ritual protocols, monetary gifts, legal exceptions, closely guarded scribal decrees from the sultan [Laroui 1977, 92–97]), so too did the material ritual practices of underclass Sufi orders reproduce sharifian hierarchy from below (Crapanzano 1973; Maarouf 2007).

For sharifian elites, material media of distinction marked the divine presence of baraka (among other spiritual qualities), along with the capacity to transmit its effects to adepts and followers (Clancy-Smith 1994; Geertz 1968; cf. Cornell 1998, intro.) But among the marginal folk especially, as Edward Westermarck's exquisitely detailed pre- and early colonial observations show, baraka's sacrality evoked the mysterious workings of jinns (Westermarck 1968, I, chaps. 1–6).[2] Sufi trance rites offer a case in point: conceived as the presencing of jinns summoned and controlled by the baraka of the shurafa', possession itself distinguished the vulgar commoners (*'amma*)—a disdained and feared source of disorder (Laroui 1977)—from the cultural, religious, political, and economic urban elites. Indeed, within the relatively stable "plural society" of Fez (Furnivall 1956), the rites demonstrated the blessed power of these latter by staging and also domesticating the madness of subaltern bodies (one Arabic term for madness, *majnun*, derives from jinns).[3] If baraka was a sign of distinction, it also named a power to summon up the distinguishing marks (jinns) of the subaltern bodies—and to control them as signs of difference and deference. What would come to be known as "Moroccan Islam" encompassed trance rites not as madness pure and simple, but rather as rituals of underclass Muslims' receptivity to baraka's call.

The early twentieth-century emergence of national consciousness witnessed symbolic continuity as well as material changes in sharifian rituals. Indeed, nationalization of Islam meant shifting controls of social difference itself. Colonial and postcolonial-era technological stagings of trance as national culture attended the formation of baraka's mass dissemination in new royal audiences (see Chapters 2 and 3). In the late twentieth century, state and sharifian elites capitalized on the global culture market, sponsoring older saints' pilgrimages, televising Sufi performances, and developing mass-market Sufi-themed "festivals" for both Moroccan and foreign tourist markets, among them the Fez Sacred World Music Festival, and the Essaouira Gnawa and Trance Festival (Kapchan 2000, 2007; Zillinger 2008, 2010). Taking the throne in 1999, Mohammed VI soon built on these efforts, replacing Hassan II's minister of religious affairs with Ahmed Tawfiq, a noted Sufi leader of the growing middle- and upper-class Boutchichiyya order. This trend found further impetus following the May 16, 2003, militant Islamist bombings in Casablanca. With the "spiritual security of the nation" at stake (Arif 2008; Kaitouni 2010), Mohammed VI and sharifian allies added the Sufi Cultural Festival of Fez (like the Fez Sacred Music Festival, developed by a Fassi sharif); a renovation of the Sufi shrine to Sidi Ahmed Tijani (d. 1815) in Fez was completed in 2007, its opening celebration publicly sponsored by Mohammed VI, who also offered a keynote message highlighting the "close ties" that Tijaniyya followers faithfully maintained toward the sharifian throne.[4] The purpose of these events, like the monarchy's new "tolerance festivals," was unambiguous: to call underclass and middle-class Moroccan Muslims to proper (sharifian Sufi) Islam and (mass) social order.[5]

These newly national (and transnational) Sufi revivalist practices symptomatize the far broader transformations of public religion, ritual practice, and ritual media. The state's appropriation and redeployment of signifying practices and bodily dispositions in technological media signals the importance of mass social formations, both public and private—broadcast audiences, anonymous urban spaces, digital media producers and consumers—as objects of national politics and statecraft. Staging historically marginal cultural practices attempts to discipline participants as specifically national subjects. Indeed, for a segment of the middle-class population in particular—those who can afford to consume these novel media—"trance" and "reception" take on both the corporeal sense of receiving jinns and the technological sense of receiving and interpreting state-sponsored and mass-market signals. To be in trance means demonstrating one's interpellation as the subject of a technologically and socially modern nation-state. It is to enter a communicative domain supported by the throne: to maintain baraka's call and its differentiating effects as a national force—as the call of the nation—rather than as that of a particular saint and sharifian lineage.

As a state and upper-class ideal, at least—one largely adopted by middle classes in Fez—the current slate of Sufi and trance festivals, as well as sponsorship of older popular saints' festivals, evidences the technological and discursive conditions of a national community in which rituals, whether performed in public or private, circulate through a (putatively) uniform homogeneous time and interconnected space of culture (B. Anderson 2006; Thongchai 1994; Pemberton 1994; Morris 2000). More pointedly Sufi revivalism speaks to the political necessity of summoning urban Moroccans as mass-mediated subjects. Through mass-mediated ritual, the state, sharifian elites, and middle-class aspirants imagine differences controlled—a mass public as one people, wholly attuned to and distinguished by one call. At its origin stands Fez medina, the renewed beacon of Morocco's disciplined and modern Sufi social order.

But the medina's status as ritual staging ground encounters the social and political realities of the underclass rural migrants and lower-middle-class families that now occupy its once splendid mansions. This new social makeup—of largely anonymous and struggling people, rather than elites—exemplifies the broad obstacles to visions of mass unity and, more importantly, to the risks of communication that such unity demands. For elites and middle classes, the reality of mass circulation means that ritual mediations of one group, and the kinds of Muslims they produce can affect everyone. The social distinctions that once marked elites (*khassa*) from commoners ('*amma*) are more porous within a mass-mediated national culture and society. Indeed, the kind of social order and consciousness to which middle-class urban Moroccans aspire is put at risk by the very technological mediations that would make it possible.

Different calls of Islam may produce a coherent "counterpublic" (Warner 2002; Hirschkind 2006). But where calls summon the urban margins by way of jinns, another possibility comes to mind among Moroccan Muslims: a contagion of proliferating calls, a network of dispersed but hidden differences, only momentarily and never finally exposed (cf. Newcomb 2009, chap. 1). Put otherwise, if Sufi saints and other elite bearers of baraka summoned and controlled jinns, and by extension, the social margins, jinns remain a force of difference—different consciousness, different status—that both defines the margins and threatens to extend their influence and presence. This difference remains one brought out by mediation, but not only by older Sufi rituals. The mass mediation of jinns takes place on national television, in mass market curing manuals, cassettes, CDs, DVDs, in new rituals and videos of Islamic exorcism, and in endemic conversations and ritual apparitions to which these give rise. Jinns are the sign of difference, not as a stable object, but rather as a possibility to be triggered—a possibility of difference waiting to be made in the act of the call.

## May 2003: The Rising Stakes of Religious Calls

The state's Sufi revivalism that started under Mohammed VI, May 16, 2003, expanded the national significance of the call, as Islamist members of al-Qaeda-affiliated Salafiyya Jihadiyya carried out multiple suicide bombings in Casablanca. The *attentats dyal*

*Casa* quickly raised the stakes of religious opposition for the monarchy and the state, as well as for a broad swath of ordinary Moroccans in Fez, who found the attacks a horrifying and grotesque turn. Forty-five people died and scores more were injured in Casablanca; the attacks, diffused in journals and television, prompted a highly public national and nationalist response. The maturing autocrat Mohammed VI delivered several national addresses recalling Morocco's 1,200–year Islamic history of "moderation and tolerance, human dignity, and coexistence with others," its "unified religious approach" and Maliki legal interpretation, and its thorough rejection of "foreign religious approaches," defined by "intolerance" of diversity.[6]

A "unified religious approach" meant unleashing security services to hunt down additional presumed Islamist militants. The violence in Casablanca, it was soon established, had roots in Fez as well. The city's marginal neighborhoods, in the medina and outside it, like the bidonvilles of Casablanca, were searched with ruthless fervency. Seemingly anyone fitting an Islamist profile was vulnerable. A large weapons cache was uncovered near the Marinid-era tombs on the edge of the medina. By late June at least 920 suspects had been arrested for questioning, with an unknown but likely high number suffering indefinite detention and torture (Santucci 2005). A friend of my close friend Mohammed was detained while selling Islamic literature and media from a small storefront in the medina. A young in-law of the family with whom I lived was arrested, tortured, and sentenced to two years of prison.

These developments could appear irrelevant to popular jinn rites in Fez—but they mattered quite a lot, and viscerally so to Islamic exorcists. The Islamic exorcists' practice was always implicitly political, and from our earliest encounters they had explicitly denounced the particularities of religion in everyday Moroccan life. In 2001 when I first watched exorcism videos, including the exorcism of Aisha, I sought out and interviewed some of the video producers in Sidi Boujida, a working-class Fez medina neighborhood, home to the Islamic *jam'iyya*, or association, where Aisha's exorcism had been recorded. Hassan and Abdelwahid, the video's producers, were also leaders of the association and known to local shopkeepers as the owners of an Islamic bookstore on a dirt side-street next to a hair salon and a télé-boutique.

The bookstore served as an informal hub for practitioners of *al-ruqya al-shari'iyya*, literally, "legitimate curing," but commonly and accurately translated into English as "Islamic exorcism." The owners kept a list of exorcists (*raqiyyin*, sing. *raqi*), seven names and cell-phone numbers, at the cash register. Like other Islamists in Morocco the men dressed in "*ikhwani*" ("Muslim Brotherhood") style, or "*libas afghani*" ("Afghani dress"), a plain white cotton or polyester robe devoid of the exquisite embroidery and silk mixes of Moroccan gowns. Their sartorial difference signaled a critical distance from recognizably local style in Fez and from "Moroccanness" more generally. The books, cassettes, and digital videos they sold told a similar story of universal Islam originating in global, or at least largely Middle Eastern—Saudi, Egyptian, and Kuwaiti—publishing houses. A substantial selection of media focused on Islamic curing itself; the Salafi and Wahhabi formulations of the dangers of jinns and traditional forms of sorcery provided a template for my interlocutors' denunciations of local Sufi jinn rites, including trance and popular talismanic writing. Behind the counter the owners kept several audiocassettes and videocassettes of live jinn exorcisms these specialists had themselves performed and recorded to sell in Fez.

The men and other young Islamists and raqiyyin at the bookstore were warm and talkative; they recommended the best mass-market manuals and descriptions of ruqya and described the nature of the practice and its emergence in Fez. They took pleasure in criticizing "Moroccan traditions" of hierarchical Sufi practice as pervasive local deviations from shari'a, not least, the unpardonable sin of idolatry or "associationism" (*shirk*), in the form of Sufi saint and spirit veneration. To that point they referred to their neighborhood of Sidi Boujida, which had been named for "My Master Abu Jayda," a tenth-century Fassi saint, simply as "Boujida," thus brashly rejecting the Moroccan Sufi honorific. They tested me on the number of Muslim holidays (*'id*) in the year, accepting only two—'Id al-Fitr, ending Ramadan, and 'Id al-Adha, the Feast of the Sacrifice—and rejecting putatively religious Moroccan holidays like the Throne Holiday (*'id al-'arsh*) or Celebration of the Throne (La Fête du Trône). They were equally dismissive of the monarchy to which the nation ritually pledged its fealty. Mohammed VI might yet be a pious and just man, but his late father Hassan II, the heir and master architect of contemporary sharifian rule, was nothing but a *"mul-hayt"*— "Master of the Wall"—a reference to his mandatory public photographic portraits but also a pun on *"mulhid"*: "Unbeliever."

I was away from Morocco during the September 11th attacks and the beginnings of the Bush administration's Global War on Terror, in which Morocco was a willing participant, with Islamists bearing the brunt of violence (Slyomovics 2008). Yet upon returning to Fez in 2003 I found the Islamic exorcists at the bookstore, their curing rites and conversations continuing unperturbed. Following the subsequent Casablanca bombings, however, the security state's targeting was broader, its gaze pervasive; in late May of that year the *jam'iyya* was shuttered. My regular interlocutor Hassan, featured in Aisha's exorcism video, disappeared. Now the bookstore staff, Noureddine and Youssef, sat in silence, abandoning their suspect "Afghani" Islamic white robes for colorful t-shirts and sweatpants. Youssef explained with astonishing candor: "This is the 'War on Terror' [*hadi muharabat al-irhab*]." Shortly after, Noureddine alerted me that two foreign Muslim schoolteachers had been detained and bluntly advised me to stay away. From Abdelwahid's nephew in the neighborhood I learned that he too had been arrested. When Abdelwahid and I next spoke in 2005, I would learn that Hassan's disappearance was due to his detention and subsequent ten-year prison sentence. If the state's seizure of the jam'iyya and the arrest of the bookstore owners had little to do with the men's jinn exorcisms, neither were they irrelevant. Their call to Islam, within which "legitimate curing" played an integral role in Fez medina, sought explicitly to eradicate not only jinns but, more broadly, the un-Islamic political culture and social hierarchies of possession or trance that Moroccan Sufism induced. It was, in other words, a countercall to the state's and the state-sponsored and -enforced culture of Sufi nationalism. To a remarkable degree, the state's response to them, as to other purveyors of Islamic "propaganda," confirmed the men's diagnosis; both through legal changes and extrajudicial arrests, the state attacked these Islamic callers as nodes of potentially uncontrolled communicative power.[7]

The competition between the two calls is horribly asymmetrical, of course. The state marshals a far larger media network, a bureaucratic organization of religious and cultural authorities, the support of cultural and religious elites—and a security apparatus to violently repress what it cannot otherwise dispute. But the explicitly national contest for Islam's call and, more to the point, for national subjects of the call, foregrounds the distinctly modern mass-communicative conditions in which these competing forces—Islamist da'wa or state Sufi command—are reproduced and disseminated. The technologized and dispersed efforts of the opposed callers mean that each assumes the other to emanate not from an individual or even a collection of individuals but from a diffuse yet coherent structure—a global "network" of Islamists, or a national "culture" of Sufism. Both calls attempt to "exorcise" the other through broadcast action, targeting individual bodies possessed by national jinns or global Islam's network and call.

## Summoning Jinns: Making Difference

Anxieties regarding Islamic networks, especially "foreign" Islamists, are shared among urban Moroccans. Anxieties regarding jinns—their ritual apparitions, attendant beliefs, and social and subjective effects—are also prevalent, most markedly among middle-class Muslims, men and women alike. The two topics overlap in particular around concerns with the social progress of Morocco as a modern nation, and more specifically with the social order presumed to mark this progress. This concern with the popular Sufi practices of others brings together vocally Sufi cultural modernists, Islamists, as well as socially conscious reform-minded Muslims. Their views differ concerning the social value and religious validity of these rites, but there is strong agreement over popular jinn rites' particular Moroccanness.

There is also little disagreement over the existence of jinns. Their presence within the Qur'an and *hadith* (the reported words and deeds of the prophet Muhammad), that is, within the textual sources of Islam's dominant discursive tradition, means that by all orthodox standards, belief in jinns is an article of faith. Qur'anic verses establish that God created jinns from fire (God created angels from light and humans from clay); they are invisible but see us; they are sentient but not more intelligent than humankind; they bear witness to the call of God, and eventually they die and stand before God's judgment.[8] In the Qur'an jinns bear an ambiguous relation to Satan (Shaytan) or the Devil (Iblis). When Adam was created, Iblis stood among the angels, but refused to bow to God's new creation, precisely because fire (from which God formed him) was superior to clay, so Iblis was cast out and cursed by God. Among the jinns are *shayatin*—the plural of Shaytan—who, in contrast to jinns, are wholly demonic and evil. Many Muslims are familiar with the story of Sulayman (Solomon), who mastered animals and jinns and who by his magical ring summoned jinns to do his bidding.

For others in Morocco, local discourses gleaned from expert curers as well as from grandparents, parents, and friends provide knowledge of jinns beyond that mapped out in the Qur'an and hadith. Vincent Crapanzano made famous "Aisha Qandisha," a "camel-footed she-demon" and threatening succubus (1980, 15). There are other jinns, other groups or "species" of jinns named Aisha, including Aisha Sudaniyya (from the Sudan, or sub-Saharan Africa) and Aisha Bahriyya (from the sea) (cf. Crapanzano 1980, 100–101). Jinns in Morocco conventionally have been identified as unnamed or named. The former appear unexpectedly, as sheer disruptions: illness, madness, and possession; the latter comprise a pantheon of "possessors," the mluk al-jinn, distinguished by color, musical rhythm, tastes, habits, and religion.[9] As Crapanzano argues, the curing process of the underclass Sufi orders is a process of assimilating the shock and disruption of the unnamed jinns to language: the ill recuperates by adopting the idiom, and thus the controlled and ritualized differences, of the named jinns, the pantheon of mluk. It is, in short, a matter of acknowledging jinns as difference, and controlling that difference within ritual, and, given the class distinctions to which the Sufi orders submit, within social hierarchy.

The mluk, including Aisha, are Muslim and Jewish, but this distinction matters only insofar as they make different, but regular and largely predictable, demands on the entranced. Particular underclass Sufi orders, including the 'Isawa, Hamadsha, and Gnawa, venerate some or all of them, placating them, and thus curing the afflicted, through trance rites and sacrifice. Mluk have shrines as Sufi saints have shrines and are often situated near them, to be visited as one visits the saint's tomb. Association with one or another marks social distinctions in urban Fez. As Crapanzano suggests, there are named or unnamed jinns, but in recent decades jinns with new names and identities have begun to appear regularly. Jinns are often foreign nationals—"Jackson" and "Robert," from the United States, for example—indicating the globally circulating media images and technologies jinn rites now incorporate.[10]

In contrast to Sufi veneration of jinns, Islamic exorcists largely consider jinns demonic and most certainly unworthy of veneration. For still other urban Moroccans, jinns are a source of intense curiosity and inscrutability. A son of the family with whom I lived described in awe his friend's possession by a jinn in a cemetery; he offered no explanation, only the limit of certitude: "With jinns, there is always a question mark." Distinctions notwithstanding, these discourses acknowledge jinns as a different force—invisible, immaterial, highly mobile—the rare presence of which produces astonishing and mysterious effects. Not fully present and accessible to the senses, they are always potentially so; indeed, it is the ritual lending of presence to such difference that gives jinns social and political significance.

The varied ritual curers offer distinct explanations for what brings forth jinns as eruptions of difference and indeed whether jinns themselves command respect or inspire loathing.[11] Yet all claim some power to summon forth and control these forces of difference: Qur'anic scholars, fuqaha', learn to control them with talismanic writing; Sufis in trance learn to withstand jinns' effects, and some men and women possessed by mluk may serve as their mediums or seers (fem. *shuwwafat*, sing. *shuwwafa*; masc. *shuwwawaf*, sing. *shuwwaf*). The most spectacular Islamic exorcisms pose the power of the Qur'an and the exorcist himself against the embodied jinn, as the possessed body's face and limbs twist and its mouth spews language and saliva.

More crucial, each of these ritual stagings—whether exorcism or trance—also *makes* a difference, gives jinns body and force within social life, ostensibly as a controllable force. Each ritual staging contributes to the ritual medium itself as a repeatable structure and thus the possibility of a future performance, a future apparition. Each ritual is a collective act, repeating the idiom by which future eruptions will be interpreted and recognized *as* that of a jinn. The jinns, in other words, have different meanings, reproduced by different rituals. Such differences mark social boundaries. As Susan O'Brien has put it succinctly in Kano, "Forms of involvement with the spirit world index distinctions of class, education, and gender" (O'Brien 2001, 224). Or rather, they *should* mark boundaries. How, after all, does one respond to difference that inhabits one's body, one's community, that by virtue of its activation produces differences of self and social life, power, and authority?

### Jinn Rites and Mass Mediation: Communicative Bodies, Responsible Subjects

Jinn rites matter politically and socially today because the differences they make are *not* contained within distinct social boundaries. Islamic exorcists launch their call on YouTube, Sufi trance specialists perform on Moroccan radio and satellite television channels; even the smallest and most marginal jinn curers contact their clients via cell phone and carry business cards. Mass circulation gives rise to nonspecialist public and popular discourses of jinns in urban Morocco, which in turn help to shape the sociopolitics of one curing rite or another. Islamist, Sufi revivalist, secular, and cultural thinkers alike emphasize the social and subjective effects of the rites—the rites as communicative practices—in what speakers or writers assume to be a technologically (if not socially) interconnected national space. These are more than structural effects. Discussions invoke the consciousness (or lack of consciousness) of Muslims partaking of jinn rites or taking them seriously; they center on the varied economic effects of jinn practices (the ill-gotten gains of the experts, or the lost fortunes of the clients). Discussions of jinn rites (like discussions of children's and teens' video-game or drug use in the United States) focus on the different kinds of person and community that such structures and acts—such mediations—generate. More importantly, however, these discussions focus on the ways particular rituals contribute to "society" as a presumably uniform, or at least interconnected, object.

Drawing on this range of discourses, my Fassi acquaintances and friends, including the young members of the household with whom I lived, discussed jinns and jinn rites in terms of differences of piety and ethical standards among Muslims. Similar discussions recur in various Moroccan media, from self-help sections in the nation's largest-circulating newspapers and popular magazines, to repeated reports and lengthy exposés on jinn rites on national television. With older, traditional practitioners (fuqaha', Gnawa, and other Sufi trance specialists), discussions concerned the demands of jinns, the techniques of ritual, and the expected outcome. In contrast, among my reform-minded friends and interlocutors, among revivalist curers both Sufi and Islamic, and in mass media, discussions centered on the social and subjective effects of the rites. While differences pertained between Islamists, Sufi revivalists, and cultural modernists, they nonetheless shared a particular point of reference and criticism of what they deemed "traditional" forms of the rites. Specifically, they emphasized that traditional jinn practitioners and patients (or, more pointedly, "clients") were "unaware" (*ghair wa' i*) and damaging both themselves and "society" (*al-mujtam'*), thus contributing to endemic antimodern conditions of ignorance and superstition, underdevelopment and poverty. Practitioners, of course, were assumed to be enriching themselves at the expense of society, but this too signaled unawareness, their lacking "education" or "formation."

In viewing jinn rites in terms of self and "society," and more specifically, "Moroccan society," my educated and middle-class interlocutors in Fez (and in Rabat where I lived and carried out similar research in 2001) shared a national frame of reference. Islamists, but also reform-minded Muslims, faulted the state itself for fostering ignorance, for example by televising the performance of an underclass Sufi order (an 'Isawa group) and provoking people "to think that they're important, a big deal"—or producing national subjects, in the words of an Islamic exorcist in Rabat, "bewitched by ideology" (*mashur bil-idiulujiyya*). The tone of such comments was especially sharp in Fez medina, usually precipitated by signs of the city's particularly difficult straits, its ruined social structure and physical and economic infrastructure, exacerbated by overpopulation by recent rural migrants. Thus a café owner in the medina could tell me, with seriousness, that the demand for magical amulets, along with prostitution and cannabis, provided the lifeblood of the medina's economy. Located in Fez, my interlocutors were particularly well placed to criticize Morocco's condition as a whole and indeed marked their own awareness by adopting a larger view of the nation and its comparative place in the world.

Discussions of religious practice and lack of consciousness reiterate colonial-era modernist criticisms of particular Muslim practices, of Sufi *dhikr*, rote memorization and recitation, as mindless repetition that is both animal and mechanical (Hirschkind 2006, 14–16).[12] Like these modernist discourses, they have emerged simultaneously with and presume the efficacy of a modern community of like subjects, potentially literate and reachable by and thus responsible to the demands of the state. They speak to the distinctly modern demands for pious participation—demands for responsibility—that apply not to particular categories of subject, either gendered or classed, but to the mass-mediated "anyone" of postcolonial nation-states' "deep, horizontal" collective (B. Anderson 2006; cf. B. Anderson 1998). On the one hand, there are the newly centralized states claiming sole communicative authority conveyed in putatively transparent, standardized transmissions (Messick 1993, 1996). On the other hand, there is a new kind of responsible subject, ostensibly present to itself, to its community, and to the state—a newly receptive but rational subject of the nation-state who freely obeys and understands its authoritative calls.

The norms of conscious and responsible ritual performance, such as trance rites in a "cultural festival," point up the fear that one's image may reach anonymous audiences and thus suffer "uncontrolled circulation" (Moors 2006, 120; see also Najmabadi 1993). However, these norms encompass putatively public and private life, indeed extending expectations for public piety and visibility into all aspects of daily life.[13] Responsible performance also speaks to the logic of pious communication in Islamic revivalism or "awakening"—a logic of piety *as* consciousness of one's communication. That is to say, in the modernist criticisms that jinn rites violate the ideal practice of Islam as "reflexive," or in Lara Deeb's words, "conscious and conscientious," we can discern not only the demand to *not* mindlessly repeat or reproduce older traditions (as, they argue, their parents did), but to manage one's communicability more generally (Deeb 2006, 5).

This communicative volatility is equally evident in Islamists' and other reform-minded Muslims' ethics that guards against jinns—an ethics of communication and one's body and consciousness as the potential point of transmission. For Islamic exorcists, jinn possession is a matter of impiety and can be eliminated by vigilant prayer and by maintaining continuous ritual purity (*tahara*). Piety concerns the calls (the particular mediating ritual practices) that one receives and transmits, and how one's response produces personhood or its opposite: either one is "conscious and conscientious," or one is reiterating and reproducing as mere automaton.[14] In this sense jinns evoke the problem of controlling one's basic social connections with others, but within particular conditions of blindness to the larger-scale systems through which influencing calls circulate. It is no accident, I think, that Islamic exorcists repeatedly cite one Qur'anic verse, which other experts rarely invoke, asserting that demons (Shaytan "and his tribe") "see you from where you do not see them." It is a position of mass-mediated anxiety that attempts to master a condition of unseeing by locating what is diffuse (as voice) as the condition for its expulsion. Islamic exorcists stage their arrest of jinns and their mass-mediated call to Islam as the countering of prior or distant ritual, or indeed, of state broadcast: as the targeting of circulation that transforms, that is, of *différance*—the movement of communication itself (Derrida 1982).

Elite cultural analysts across mass-media outlets similarly emphasize exposure of what remains hidden but endemically present, in a national society subject to global flows.[15] Here, authorities tend to adopt a uniformly modernist view that acknowledges jinns as a fact (or avoids stating the contrary), but questions the religious propriety and bodily and social consequences of established underclass practices. A repeated theme of television reportage is the fact that saints' tombs still summon jinn-sufferers and their families, with the suggestion that a psychiatric cure would be more humane. If the tone of these programs is pity, another distinct theme more passionately focuses on urban purveyors of sorcery (*sihr*) and charlatanism (*sha'wada*)—jinn mediums, or seers, and fuqaha'—as purveyors of the ritual calls that reproduce jinns as objects of endemic fascination and practice. Sorcery and charlatanism are usually described as a pair, which acknowledges the reality of an evil and otherworldly power (sorcery) in which jinns are often instrumental, as well as its this-worldly social effects (charlatanism) on recipients, clients, and patients.

These programs are exposés in the true sense—an implicit call to awareness of what constitutes a shared Moroccan society but remains hidden to its occupants. The problem is communicative force undisciplined. The call is meant to expose hidden powers *of* circulation in Moroccan society, which begin by experts' relaying the jinns' presence or giving credence to its demands. Proliferating and ostensibly authoritative communicative media exacerbate the problem: fuqaha' and mediums inevitably use cell phones to contact clients, and some even advertise in the proliferating downmarket weekly press. They permit an aura of respectability to which (such analysts comment) even ostensibly intelligent and "modern" people succumb. Thus do the rites and their attendant media resist full integration within the reformist dream of a unified public; mass social belonging should preclude the occult powers of jinns, but in fact it makes their tiniest manifestations matters of national importance.

Mass mediation is, in other words, double-edged. The ongoing constitution of a technologically interconnected space promotes the fantasy of a unified and uniform— which is to say, transparent—sphere, and uniform subjects of communication in which rituals take place. Mass mediation accompanies an ethics of transparent, self-present subjectivity as a condition of modern belonging. In doing so, it highlights difference *as* communication: precisely those communicative rites, both secretive and mystifying, which can now be said to "resist" integration and total oversight. The politics of jinns and jinn curing is thus a politics of difference and the acts of ritual communication that confer difference, deference, and authority.

At the same time, cultural modernists express full-throated support for the state's Sufi revivalism, especially after the Casablanca terrorist attacks of 2003. Mass-market forms of trance, such as the highly popular Gnawa Festival in Essaouira, differ from private rites, namely, in the kind of visceral response jinns produce. Here, the norm is not total loss of consciousness, but "conscious and conscientious" trance—a ritual reception of the call that equates to its consumption as mass-produced signifiers of belonging. Here, rather than differentiate lower from upper classes, trance supposedly stands for a shared Moroccan unity across difference—a hospitality in which subjects control their own communications rather than rely on someone else, literally, to control and support their bodies. That these rites assiduously strip the practices of actual spirits in favor of a putatively shared national Spirit is all to the point: bringing marginal practices closer to center and summoning Muslim masses by way of such practices involves new pious expectations of cultural representation rather than transmission, of conscious consumption rather than unconscious submission.[16]

And yet, cultural representations cannot wholly guard against transmissions that exceed the subjective and social structures upon which representational mediation is founded (Morris 2000; see also Siegel 1997). This concern is shared as much by reform-minded Muslims as by Islamic exorcists, Sufi revivalists, and cultural commentators. My introduction to jinns in Fez were in trance rites presented precisely as cultural entertainment, when in 1998, among the family with whom I lived, Fatima and Abdelqader invited Gnawa musicians to play for me and my visiting sister. Hiring Gnawa musicians not for ritual but for entertainment is typical of more upper-middle-class Fassis, to which my host family aspired. But one of my host brothers was also a drinker and a friend of the musicians with whom he caroused—I had already spent a few evenings with musicians sitting in my bedroom, far later than I had planned, eating, smoking, drumming, and singing—so the family paid little more than a meal—the baraka of a donation. The evening was fun and light—a cultural demonstration for a foreign guest and a party for the family and their friends. In the midst of the drumming and the incense, however, a young Moroccan woman sitting quietly on a low couch lurched forward onto the floor, convulsing and violently snapping her head and hair back and forth. The woman's transformation shot adrenaline through the room. Another young woman fell to her hands and knees, head and hips gyrating. Two older plump matrons quickly stepped forward, looping a scarf around the waist of each trancer, as if holding back horses, trying to keep their heads and limbs clear of one another and the low tables and couches. Another woman lit a stick of sandalwood and wafted it around the women's heads. I was clearly not alone in feeling some danger. But I was more unnerved by Abdelqader and Fatima's eldest son grinning, gesturing to the musicians to play faster, harder. "Go, go, go! *Yallah!*" with the object of pressing the women's bodies harder and harder. I worried that a controlled performance had turned pornographic—in the sense Susan Sontag describes, of the "violation of an attractive body," with the women subjected both to spirits (I presumed) and to the men summoning them (Sontag 2003, 95).

But others in the room did not share my concern. "What is happening?" my sister asked Fatima's daughter, Fatiha.

"They have been taken over by a color," Fatiha whispered, watching.

I would later come to understand "color" to be a circumlocution. Like "the Others" or "them," it refers to jinns that one cannot see but may well be present. "They" occupy what the Qur'an and Muslims call *al-ghayb*, or *'alam al-ghayb*, the Realm of the Unseen Unknown, meaning spiritual truths, which only God sees and knows, and only God reveals (Qur'an 2:2; 2:33). The circumlocution mitigates the risk of attracting jinns to oneself, unwittingly summoning them into one's presence and one's business. Indeed, in Qur'anic and contemporary Moroccan interpretations al-ghayb also surrounds one in a material sense, as that which evades the naked senses (R. Khan 2008, 38). Whereas I was obsessed with the women's vulnerability, Fatiha focused on that sovereign power, summoned by the men's chants, rhythmic drumbeats, iron castanets, and burning incense. I need not have worried, in Fatiha's view. "They" were in control—or more specifically, their power was contained by the shared conventions and acts of the musicians and the older women in the audience. Indeed, the music, incense, and trance eventually "cooled" the jinns, and the women, still dazed, settled on the silk-embroidered cushions.

If my initial impressions and worries over trance were misplaced among the participants in my household, I subsequently recognized variations of my anxiety in the modernist discourse of others, and more specifically in judgments of the loss of control I interpreted as erotic. Certainly my concerns were shared by other friends who expressed some discomfort with the family's habits and also their concerns for me as a Muslim exposed to the rituals both there and during my research. For Mohammed and his wife Najia—who were both struggling middle-class parents in their late forties—trance rites could be at best entertaining, which is to say, a cultural representation before which one stood back, unaffected and self-controlled. But such a posture of control is not guaranteed even in the ostensible privacy of home.

Such behavior might stay in the home. Or it might enter the home from outside. When Mohammed and Najia's teenaged son, returning from school, breathlessly repeated a story that a friend had seen a jinn, Mohammed intervened, cutting off and also discrediting a potential mechanism of repetition: "Enough!" Mohammed said, "that's superstition [*khurafa'*]—all that talk is junk [*tkharbiq*]." Mohammed's extended family did not share his view, however, underlining the stakes of his intervention with his own son. When his cousin suddenly fell ill with an aneurism, his aunt and uncle called one fqih after another to exorcise him, before finally taking him to a hospital. He died there, in Mohammed's view avoidably so, had the family sought medical help immediately.

The stakes, in other words, are life and death, and they rest on what other people are saying elsewhere, on repeated stagings that exceed their frame. Such communications may occur elsewhere, but their effects are felt nonetheless, in some cases unknowingly, as the result of secret exchanges. One of Mohammed's regular acquaintances, al-Hajj (he had made the pilgrimage), warned me against researching jinn mediums at all, precisely for their powers of persuasion. He offered a cautionary tale of a robbery in his home, and al-Hajj's wife's suspicions of him that had only belatedly come to light.

Some years ago al-Hajj traveled for business from Fez to Rabat along the coast. On the first night of his trip, a thief burglarized his home, where his wife and her friend were staying, taking valuables belonging to both women. Al-Hajj's wife paid a *shuwwafa*, a female jinn medium or seer, to divine the thief and locate the stolen property. The seer assured her, "Someone stole and is now traveling, is close to the ocean, is on the beach. It was someone close—from inside—who stole your things." Al-Hajj explained to me that when he returned home no one mentioned the theft. "A year passed and the police caught the thieves, and recovered some of the property. *Then* my wife told me about the theft, and what the seer had said. For *one year* she had suspected *me*. The entire time, *I* was the accused." Al-Hajj looked at me, questioning my wisdom (it seemed to me) in engaging with such people. "Don't waiver—go straight." Later Mohammed would assert rather casually, "If a seer were here now, I would gouge out her eyes."

To whose call does one respond, to which authority does one turn? To the state, or the jinn (speaking through the seer)? To a medical doctor, or a fqih? With what consequences for health and social order and domestic tranquility? For knowing? For controlling one's social environment?

All of these authorities, we should note, claim some knowledge of the difference as unseen—whether internal to the individual body or the spatialized social body. But in al-Hajj's case, his anticipated hierarchy of the knowledge and authoritative knowing was overturned. His wife heeded the jinn's command—extended by the jinn medium—instead of the state's. At the same time the boundaries between the community of the entranced clearly intersected with his, to his detriment; it invaded his home. Which is to say that the medium's act of differentiation, her trance, did not stop with her, but influenced al-Hajj's wife who had been in her own way "entranced." If only the public were there and the private here, but the boundaries are difficult to discern or protect, violated by intersecting calls, all the more dangerous for their secrecy. Mohammed's (unusually harsh) response was to attack the messenger. Al-Hajj advocated personal morality; if one cannot eradicate the call or the caller, one can try to remain immune to its compelling power.

We might wish to see in jinns a demonstration of Jacques Derrida's ethics—of making room for the other as other, as Amira Mittermaier has viewed the place of dreams in Egypt (Mittermaier 2011, 5; Derrida 1995). This is an ethics of mediation as hospitality, and, indeed, Sufi trance rites do make room for some jinns (the mluk, or possessors) as sovereign guests. But the politics of jinns evokes less this skillful hospitable and skillful handling—domesticating—of the difference than its potential and actual failures. These excesses of communication rather call to mind Derrida's emphasis on the irreducibility of difference as it emergences in material processes of mediation and, specifically in this case, in technological reproductions of trance and exorcism rituals. For it is precisely when difference *cannot* be securely mediated and thus domesticated by social hierarchy that it appears as a force of communication—of *différance*, or dissemination—demanding new technological, social, and subjective controls and, above all, new calls.[17]

With repetition, in other words, comes transformation—in new media that newly extend the ritual call. If, in Durkheimian or Geertzian logics, ritual practices were once presumed to stage the call of a relatively closed community to itself—to "tell themselves about themselves" (Geertz 1973, 448; cf. Bell 1997, 67)—technologically reproducible rituals both expand the potential scope of "community" and undermine any assurance of a unified "themselves" who would respond to it. Contemporary jinn rites in urban Morocco habitually circulate across mass-mediated circuits of practice, in which small media technologies and marginal bodies intersect with big media, and unpredictably so. Via mass mediation, ritual mediations of jinns find new significance in occupying national space and discourses—in provoking and questioning the communal norms of a nationally defined Islam. Thus, national discourses of jinns often emphasize the dangers of indiscriminate communication across mass fields, rather than within older hierarchical distinctions and channels. Whereas, on the cusp of modernity, the calls of Islam addressed to the margins once stayed in the margin by virtue of its obedience to the center, Muslims knew that different pious norms applied to different kinds of people. The anxiety of the reception of the jinns—always mediated by material ritual—is thus an anxiety over the call itself at the point where hierarchy is uncertain and does not manage the connections between people.

Who controls communication and the differences it makes and distinctions it marks? Who claims the power of the call and all that it portends for the construction of national authority, and the order and texture of social and pious subjects?

These questions have a distinctly modern history in urban Morocco, to which we turn in the next chapter. They emerged with the influx of Islamic reformist (the modern Salafi movement) and European modernism in colonial-era Fez and with the changing perceptions of underclass Sufi ritual these brought—in particular the public trance rites. Just as fundamentally, these questions took shape with the formation of national consciousness and the simultaneous capacities of mass communications to realize a technologically, if not yet socially, connected "people." They emerged, that is, with the technologization of jinn rites and with the political disruptions of piety and communication that mark the politics of popular Sufism today. As today, such disruptions, and such promises of closure, rendered the practice of the call paramount.

# 2 Nationalizing the Call

## *Trance, Technology, and Control*

The Aïssaoua depart for Meknes three days before the Mouloud. All the Fassi teams follow one another up the *Talaa* to reach the Sais plain. They pass by in a slow procession, one behind the other—and a favorite yearly spectacle it is for Fassis, who crowd the streets as the *foqara* [Sufis, lit.: poor men] pass, while women line the terraces. . . . First to come are the ferocious members of each team, those who received the names of animals at their initiation, and who abandon themselves to all the excesses of their calling. It is utterly repugnant to see them devour a raw sheep thrown to them—its throat cut the moment before—from a neighboring house. In a moment they rush on the gasping animal, fiercely tearing up its flesh, disembowel it, and the pack of human hounds divides the strips of meat beneath blows of the leader's stick. These madmen precede the ordinary *foqara*, who form a circle, howling and dancing as the musicians urge them on with the din of their crude instruments.

—Eugène Aubin, *Le Maroc d'Aujourd'hui*

After twenty-five years of the Protectorate, scenes of such a Morocco should no longer be displayed to the eyes of the world. Rather, one should show the other Morocco, the modern Morocco, that of a new generation, who, being responsible and conscious of their duties and their rights, would never permit such open insults and attacks on their honor.

—El-Meknassi, "La Caméra dans nos murs," *L'Action du Peuple*, June 17, 1937

THE EMERGENCE OF the modern reformist call to Islam, centered in Middle Eastern and South Asian Muslim communities in the late nineteenth and early twentieth centuries, came to fruition in North Africa and Morocco decades later in the early 1920s and 1930s. Similar issues and conditions marked the movement's immediate prehistory and subsequent spread: anger precipitated by European economic and military aggression and outright colonial takeover, and humiliation at the inadequacies of Muslims' collective response. The early modernist Islamic efforts in Muslim states, from Turkey and Egypt to Morocco, focused on institutional, political, and military reforms, the rearrangement of bodies in new formations and orders. This not only meant functional efficacy in military tactics or political negotiations with the new European powers. As Timothy Mitchell has argued, the Egyptian disciplinary efforts held a communicative aim, namely, that individual bodies properly arranged signify a vast, if absent (abstract), order (Mitchell 1988; cf. 1992). For Mitchell, order claimed by newly consolidating nation-states constituted a central Logos, of which the disciplined bodies or built environment were the outer, if wholly transparent, representatives. Put otherwise, the national Logos was the source of the call and command that the disciplined bodies or built environment received and transmitted to both domestic and global audiences.

Not surprisingly, then, as Mitchell and others have demonstrated, Islamic reform movements emphasized both the powers and dangers of new techniques of communication, the telegraph and mass print, through which "the general public—that curious body—could be formed and entertained, and a modern political certainty produced" (Mitchell 1988, 130). For indeed, as prior hierarchies of transmission failed to delimit and control the circulation of messages and commands, these new media presented ambivalent possibilities to perhaps extend and consolidate authority or attenuate and pervert it (Skovgaard-Peterson 1997, chap. 3). Communication appeared as a material force—creating confusions and summoning responses beyond the intentions of the authors and authorities. As Skovgaard-Peterson relates, arguments among established scholars in favor of such media, which won the day, were premised on denying this ambivalent materiality, on emphasizing media as instruments and thus servile messengers. In short, by claiming to reduce material effects of the new media to mere transparency, guardians of old religious (scribal and oral) media reestablished social hierarchy on a new scale.

Islamic modernist movements, which arose contemporaneously with political reforms, also sought to discipline and reorder religious institutions and practices, ultimately in the name of the nation-state (Moaddel 2005; H. Laoust 1932). Their calls were social and cultural as well as explicitly political, as leaders sought to redefine the moral parameters of practice within newly nationalized populations. The media of concern were not only technological or wholly novel. Reform also took seriously the old media—the Sufi hierarchies and structures of ritual communication—that now, in the wake of new transmissions, appeared as material impositions to the hierarchical flow and potential reach of the call.[1] To awaken Muslims from their wooden slumber meant expelling Sufi accretions to Islam's original call—rituals of excess that now compelled new forms of attention. As a writer lamented in the June 3, 1905, issue of pan-Islamist journal *Al-Mu'ayyad*, "The public festivals [of Egypt's Sufis] are no longer but profane celebrations and objects of curiosity for infidels." This lament of Sufi practice was a demand for communicative order, indeed, a call to order—by which authority and hierarchy might extend across necessarily mass political, mass-mediated, subjects and society. In short, religious and political *re*-form required new ways to *per*-form.

In urban Morocco Islamic reformist condemnations of popular Sufi trance arose contemporaneously with a popular Moroccan nationalist movement. In the early 1930s, nationalists sought a symbolic nationwide ban on underclass trance rites to be articulated by the rising political figure of the young sharifian sultan Sidi Mohammed

(Mohammed V); in the same year, nationalists staged a novel national ritual, a "Royal Holiday" ('*id maliki*) in honor of the sultan. These two simultaneous calls for reform were strategically intertwined. On the one hand, Moroccan nationalists sought to expel an old Sufi social order based on separate and distinct practices and pieties for separate classes; on the other, they sought to summon modern Moroccans, "responsible and conscious of their duties and their rights" ("El-Meknassi" 1937, 1). Both calls—the one to expel, the other to summon—signaled Moroccan nationalists' adoption of new communications media and imagined national society of unified and conscious subjects of the call.[2]

## Sufi Nationalists, Colonial Rule

The inaugural issue of the nationalist journal *L'Action du Peuple* based in Fez reported the interdiction "across all of Morocco of the contemptible Aïssaoua and other similar Sufi brotherhoods" ("Une grande réforme sociale," *L'Action du Peuple,* Aug. 4, 1933, 4). Two issues later the newspaper provided further details:

> *L'Action du Peuple* is pleased to announce and record this reform, which constitutes a notable achievement in the social evolution of the Moroccan people. The measure was taken with dignity, energy and firmness, and not without some resistance, by His Majesty the Sultan, to definitively prohibit across all of Morocco, the Aïssaoua and similar Sufi brotherhoods: Hamadsha, Dghoughiyyin, Gnawa, Oulad Milianis, etc., each surpassing the others with practices that are barbaric, savage, and, let us not forget, contrary to the spirit and the prescriptions of Islam. ("L'Interdiction des Aïssaouas et des confréries similaires," *L'Action du Peuple,* Aug. 18, 1933, 2)

The unsigned article condemned the broad swath of underclass Sufi orders. More specifically, the author criticized the groups' practices as "barbaric, savage." They violate the "spirit and prescriptions of Islam." Yet this concern was secondary ("let us not forget"). The object of the reform was social and, more specifically, national. The ban would promote "the social evolution of the Moroccan People."[3]

As with discussions of ritual, reformists' concern with underclass orders was not new; nationalists specifically drew on an early nineteenth-century sermon by the 'Alawite sultan Mawlay Sulayman seeking to regulate the behavior of 'Isawa adepts in particular around the shrine of Muhammad bin 'Isa in Meknes.[4] But times had changed. The problem was not behavior around a local tomb; neither were its consequences a matter of reward or punishment in the afterlife. Nationalists lithographed copies of Mawlay Sulayman's sermon for broad distribution not only within Fez but also in the outlying countryside. They addressed rural and urban underclasses not as members of families, tribes, or Sufi orders, but rather as "destitute popular masses," with the aim to "free [them] from imperial imposters who exploit their ignorance and poverty, who wish only to keep them indefinitely in their current state of inferiority and unawareness and to hinder their intellectual and social emancipation" ("L'Interdiction des Aïssaouas" 2). Young reformists had, in Jamil Abun-Nasr's view, shifted from a "social and political program of the Salafis . . . based on traditionally Muslim arguments, to a modern nationalist movement in its objectives and tactics, [presented] inside a religious framework" (Abun-Nasr 1963, 105).

Nationalist reformists responsible for the publication of *L'Action* were Fez elites connected culturally and institutionally with circles of like-minded nationalist youth in Rabat and Salé in the French Protectorate zone and in Tetouan in the Spanish zone. They were products of early Salafi "free schools" (*madaris hurra*)—misnamed "msids *renovées*" by French officials—but also of French elite educations, including franco-phone *collèges musulmans*. From the end of the Rif War (1921–26) to 1930 especially, they formed local theater clubs and literary circles (Rachik 2003; Brown 1973; Rézette 1955, 68–83), as well as a clandestine nationalist press. In Fez medina, nationalists grouped around two leaders and two institutions. At al-Qarawiyyin mosque-university, Allal al-Fassi preached "*neo*-Salafiyya" (*al-salafiyya al-jadida*); at the Collège Moulay Idriss ("the Eton of Morocco"), students and alumni, led by Mohammed Hassan al-Wazzani, Morocco's first diplômé from l'École libre des Science politiques in Paris and the Arab nationalist Shakib Arslan's personal secretary in Geneva, aligned under the name "Jeunes marocains" (Halstead 1967, 206–8). Both threads of reform were conservative in their demands, rhetorically aligning themselves with the Protectorate, rather than seeking anticolonial independence, and calling repeatedly for France's faithful guidance of Morocco toward modern statehood, as outlined in the 1912 Treaty of Fez (Comité d'Action Marocaine 1934, xii–xvi).

These efforts were radical enough, however, and beginning in 1930, with nationalists' protest of the Protectorate's "Berber Policy"—a policy placing so-called Berber customary law (*'urf*) under French legal authority rather than Islamic courts—Protectorate "pacification" focused increasingly on urban rather than tribal unrest. The "Berber Dahir" protests, although attracting global attention, were nonetheless limited in scope and effect, and subsequent efforts turned to the development of a nationalist press. Not surprisingly, the French Protectorate had effectively blocked an independent local press, with Moroccan-owned Arabic papers prohibited and a French cosignatory required to publish any French-language journal. But nationalists (now organized as a nascent political party, the Kutlat al-'Amal al-Watani [Fr. Le Comité d'Action Marocaine; Eng. National Action Bloc]), drew on international connections.[5] With the aid of Shakib Arslan, the group enlisted Jean-Robert Longuet, grandson of Karl Marx, to edit the francophone journal *Maghreb* in Paris in 1932. In the same month in Rabat, Mohammed al-Salih Missa, an Algerian national employed by the Protectorate as a court translator, established an Arabic literary journal, *Majallat al-Maghrib* (The Maghrib journal). Although officially unaffiliated with nationalists (and thus free of the restrictions they suffered), the journal soon found a compatible nationalist readership across North Africa and in multiple cities inside Morocco (Baida 2005). During the following summer in Fez, Mohammed Hassan al-Wazzani began editing *L'Action du Peuple* [Ar. *'Amal al-Sha'b*, or The people's action]. Like the Parisian *Maghreb* the paper appeared in collaboration with French socialists, evading Protectorate suppression by enlisting George Hertz to sign as the paper's publisher. In both cases, however, the French leadership was nominal. Moroccans researched, penned, and edited the journals, with some adopting pseudonyms (Halstead 1964).

The nationalists' critique of Sufism was part of the larger project, of course, one seeking parity of educational and agricultural resources, unity of language, and modernization of Morocco's nascent industrial sectors (Comité d'Action Marocaine 1934). But it was a passionately held critique, directed at fellow nationals and Muslims as much as at the colonial policy of supporting popular religion. Attacking Sufi practice at all might have implicated nationalists' own religious affiliations and authority. The Wazzani family were shurafa' and enjoyed both the social prestige and political sovereignty afforded under the sharifian state. Other nationalists were devout Sufis, and Allal al-Fassi would go so far as to suggest that Morocco was predisposed to salafiyya reformism by virtue of its Sufi heritage of piety and rigor (al-Fassi 1954, 111). Rather, the substance of these critiques accented the immense class differences within the sharifian culture of urban Morocco; as Jacques Berque has observed, nationalists were themselves elites, and their critiques did not put that at risk so much as focus on highly public practices that distinguished underclasses as such.

Sufi orders in urban Morocco incorporated men and women across social classes; the range of ritual acts was also vast, from orderly recitation of a saint's prayer (*wird*) and mild states of ecstasy in dhikrs to public and private trance rites among women and bloody self-mutilation and sacrifice among subaltern men. Subtle differences among these concerned the saint whom they venerated. But more stark differences of practice marked fundamental sociocultural and economic distinctions. As Geertz (1979, 158–59) observed in Sefrou (Fez's way-station in overland trade), from upper class to lower, the Sufi orders and the crafts comprised a spectrum of symbolic cleanliness or dirtiness. Similarly, in early colonial Fez, elite and upper-middle-class orders, such as the Tijaniyya, Wazzaniyya, Darqawa, and Kattaniyya, included religious scholars of the Qarawiyin, rich merchants of the overland import trade, as well as artisans handling silk, gold, and other luxury goods (Le Tourneau 1987 [1949], 606; Salmon 1905, 101).[6]

The underclass orders that provoked concern, the 'Isawa and Hamadsha, were, like other orders, composed of an internal hierarchy. 'Isawa members included elite shurafa', or male and female descendants of the founding saint, middle-class adepts, literate bearers of the saint's special prayers. But the vast number of adepts came from the lowest of the Fassi social classes, those who occupied the dirty end of the spectrum: blacksmiths and butchers, basket and cord weavers, peddlers, public furnace and bath workers, as well as more menial laborers, freed slaves, and the waves of refugees from the starving countryside (Brûnel 1926, 51–52).

The object of nationalist concern was specifically the public rituals of the underclasses, not least the spectacular trance rites of the 'Isawa, described with a combination of fascination and horror by European visitors to North Africa. In the "*frissa*" (meaning *prey* in dialectal Arabic) adepts took on the character of animals, ripping apart sacrificial sheep or goats given by devotees as tribute to the founding saint Muhammad bin 'Isa and his descendents.[7] It was extremely popular in Fez, being held as many as thirty times a year by an individual team (Brûnel 110).

For Fassi audiences trance fascinated as a visible moment of madness contained by social hierarchy. Within the order trance was strictly limited to followers of the saint, rather than to shurafa' or to middle-class adepts.[8] The rituals indeed staged a sharifian immunity to trance; although the entranced adepts were said to attack the color black, shurafa' would wear the color without fear, striding serenely amidst the chaos as sovereign centers to the demonic margins. In that vein, 'Isawa trance partook of larger ritual parameters, for example, providing a climactic end to the procession of other Sufi orders during the citywide celebration of the Fassi saint Moulay Idriss (Le Tourneau 1987, 303). It fit within the larger urban socioeconomic hierarchy defined by spiritual receptivity to one call or another, that is, by a structure of ritual practices appropriate to and effectively summoning one class rather than another. Indeed, the rituals confirmed and solicited support for the sharifian order: they summoned crowds, providing a larger circuit of exchange by which the Sufi orders distributed the blessings or baraka of saints to the broader urban population (Crapanzano 1973). Trance, in short, enacted the sharifian call by which the sultanate's margins were brought into communication with the center.

Thus, not surprisingly, while these practices had previously garnered criticism, they were hardly the focus of prenationalist reform efforts. For the mainstream of fin-de-siècle Muslim thinkers in Fez, the major religious disputes of the moment concerned, rather, the elite classes: the legitimacy of the sultan Mawly 'Abd al-'Aziz himself (described as "Christian" for his violation of sharifian sanctuaries) and the ostensibly heretical claims of Muhammad al-Kattani, a sharif "attempt[ing] to redefine the parameters of shari'a and innovation, of orthodoxy and heresy" (Bazzaz 2010, 56). As Bazzaz notes, the most extreme rituals of the 'Isawa and Hamadsha orders warranted little concern. One could surmise that these rituals, unlike the claims of al-Kattani, did little to threaten the social or political order, and one would be correct.

That nationalist efforts to ban the rites in the late 1920s met with significant resistance in Fez from both participants and spectators signals the rites' embeddedness within the sharifian hierarchy of the city (Brûnel 1926). That these efforts emerged *only* in the late 1920s is no less indicative, however, of the shifting circuits of power and communication under colonization. The problem was not a matter of doctrine, practice, or class alone, but rather of rituals' communicative effects as calls. Nationalists were responding to the colonial appropriation of the rites and of the sharifian call itself, which these rituals extended and gave social force.

## Cameras and the Colonial Gaze

Nationalists' reference to "imperial imposters who exploit [the masses'] ignorance and poverty" reflected a truth of French policy of indirect rule, and more specifically its international pledges as colonial "protector" to respect and preserve the 'Alawite "Sharifian State's" (*al-dawla al-sharifiyya*) "religious customs." This approach of course thoroughly instrumentalized religion; far from novel, it drew on France's strategic appropriation of and "obsessive interest in the political dimensions of spiritual cartography" in Algeria, grounded in the ethnographic studies of *Bureaux Arabes* (Clancy-Smith 1994, 39; cf. Clancy-Smith 1990; Berque 1957). So too for French Protectorate technocrats in Morocco, buttressed by the ethnographic *Mission scientifique au Maroc*, the "religious throb of the crowds' soul" offered a mysterious but useful lever of social order (Le Glay, cited in Rivet 1988, 148).[9] In practice this meant reframing old rituals and generating new stagings in new media as well. On the one hand, Protectorate officials supported Sufi rites under strict police control for colonial political and economic benefit, including a burgeoning tourism industry.[10] At the same time, they reimagined and restaged trance rites for touristic consumption in place. A 1932 Christmastime "exhibition d'Orient" was a typical event; staged for ease of local display, and photographed for consumption in the metropole, it featured an "Aïssaoua snake charmer" and "les Gnaoua des Mesfioua" standing on a large square stage decorated with local carpets, facing the audience in an orderly row ("Un Noël de joie dans les palmes," *L'Afrique du Nord Illustrée*, Jan. 7, 1933, 12). For colonial observers, these stagings could simultaneously permit social control and fantasies of authenticity, as a "raw [inédit] and decidedly local spectacle" ("Un Noël de joie," 12).

Such stagings were not simply photographed, but rather staged to be photographed. Other rituals, including large-scale trance processions, could not be so thoroughly documented, but nonetheless took on new life in the photographic medium—a point of particular concern for nationalist critics of trance. Building on familiar Orientalist scenes (Eugène Delacroix's "*Les Fanatiques de Tanger*," painted during his 1837–38 tour of Morocco, and European tours of 'Isawa adepts from the 1867 Paris World Expo onward), Protectorate functionaries now reproduced trance images in *cartes postales* and business and cultural magazines (*Maroc Illustré, France-Maroc*).[11] A regular feature in *France-Maroc* (the trade paper for the Protectorate Bureau of Commerce) titled "La Vie sociale" repeatedly covered the underclass Sufi orders, authored in several instances by André Schelcher, a prior director of the Service des Beaux-Arts, charged with identifying and restoring Morocco's architectural heritage (Abu-Lughod 1980; Rabinow 1989; Wright 1991). Articles included at least one photograph, usually several, and in one case a montage of fifteen. Other pictures of trance rites dotted the magazine's empty spaces.

A typical dispatch from Fez entitled "Le Joyeux Miloud" (*France-Maroc*, Nov. 21, 1920) reproduced the procession of the 'Isawa in black and white with brief captions: "Aïssaouas carrying the debris from the sheep they devoured," and a "group of jackals covered in blood." The article addresses both the performers ("filthy and howling . . . seminude men and women") and the crowd of spectators ("out in their finest to watch them"), with the spectators' "insatiable" appetite matching the savagery of the spectacle. Indeed, this was the point; insofar as trance rites attract a crowd they were not the excesses of a small minority, but rather the defining feature of Moroccan society and Moroccan difference: "We should note that these poor devils, most of them poor and hideously ugly, are a huge success in the public eye [*sur la place publique*]. Everyone is out in their best to watch them, and the Europeans who come for the processional would, in seeing them, need a hundred eyes to believe that they are not dreaming" ("Le Joyeux Miloud," 50).

As Mitchell suggested in Egypt, colonization involved staging and display of bodies in space. But rather than respond to the call of Order, the crowd—adepts and audience alike—here responded to a mysterious call beyond the comprehension (but not the control) of colonial observers. The author acknowledges both the mystery and the colonial penal mechanism: "Like a police report, [this article] neglects the feelings and the religious beliefs of the crowd—the mystery that lives under the appearances" ("Le Joyeux Miloud," 52). That mystery may be invisible, but it submits to surveillance; in responding to it, the Moroccan underclasses—wild animals all—submit as well. Moreover, this defines Moroccan society—"la vie sociale" of France's colonial subjects. If historically such rites had been disciplined within precolonial sharifian hierarchies—the call circumscribed by those upper classes who remained immune to it—now the colonial French occupied that position, claiming the call by controlling its reception and reproduction.

## *The Problem of Trance: Technologizing the Call*

Nationalists were well aware of colonial tactics and complained specifically of the damage such representations brought to Morocco's international reputation. But technologization of the rituals also contributed to their reinterpretation of the rituals as acts of communication. Now, if that call had in fact gone awry under the colonial gaze, this merely supplemented an older process of miscommunication and perversion of the original call. *L'Action*'s author, likely Mohammed Hassan al-Wazzani, began a longer meditation on the problem of trance by affirming the piety of the 'Isawa's namesake, Muhammad bin 'Isa (Sidi M'hammed Ben Aïssa), along with the "primitive founders" of the "similar brotherhoods" *despite* "acting in the margins of Islamic dictates" ("L'Interdiction des Aïssaouas" 2):

> Sidi M'Hammed Ben Aïssa lived in Meknes under the reign of Mawlay Ismail and passed for a saint. His activities were given over to reciting prayers, which he taught his disciples. One of them, Sidi Ben Rouayène [Abu Ruwayin], attended the death of the "Master" and having acquired, he believed, indubitable proof of the latter's sainthood, fell to wandering the alleys of Meknes, beating a tambourine and chanting the following phrase to whoever wished to hear it: "Rejoice! My master and yours has died a good Muslim." The use of the tambourine and, later on, the flute, as indispensable accessories to the recitation of the prayers, became itself de rigueur; it is thus posterior to the death of Sidi Ben Aïssa. (2)

The point is clear: if Bin 'Isa responded to God's call with piety and transmitted that call to his disciples, then that transmission only subsequently went awry with his death and public circulation of his call. In one sense this could be Abu Ruwayin's fault, but the author emphasizes rather the force of reception, that is, the anonymous reception of the death announcement by "whoever wished to hear it." *L'Action* imagines a situation that originates with no one in particular and leads to no one's control.

This is still a small phenomenon that does not explain the "popular masses." However, the effects of circulation continue to grow well beyond the original call to now include women and jinns and even to constitute an institutional, recognized structure of authority and authorial repetition—"sainthood":

> With the passage of time that distanced the adepts more and more from their master and made them forget his teachings, the cult of the "Saint" and the legend attached to it acquired some importance. Unfortunate and extravagant innovations followed the same course, enriched by the superstitions of women, by imaginary visions of demons and deliberately encouraged by the sad initiatives of the "Children of the Shaykh" [that is, *awlad al-shaykh*, or *shurafa'*] desirous of securing, by abnormal means, the exploitation of ignorance and human stupidity that followed from it. (2)

By now, the author might say, it is not God or his pure medium, Bin 'Isa, who calls, but an excess ritual and cultural structure, from which the author distances himself by quotation: Bin 'Isa is not a Master, but a "Master," not a Saint, but a "Saint"; the shurafa' are not Children of the Shaykh, but "Children of the Shaykh." The author's objectification of cultural terms *as* terms is important; it emphasizes these cultural symbols as repeated and recognizable sources of the call and thus as that which summons up "destitute popular masses." There's more. If the "Children of the Shaykh" signal an excess structure that summons, there are also strictly colonial and modern technological structures at work:

> Before the establishment of the Protectorate these exhibitions of the possessed [*énergumènes*] were almost exclusively limited to the city of Meknes, where Sidi M'Hammed Ben Aïssa is buried and where, moreover, they hadn't the pomp they have today and were not propped up as official festivals. The other urban and rural centers of Morocco produced only undeveloped demonstrations [*manifestations larvées*]; rare were those who wished or had the means to make the pilgrimage as far as the tomb of Sidi Ben Aïssa. [But] with the establishment of the Protectorate the means of transport multiplied and the bloodthirsty throng of Aïssaoua, each year more reckless, could stream into the unfortunate city of Meknes, pillage the cemeteries and perform before a shocked humanity the most repugnant and most shameful demonstration that history has ever recorded. (2)

*L'Action* suggests that before the Protectorate and apart from Meknes, the 'Isawa rites (here called "demonstrations") were merely "larval" in form. They were already in motion, according to *L'Action*, as communicative performances; only then did Protectorate policies of "propp[ing] up" the rituals bring them to maturity. This supplemental

power links cultural practice with technological infrastructure: the French Protectorate's transportation network of railways and roadways, which, rather like Abu Ruwayin's
tambourine, is indiscriminating in its effects. Before, 'Isawa performed in small, separate, local settings, but now the transportation network precipitates the mass.

Again, trance rites were always repugnant. But if this now naturally appeared as
a function of their *communicative* excess, the reading nevertheless took place in the
present—after supplemental forces, intentional or technological, had made them so.
From within the dominant logic of communication, and more specifically technological communication, the problem of trance is the communicative power, the call, that
precipitates it. Piety is to be defined by virtue of one's responsiveness to a call and, in
responding, one's further reproduction of its structure.

But piety is also being defined nationally. Trance in its technological form, as nationalists well know, has national implications. There is now national infrastructure; purely
local—indeed marginal—practices now amass to form a national practice. As such
they matter to the nation. Indeed, the nation's reputation is at stake on a global stage.
*L'Action's* critique sees the 'Isawa masses communicating something to be recorded by
"humanity" and "history." That is to say, trance sends a message to others. As "demonstration [*manifestation*]" the rites anticipate or compel their further travels as image:
"Beyond the Aïssaoua who head toward Meknes the number of sadistic spectators has
risen steadily. The zeal of tourists and filmmakers has transported the image of these
ignominies beyond the hills and seas to all four corners of the world, as if it were the
present style in our country and defined the evolutionary social stage of our people" (2).
Here the global view is explicit; in the view of the newspaper, which comprehends other
nations' views, trance rites are bad publicity.[12] From this perspective the communication
that forms the "bloodthirsty throng" continues with momentum. Energy seems to be
unleashed, transferred from the 'Isawa to those who, sadistic and zealous, take pleasure
in Morocco's humiliation. The problem of trance is the lack of awareness or self-presence
that it induces and, more specifically, the lack of awareness of a message and call those in
trance are conveying through new global circuits of communication.

At the same time, this unconsciousness does not implicate just one Sufi order or
even the underclasses. Indeed, whatever hierarchy should be in place, setting upper-
class nationalists over underclass masses is reversed, such that the underclasses send
powerful messages and do so, by virtue of the camera and its captions, in the name
of *all* Moroccans, the Moroccan People. The sultan's prohibition would thus not only
"free the destitute popular masses from imperial imposters who exploit their ignorance and poverty," but also "rehabilitate the international reputation of Moroccans"
now bound to one another technologically, if by nothing else.

## The National Call to Conscience

What kind of national subject and what kind of national society did Moroccan nationalist reformists wish to see? In complaining of colonial representations of trance, one

nationalist author, "El Meknassi" (quoted in the epigraph to this chapter), spoke of another Morocco, an appropriate representative: "Rather, one should show the other Morocco, the modern Morocco, that of a new generation, who, being responsible and conscious of their duties and their rights, would never permit such open insults and attacks on their honor" ("El-Meknassi" 1937, 2). The "new generation" is modern; being modern means being "responsible and conscious of [one's] duties and their rights," which is to say aware of one's place within contemporary social exchanges—responsive to the calls to which one must respond. Being modern also means grasping the effects of communication that exceed one's control.

The theme of consciousness runs throughout. Al-Fassi, with other salafi reformists of the day, articulated the aim of a society purified of trance rites and of the state of mind—superstitious, ignorant—that such ritual practices induced. Al-Wazzani's writing on trance emphasized the problem as one of communication and its subjective and social effects—again ignorant masses, but forceful in their communications. It is a problem, as I have characterized it, of the uncontrolled call of a cultural structure that, being newly colonized and technologized, now exceeded the prior social order of its recipients. Much as modern urban observers and media theorists defined the 1930s' urban masses by their heightened receptivity to messages, nationalists viewed trance as a kind of contagion, and entranced masses as hyperreceptive, hypercommunicative bodies. For nationalists, consciousness would require management of the call by way of receptive bodies, that is, by eradicating trance rites.

The new nationalist journal, *Majallat al-Maghrib*, offered a different suggestion. In an article criticizing the annual gathering or moussem (Ar. *mawsim*, pl. *mawasim*) of 'Isawa, a letter from Mohammed bin Yahya al-Sqalli is quoted:

> This year I estimated the number of participants gathered at the rendezvous at no less than 200,000. If we further estimate the expenditure per person, including the round-trip transportation, at 100 Francs, we reach a total of 20 million Francs (20,000,000).
>
> This is a significant fortune, which, if spent on science and charity, would surely bring great benefits. But "Indeed, [O Muhammad], you do not guide whom you like, but God guides whom He wills." ("Mawsim al-'Isawa," *Majallat al-Maghrib*, July 1933, 9; Qur'an 28:56)

Al-Sqalli notably condemns the 'Isawa's rituals, drawing on the Qur'an for at least rhetorical support, but without reference to ritual practices. The language is wholly modern: the event is discussed only as the formation of the numerical mass, that is, abstracted and quantified, as Simmel identified the modern metropolitan and money-based consciousness (Simmel 1950b). Like al-Wazzani's views of trance, al-Sqalli sees uncontrolled communication, or more precisely, systematic communicative waste, to be recuperated for social benefit.[13] If al-Sqalli neglects explicitly to criticize Bin 'Isa's followers for their lack of consciousness, he does so, nonetheless, implicitly. The followers do not see themselves as part of a larger system and mass body. They no doubt experience themselves as a part of a crowd, but they lack consciousness of their own massness and thus their impeding of the nationalist mass movement.

Other nationalist reformists explicitly emphasized popular Sufi followers' unconsciousness, and thus irresponsibility, as a result of receiving a detrimental call. Ritual trance meant abandoning consciousness in response to a ritual structure of baraka and its dissemination; the nationalists would stage a countercall to awaken masses to their responsibility *as* a coherent and self-conscious mass. Newsprint was assumed to be a viable and effective medium for stimulating national consciousness—"the life of the press," the first issue of *Majallat* intoned, "is the best indicator of the life of the nation" (*Majallat al-Maghrib*, July 1932, 9). Indeed nationalists' criticisms of trance appeared simultaneously with *Majallat*'s and *L'Action du Peuple*'s calls—"a call to reform" (*da'wa li-l-islah*) is *Majallat*'s phrase—in the name of "society" (*mujtam'*), "the nation" or "homeland" (*al-watan*), and "the general public" (*al-'umum*). To be sure, both journals addressed educated people (in either French or nationalist "free schools") literate in French and familiar with these newly minted Arabic terms of political discourse (Stetkevych 1970, 25; Asad 2003, 19).[14] In the journals' views, however, to be educated did not yet mean to be fully conscious of one's place and duty to these new sociopolitical bodies.

An early issue of *Majallat* was themed the "duty of the wealthy to the nation [*al-watan*]," its aim being "to publically address the wealthy" regarding the needy (Sept. 1932). One article quotes the Egyptian poet Ahmed Shawki: "The sustained life of nations rests on their good morals; when they lose those morals, they vanish." It continues, echoing a prophetic hadith: "Indeed, whoever harms one [person], harms the group of which he is necessarily a member and a part, for each [person] calls upon the other [*yatada'i*] according to that community's nature and its relationships" ("May God unite us, by our morals, in total unity," *Majallat al-Maghrib*, Sept. 1932, 6). To be moral, as El Meknassi also describes it, means responding to others' calls and ultimately to the collective call of the nation. The newspaper claims to voice that call, or what amounts to the same, to alert readers to the fact that they are called.

But the wealthy are not responding: "Why has the community shrank from obeying our call [*ihjam al-umma 'an talbiyat da'watina*]?" the author asks (4). It is a matter of awareness, but also, like the poor and entranced, of responding to the *wrong* call, one defined by cultural habits. The wealthy of Morocco today are profligate, spending on worldly pleasures and self-aggrandizing acts rather than sacrificing, or responding to the needs of others. The author points to saint veneration: "They spend generously for the tombs of the dead and spare little for the shacks of the living" (4). The wealthy of Fez—the city named as the Idrissid Capital (*al-'asima al-idrisiyya*), the exemplar of specifically *sharifian* morals—are criticized in particular; the author exhorts them, with a Qur'anic reference, to think of divine reward for generosity, in which God "'raises high your esteem [*raf'a laka dhikrak*]'" as God raised high the prophet Muhammad's name (6; Qur'an 94:1). The wealthy (*shurafa*') of Fez may be the bearer of an older ethical standard, but today they are ignorant. Their failure to respond comes "not from miserliness, nor incapacity," but from a lack of understanding of the value of dedication to the "general public [*al-ʿumum*]." (The term is distinct from an older term for "commoners" [*al-ʿamma*].) Wealthy Moroccans' "sacred responsibility" to this body is, in the author's view, the basis for collective awakening and progress:

> Truly exertion for the good of public works [*fi sabili al-mashariʿ al-ʿumumiyya*] is the first condition for awakening and the strongest foundation for progress. Indeed exertion is the first duty we teach the self [*al-nafs*] to accept. We Muslims will not cast off our gloom but by our charitable giving and sacrifice of money. Now, to lead the nation to this sacred responsibility we should seize all opportunities and means to demonstrate sincere dedication to society [*ikhlas li-l-mujtamʿ*]. (5)

The author is calling readers (in Sufi terms, al-nafs) to new morals appropriate to a new community by which, in receiving it, readers may expect divine reward as well as a national good. Indeed, one's divine reward is defined in terms of national recognition, that is, as public esteem. God's reward is a national reward; God's call is the nation's call. Just as God calls, so must the nation, and the author is teaching readers to recognize the origin of the call in the "general public." Readers must learn to respond to a call the origin of which is no place in particular, thus requiring a new kind of awareness. To recognize that you cannot see the origins of what calls you is to develop consciousness of this new, distinctly mass-mediated, national community.

## The Sultan's Call

That advocates of these novel sociopolitical forms sought inspiration in the perfect unity of the "al-salaf al-salih" surrounding the prophet Muhammad is no accident. In Islamic modernist imaginary, both the ideal modern society and that of the Prophet's day comprised subjects abstracted from particular social relations and refitted in unified responsibility to God and the Prophet's all-encompassing call. It is a very different image from the explicitly hierarchical society into which nationalists were born, the society of the "Old Turbans" and unquestioned Sufi orders. Just as crucial, it reflects a society defined by different circuits of communication, mass-mediated technologies that, for all their distancing, could nonetheless (by nationalists' logic) bring people into perfect unity, as "*the* People."

To be clear, however, Moroccan nationalists did not disavow sharifianism itself. Indeed the movement's explicit embrace of the sharifian sultan turned nationalism from a largely elite enterprise to a popular call. *Majallat al-Maghrib* and *L'Action du Peuple* converged around a tactical call articulated in 1933, to which, they hoped, Moroccans across classes and social differences would respond: a new "Royal Holiday" (*ʿid maliki*) in 1933, publically celebrating the then-sharifian sultan, Sidi Mohammed (Mohammed V). In the July 1933 issue of *Majallat al-Maghrib,* in which al-Sqalli's critique of the ʿIsawa appeared, "A Moroccan" (the pseudonym of Mohammad Hassar, a young Salé nationalist involved in the Berber Dahir protests) criticized the Protectorate's treatment of Moroccans ("Hukumatuna wa-l-ʿiyad al-islamiyya" [Our government and Islamic holidays], *Majallat al-Maghrib,* July 1933, 12). The article recalled the Protectorate's founding legal responsibilities to respect the religion, including the religious holidays, of the Sharifian empire. But it recommended an additional celebration as well, to recognize "the day of His Majesty's ascension to the throne as a national holiday [ʿ*id watani*]" ("Hukumatuna," 12). The editor, the Algerian national, Mohammed al-Salih Missa, added a note of support, praising the sultan for ruling over Morocco in an "Era of Renaissance and Reform, by which [the nation (*al-umma*)] has become one heart, with love for his High Honor, and one tongue praising him and supplicating God for his protection and providence" ("Hukumatuna," 12).

The idea of celebrating the sultan provoked much interest, and the September 1933 issue of *Majallat al-Maghrib* ran with an explicit call for the "Royal Holiday [ʿ*id malaki*]," outlining not only the specific steps to be taken in preparation for the event but also its significance for Morocco's developing unification. *L'Action du Peuple* quickly joined the call, and articles detailing and heralding the holiday (La Fête du Trône) appeared in the two journals for the next six weeks.

Like the sultan's interdiction of underclass orders' ecstatic rites, the "Throne Holiday" would involve the nation as a single unified body. The nationalist press emphasized the customary quality of the new holiday it was creating, its fidelity to tradition, while also calling attention to its novelty—Morocco's "new era" under Sidi Mohammed. Designed as a set of multiple rallies held simultaneously in major cities across Morocco, the holiday would require equally national organization and publicity—a call for participation ("La Fête du Trône," *L'Action du Peuple,* Nov. 4, 1933, 1). Certain hierarchies would be required in order for the call to reach a popular audience. *Majallat* recommended the formation of a "national council of notables to communicate in official circles [*mukhabarat al-dawaʾir al-rasmiyya*], forming a program of celebrations, and then spreading the word [*idhaʿa*] among the general population [*al-ʿumum*]" ("Al-ʿId al-malaki" [The royal holiday], *Majallat al-Maghrib,* Sept. 1933, 3). Although no particular media were assigned to the project, a variety of technologies would serve in the celebration itself.

Local organizing committees were thus formed in numerous cities, including Fez, Meknes, Tangier, Marrakech, Casablanca, and Oujda, and a central committee composed of delegates from the local committees was formed in the colonial capital city of Rabat. In keeping with nationalists' alignment with Protectorate power, the organizers actively solicited French support, with the Rabat central committee inviting the still-new Resident General Henri Ponsot and Grand Vizir Hajj Mohamed El-Mokri to accept jointly the honorary title of Committee President ("La Fête du Trône," 3). There were limitations certainly, including an unscheduled visit of the Resident General Ponsot to Paris (committee members feared potential political fallout from celebrating in the absence of the colonial authority), and an attempt to cancel the event by the unpopular Pasha, the city executive of Fez. Nationalists also noted a lack of preparation time; *L'Action* had envisioned the holiday as "at once an imposing popular demonstration and an official grand celebration," with the decoration of markets and city streets, the closing of shops, and "popular rejoicing" ("La Fête du Trône," 1). But the new holiday could risk delivering less "pomp" than was promised.

The celebration nevertheless succeeded in individual cities and on a national scale: in Marrakech charitable foundations (*mu'asasat khairiyya*) succeeded in obliging the wealthy to aid "the nation," providing new clothing for three hundred poor folk and feeding many hundreds more. In Salé the Pasha Sbihi opened his home to visitors, serving cookies and tea. Even in Fez the absence of official recognition (and much wind and rain) did little to dampen spirits. Shops and nationalist free schools (*madaris hurra*) closed. The editorial committee of the *L'Action du Peuple* provided tea and cookies and sodas to "Young Tarbouches" and "Old Turbans" who crowded "two to a seat!" onto the terrace of Boujeloud Garden Café (*L'Action du Peuple*, Nov. 25, 1933, 4). These two previously divided generations unified in reciting a new anthem, "Sultan al-Shabab" (The sultan of the youth), honoring Sidi Mohammed, and as audiences and agents of new technologies, they looked on at portraits of the sultan and little Moulay Hassan, dressed in a French scouting uniform (both previously printed in the nationalist press) that adorned the balcony, while a phonograph played Middle Eastern and North African hits. The celebration closed with more than two hundred attendees signing a telegram of support addressed to the sultan.

By all measures, the call succeeded. Despite the short time available for organization, nationalists managed not only to stage their loyalty and love for Sidi Mohammed but, more fundamentally, to summon the masses across disparate urban centers.[15] Following the holiday, *Majallat al-Maghrib* opened with a lengthy paean to the sultan, penned by the head of the 'Alawi shurafa' (*naqib al-ashraf al-'alawiyyin*), Mawlay Abd al-Rahman bin Zaydan, and featuring hand-drawn European portraits of 'Alawite rulers, and photographs of Sidi Mohammed, including one in the classical posture of the royal audience, on horseback, with a parasol ("'Id julus sultan al-bilad" [Holiday of the sultan's enthronement], Nov. 1933). An additional editorial expressed gratitude to "the Moroccan people as a whole for its acceptance of and service to the call [*talbiyatihi li-l-nida'*]," and to other nationalists as well, including the editors of *L'Action du Peuple*, Mawlay bin Zaydan ("Ada' wajib" [Completing your duty], Nov. 1933, 12). The prominence given the 'Alawite lineage and to the gratitude expressed to the Moroccan People for responding to the call repeats themes of the holiday itself: the reproduction of sharifian ritual (the royal audience) in newsprint, camera, and multiple simultaneous crowds to summon a new and dispersed national body. Of course, the new ritual also reiterated the Protectorate's own deployment of religious custom; not surprisingly, it soon received legal recognition by the colonial government, which praised the holiday as the continuation of a "tradition established by the ancient Sultans," with "the double merit of satisfying the natives and of celebrating the benefits of the French Protectorate" (*Bulletin Official* no. 1149, Nov. 2, 1934, 1124). That is to say, the nationalists' construction of the Throne Holiday, while maintaining a sharifian Sufi ritual tradition suitable to French rule, assimilated the sociopolitical conditions of mass consciousness.

## Nationalist and Reformist Legacies

In 1934 nationalists could still celebrate basic elements of colonial rule. Foremost among these was the spread of sovereign power over the territory—the "pacification" of the tribal "lands of dissidence" (*bled al-siba*)—by French military forces in that same year. *Majallat* vigorously supported the end of tribal "dissidence" (*siba*), and the "extension" of Sidi Mohammed's "effective authority [*nufudh*] over the farthest reaches of the kingdom." It was, after all, a step toward "national unity . . . the importance of which cannot be overstated" ("Nazra 'ama 'ala al-'am al-madi" [Overview of the past year], *Majallat al-Maghrib*, April–May 1934, 5). In John Waterbury's words, "The admistrative authority of the sultan [was now] coextensive with his baraka" (Waterbury 1970, 35).[16]

This very desire for the extension of power and coherence of the nation marked the specificity of the age newly centered on communication "as a system of thought and power and as a mode of government" (Mattelart 1996, xi). As Armand Mattelart has described the "invention of communication" in European thought—"both the unleashing of movement and the consolidation of the center with the support of the periphery"—so too did nationalists' intervention refigure the Moroccan sovereign's power, his baraka and its effects, a particular kind of call, one simultaneously reaching a homogeneous territory. In conjunction with this redefining of political power in modern mass-communicative terms was also a very different staging of the sultan's baraka and presence—one marked by his *absence* from the reverent audience.[17] Sidi Mohammed's absence would not, after all, be incidental to the holiday, but rather would be a constitutive feature of simultaneous celebrations in multiple cities (cf. Gelvin 1998, 276). A national territory made possible by long-distance communications demanded such new stagings of baraka, power, and presence (absence) that recast the old sovereign-subject (or master-disciple) relations of proximity and distance.

Yet, if the Throne Holiday showed the possible appeal of the young sultan as a national symbol, his stimulating effects on urban crowds in Fez soon exceeded the limits of colonial tolerance. On May 10, 1934, the sultan's official visit to the city resulted in a popular outpouring. Writing in *L'Action du Peuple*, al-Wazzani described the novelty of the scene. An "imperial motorcade" replaced the ordinary sharifian procession on horseback; crowds of more than fifty thousand—nearly half the estimated population of the medina—rippled with waves of "indescribable enthusiasm": "From everywhere resounding shouts and cheers arose: 'Long Live the King! [*Vive le Roi!*] Long Live the Crowned Prince! Long Live Morocco!'" (al-Wazzani 1934a). Although al-Wazzani was clearly invested in the occasion's success, perhaps even overestimating the crowd's size, other sources concurred that "Fassi annals have never witnessed a comparable out-pouring [*affluence*]" ("Les résultats de l'enquête d'un temoin impartial," *Soir Marocain,* May 12, 1934, 3; cf. Halstead 1967, 55–56). Something new had arrived. The notables of the medina paid tribute to the sovereign, but "the Youth," a new social category, greeted him next, which went against protocol. Jacques Berque described the composition of the crowd itself as new: "They included all sorts of incongruous elements, with noth-ing in common, apparently, but the disruption of their social background: bourgeois who had lost caste, dispossessed and uprooted peasants, unemployed artisans. A few years earlier these individuals in revolt against tradition, these outsiders, would have found shelter in the silent fold of mysticism. Now they were welcomed by working-class movements and political parties" (Berque 1967, 104–5). Berque rightly notes the liminality of people uprooted and seeking new modes of belonging. We should equally emphasize that the "welcome" of the dispossessed into new social structures rested on a call, an incitation and implantation of desire to turn toward the new.

If Protectorate officials had successfully claimed the force of the conventional Sufi calls, they described the effects of this call as insurgent chaos. Rumors flowed that the French flag had been torn, the Pasha beaten up, and the sultan himself assaulted (al-Wazzani 1934b). On the premise that the sultan faced grave bodily danger, officials cut short his visit. For Protectorate officials, the nationalist press had summoned the crowds—specifically *L'Action du Peuple,* its office in the medina adorned with photo-graphs of Sidi Mohammed and Moulay Hassan (the future Hassan II):

> The balcony [of the office] was decorated with Sharifian colors and . . . two issues of the journal, with portraits of His Majesty and the Crowned Prince even posted. Well before His Majesty's procession more than two hundred people of all conditions, and especially the youth, had amassed, waving flags and chanting hymns in honor of the sultan and Islam. . . . When the sultan appeared the applause roared, *vivats* erupted, and the monarch was engulfed in the youth who acclaimed their faith in him and waved their flags. ("La vérité sur les événements de Fez," *L'Ordre Marocain,* June 2, 1934)

In the following days the Protectorate prohibited publication of *L'Action du Peuple, Maghreb,* and two new Arabic-language nationalist papers in Tetuan, *al-Hayat* and *al-Salam.* From "the events of May 1934" until 1937, no nationalist press was permitted in the French Zone (Rézette 83, 102).

Uncontrolled communication threatened both the nationalist project (as rumor) and the Protectorate (as hyperreceptive crowds). The receptivity of the crowds to Sidi Mohammed was not limited to one city (Fez) or to one section of the city (the medina); rather, it reflected a mass movement, in which crowds could imagine their own simultaneous replication elsewhere. For the Protectorate the "events of Fez" also highlighted the powers and potential dangers of the now-codified Throne Holiday: "Rare were the ancestors of Sidi Mohammed—in fact he may be the only one—whose

Vizirs were able to order the commemoration of such an event *on the same day, in every city of the Empire*" (Mohendis 1935, 92n2; emphasis in original). The new holiday's power derived just as much, however, from its repetition of old rituals. The Throne Holiday was, in short, a "new Mawlid" (Mohendis 1935, 92).

This assimilation of old feelings into new forms helps to explain the Protectorate's acceptance and then regulation of the Throne Holiday. In defending the sultan's May 1934 visit to Fez and, more specifically, in defending the crowds' enthusiastic reception, al-Wazzani cited the same Sufi culture: "[At] the diverse shrines of Fez . . . the people have the most absolute right to approach the Sultan to kiss his hands or the hem of his garments in homage and to partake of his 'baraka'" (al-Wazzani 1934b, 2).

Al-Wazzani's writing of baraka as "baraka" suggests both a continuity and a transformation in older ritual affect and effect; it is a citation of an old effect in a new medium. But in drawing on a term dear to Protectorate powers, al-Wazzani also elided nationalists' mass political strategy. Indeed, al-Wazzani's and other nationalists' advocacy for the sultan's centralized power may be best understood as a desire to mass mediate baraka. It is baraka reduced to its most elemental, that is, to a call that controls the underclass Muslims it summons; it is likewise a call that, unlike older ritual calls, should produce not trance but rather consciousness of oneself as part of the new Moroccan mass body. In short, medina elites recast their prior doctrinal and upper-class disgust with the ecstatic orders in terms of communication. The production of the sultan as the singular source of the call accompanied nationalists' refiguring of the Sufi trance rites as its impediment—as the destructive communication of other calls provoking other political and social effects.[18]

It may thus be surprising that trance rites so thoroughly disparaged by nationalists would return in 1990s and 2000s Morocco in technologically disciplined forms, akin to their colonial staging, to further stage a Sufi nationalist call. The more immediate legacies of the nationalist intervention are perhaps less surprising. If nationalists and the colonial administration competed with opposing calls—or, rather, competed for the power of the sharifian call—by independence its power would exceed both groups. While al-Fassi's Independence Party drew immense support in the 1940s and early 1950s, in the prelude to independence and in its wake, nationalists found their position largely diminished; it was to the king's call, rather than nationalist intermediaries', that Moroccans responded en masse. Now Sidi Mohammed's presence to his subjects largely bypassed print for radio and photographic forms of mediation, just as it bypassed political parties for putatively direct rule. His face, if not his voice, was iconic, made recognizable through widely disseminated and enthusiastically received photographic reproductions, the display of which, for Moroccans and French alike, now came to signal a proliferating nationalist sympathy.[19] In the summer of 1953, French Protectorate officials' exile of Sidi Mohammed and the royal family to Corsica prompted mass visions of the sovereign's face in the full moon (Berrada 1992).[20]

By early independence, a popular illustrated magazine polled readers about how they wished to see Sidi Mohammed posed, in traditional or Western garb (Lacouture and Lacouture 1958). At the same time, laws regulated the circulation of his image and the mode of its display in press and public spaces. In a word, the monarchy sought to recuperate its own call, its own technological extension of baraka. The power of that call provided a framework for the monarchy's religious legitimacy and power in the postcolonial period, just as it does today.

# 3 Our Master's Call

## *The Apotheosis of Moroccan Islam*

COLONIAL-ERA MOROCCAN NATIONALISTS reinterpreted the powers of popular Sufi (sharifian) rituals to foreground their material properties as media. More precisely, placed in the context of mass-mediated communications by which national subjects could be summoned, Sufi rites appeared in new light as the call of competing media, generating demonstrably different forms of piety and society: on the one hand, exploited masses; on the other hand, a coherent public, "the Moroccan People." Yet the distinction between these two has remained tenuous, both for postcolonial nationalists, such as al-Wazzani, who sought a democratic alternative to the authoritarian monarchy, and for postcolonial theorists of "Moroccan Islam." What scholars have described as "Moroccan Islam" explicitly evokes a mass public unified—enthralled, or indeed, entranced—by a culture of saint veneration, and expanded to a national scale.[1]

But if theorists have acknowledged the ritual and communicative power of saints by which a public forms—Clifford Geertz describes baraka as "spiritual electricity" (1983, 136)—they have neglected to describe precisely how technologically mediated rituals have summoned such a public into being.[2] I do so in this chapter by examining a watershed event in postcolonial Moroccan politics: the Green March (*al-masira al-khadra*) of 1975, when King Hassan II summoned 350,000 men and women to walk en masse and unarmed into then-Spanish occupied Western Sahara to reclaim the territory for the Moroccan nation-state. Hassan II's command, which marchers describe as *"nida' sidna"* ("the King's Call," literally "Our Master's Call"), succeeded in reclaiming the territory, though not without continuing conflict. More importantly, his call provoked mass enthusiasm and at least temporary national unity across social and political differences; it remains a critical current reference point in the state's assertion and enforcement of national unity and "spiritual security" (Arif 2008; Kaitouni 2010).

Examining the Green March sets the stage for post–May 16 calls of Islam by mapping out the distinctly national identity of the religious field in which these acts of the call take place (Tozy 1999). The tremendous power of the event itself, its continuing significance to political life for Moroccans as mass-mediated subjects, helps explain the predominance of the specifically sharifian, national call of Islam in contemporary Fez. It helps us grasp the social stakes of aligning oneself with or against the dominant Sufi call in urban Morocco, of belonging to the imagined community or not. At the same time, it establishes specifically mass-mediated conditions under which that call was established. In the Green March we see a regime (like the Arab-Islamic regimes in Syria, Egypt, Iraq, and Libya) at the height of its technological and social control of Islam's call, of national television and radio not yet perforated by digital communications or small media, nor yet fully challenged by an Islamist countercall. These historically specific media conditions, rather than symbolic power alone, give credence to claims of a specifically national "Moroccan Islam," while at the same time examining what is required for its consolidation and maintenance.[3]

## "My Dear People"

On October 16, 1975, at 6:30 in the evening, the king of Morocco, Hassan II, addressed the nation via state television and radio regarding Morocco's claim to sovereignty over then Spanish-occupied Western Sahara. The address followed more than a year of extraordinary diplomatic action by Morocco to secure recognition of its claim, including sending left-wing emissaries to convince European leftists of Morocco's rights, and public and secret negotiations with Mauritania, Spain, and Algeria. Hassan II's address referred more immediately to that morning's judgment by the UN International Court of Justice (ICJ), which acknowledged the historical allegiance of Saharan peoples to the ʿAlawite Sultanate, the ancestors of Hassan II, but nonetheless denied Morocco's historical sovereignty (Vermeren 2002, 69; Dessaints 1976, 460). Sitting in an ornate chair, in an elegant blazer, before a bank of microphones and speaking to his "dear people" (shaʿbi al-ʿaziz), Hassan II, with punctuated vehemence and godfatherly calm, demanded a national act: "It is incumbent upon us to carry out a green march, from the north of Morocco to the south, from the east of Morocco to the west. My dear people: We must stand as *one man*—orderly and systematically [*bi-l-nizam w-al-intizam*]—to reincorporate the Sahara, and to revive our sacred bond with our brothers in the Sahara [*li naltahiq bi-l-sahara wa li-nasil al-rahim maʿ ikhwanina fi-l-sahara*]." Looking straight ahead into the television camera he called upon 350,000 Moroccan men and women from among "the people" to carry out an unarmed mass civilian seizure of the Spanish-occupied territory to establish Moroccan sovereignty.[4]

The response was enthusiastic; within two days 350,000 Moroccans registered at local state offices, as an estimated 500,000 to two million in total attempted to do so, necessitating a lottery to choose marchers (Weiner 1979; *Lamalif* 1975, 6).[5] The result-ing swift mobilization prompted intensive public negotiations with the UN and Madrid, with France and the United States secretly pressing a weakened Spain, roiled by Gen-eral Francisco Franco's lapse into coma, to cede the territory to Morocco (Mundy 2006; Hughes 2001, 239). Meanwhile Hassan II's Ministry of the Interior coordinated the oper-ation, assembling food, water, tents, and communications outposts, and commandeer-ing private trucks and scheduling trains to move 350,000 marchers from thirty cities across Morocco down to the border towns of Tantan, Tarfaya, and Tah (Weiner 1979, 27–29). To the east around Mahbès, Moroccan and Algerian forces clashed as Morocco attempted to seal the border (Howe 1978, 84; Mundy 2006). One week later, on Novem-ber 6, Hassan II addressed the marchers via state radio, ordering the advance of two blocs of marchers into corridors hemmed in by Spanish forces. The marchers advanced only a short distance beyond the Spanish borders, but the king's strategy worked; Madrid disavowed its previous support of Saharawi independence and agreed to partition the Western Sahara between Morocco and Mauritania. Hassan II, still broadcasting from Agadir, commanded the marchers to halt and return to their home cities.

As much as Hassan II's gambit astonished domestic and international political observers, yet more shocking was the intense collective enthusiasm which Hassan II's address stimulated across the nation's geographic, class, and political spectrum (Weiner 1979, 31). Zakya Daoud, editor of the leftist *Lamalif*, and target of Hassan II's political repression, wrote approvingly of the "unbelievable mobilization" his call precipitated: "people screaming, shouting, singing, and climbing onto the trucks with their red and green flags flapping in the wind" (Z. Daoud 2007, 272). "A national frenzy seized the entire country," *Lamalif* wrote, as unbelievable and awe-inducing as film or fable: "Technicolor production or images from an ancient tome!" (*Lamalif* 1975, 6). Marchers and other firsthand observers, foreign and Moroccan alike, found similar difficulty comprehending the event (Hughes 2001, 240). A veteran French journalist described the euphoric mass of marchers as "the most astonishing spectacle" he had ever witnessed—akin only to Gamal Abdel Nasser's funeral (Desjardins 1977, 88; cf. Hughes 2001). Politically, however, Nasser's funeral at least made sense, whereas this did not. Given Hassan II's authoritarian repression, the masses' and even the left's enthusiastic response was unfathomable, a kind of mass delusion (Desjardins 1977, 82).[6] Abdellah Laroui, attending the march with Daoud and likewise supportive of it, described a psychic transformation: "a moment of the Moroccan people's conscious-ness," a "psychological reality," "an epic" (M. Daoud 1992, 147, 148). He too struggled to analyze it: "The Green March was not only a political act; it was something else. But what? It's not easy to find adequate qualification. Using a formula familiar to French thinkers since Charles Peguy, we will say that it was also a *mystical* act" (M. Daoud 1992, 148, emphasis in original). Finally, Laroui said, the Green March was a *moussem* (Ar. *mawsim*), or saint's festival, "comparable to those organized by Sufi orders, which brought together members from all corners of the country" (M. Daoud 1992, 158).

"Mystical act" or Sufi "moussem." Laroui's comment echoes the French colonial official's assessment of the Throne Holiday as "the new Mawlid." Certainly the monarchy infused the event with religious symbolism. Hassan II evoked a Qur'anic concept of sacred familial (blood) connection (*silat al-rahim,* a connection by womb) to describe the primordial belonging of Saharans with Moroccans. He chose to term it the *Green* March to signal its Islamic significance and provided copies of the Qur'an, along with Moroccan flags, to be held aloft at given points in the march (Combs-Schilling 1989, 325; Entelis 1996, 59; Hammoudi 1997, 20; Rollinde 2003; Waterbury 1978, 416). Yet what struck observers were the scale and scope of the event, as well as the patterns of social and political participation.[7]

Here rather than reading the symbols themselves, we must examine the mass media through which participants of the march received the call and felt compelled to respond. These communicative conditions matter to a call addressing audience members not as Muslims, or as members of a region, or even as objects of bureaucratic control, but as a national body: "the people"—"My Dear People [*sha'bi al-'aziz*]" in Hassan II's preferred terms. In this case the very historically contingent possibility of this communicative exchange provides rather more explanatory power. Hassan II's simultaneous call to listeners and viewers, the technologically reproduced gifts of recognition: a photographic portrait of Hassan II himself, ID cards and medals signifying one's belonging—all of these sought to summon a body of mass subjects emergent only from nationalists' stagings of the monarch onward. Prior to mass politics in Morocco, who could be worthy of such an exchange with the king? Certainly not commoners (*al-'amma*), a category that, in any case, utterly fails to translate "mass."

The Green March invoked a particular kind of relationship between the king and his listener: a call and command as invitation to exchange, that is, as gift of spiritual and material recognition. And it did so on a *mass* scale, drawing on the familiar discursive figure of "the People" as a national collective recognized by the king. The Green March's success—the enthusiastic mass response it sparked more than anything—rested on the promise of their fusion: if the material conditions of the call were technological, it promised to sustain older cultural modes of contact and closeness. The call, we could say, was baraka technologized, the promise of its person-to-person transfer on a mass scale. This was popular Islam and Moroccan Islam properly speaking: the Islam of "the Moroccan People."

## Talking with Marchers

Relatively little has been written by or about participants in the Green March. A small number of short memoirs, published individually and under the auspices of the monarchy, have given voice to a few state-affiliated elite participants. Scholarly treatments of the march generally draw on these but especially on Hassan II's recollections (Hassan II 1976). His orders for the march specified that 350,000 Moroccans volunteer, among them 43,500 government ministers, local leaders—*caids, shaykhs, muqaddams*—doctors, nurses, ambulance drivers, and youth scouts. Middle- and professional-class people—"lawyers and Casablanca businessmen" (Z. Daoud 2007, 274; cf. Laroui 1992) volunteered, as did well-known political figures (Aherdan 1976). Urban and rural underclass Moroccans, however, constituted the tremendous mass of volunteers.

The marchers whose stories I draw on here, twenty-one men and five women, belonged to this latter group. Most had registered for the march in Fez or Sefrou, with one each in Taza, Errachidia, and Rabat. At the time of the march, the two youngest among them (Na'ima, a woman from Sefrou, and Hussein, a man from Fez) were sixteen years old; the oldest (five men from Fez and two men from Sefrou) were thirty years old. As of July 2008 all lived in the lower-class and lower-middle-class neighborhoods of Fez, including the medina, and in recently built neighborhoods to its north. (None lived in the wealthier Ville Nouvelle or in the middle-class villas growing southward toward Sefrou.) In the words of one, Abdelhafid, other marchers he knew are now "very poor, living in shantytowns"—or they are dead. The most educated men among them completed secondary school—the women were all illiterate. These two men, Si Sbai and Si Alawi—the respectful "Si" for "Sidi," the rough equivalent of "Sir," signals a degree of status—are perhaps the closest to the middle of the struggling middle class in Fez. They and three other men are formally employed—three as doormen, one at a tourism company, and one as an assistant at a government office (*baladiyya*). Four men are retired (two bereft of pensions owed them); the rest, including all the women, are unemployed or underemployed, a common situation in Fez's weak official economy based largely on tourism and artisanal crafts.

Marchers described themselves in 1975 as poor and unemployed or struggling on their single salary to support siblings and parents. Si Sbai was the sole breadwinner for his ill father and ten siblings. Si Alawi was marginally better off, but of his seven family members who marched, three were illiterate. Reflecting on their motivations some thirty-three years after the fact, interviewees were candid about their material need and their anticipation of a reward—a house or a shop (*mahal*)—for reclaiming a wealthy Spanish colonial territory, and especially the city of Laayoune. Yet, Si Sbai and Si Alawi both viewed such motivations as "uneducated, unaware," and lacking "conscience" (*damir*). Si Alawi said of his own family's uneducated volunteers, "they expected to go and be given everything." Middle-class Moroccans have made similar comments to me during my fieldwork—that marchers thought the Wadi al-Dhahab, Golden Valley, was in fact gold. The implication of these criticisms is that the uneducated poor were motivated by self-interest rather than by some higher ideal that the march ostensibly demanded.

But we must consider the cultural, historical, and technological circumstances in which simultaneously hundreds of thousands of poor Moroccans—and not just elite "notables"—could anticipate a reward or a gift from the king—"to be given everything"—for their service. Underclass marchers emphasized this sentiment of service to the king, referring to material motivations and yet, without contradiction, to having "responded to" or "obeyed" (*talbiya*) the king's call, that is, "our master's call" (*nida' sidna*), as one complies with a command or obliges an invitation. Mohamed H. said, "We were illiterate people who said 'Yes' to *Sidna* [bows his head]." Mohammed W. said explicitly, "I went there for two reasons: because of the king's call, and also to stay and live there." These and similar comments made clear the logic of the event as something involuntary, a call to duty— "I did my duty [*adit al-wajib*] and returned," Abdelhafid said—but no less meaningful for being obligatory. That meaning derived not from the king's call alone, but from marchers' sense of a collective who were addressed by the king and who recognized the call's value. As Si Sbai put it, "When the king calls you—you have to obey him. [It's] the nation's call." That duty to obey derived from the collective to which one, in responding, belongs. The king *and* the nation were calling. The call is both a command and recognition of one's belonging.

Middle-class criticisms that reduce marchers' motivation to idiocy or greed miss the broader significance of the call as a promise and material gain as *gift*, that is, as recognition of Moroccan underclasses' more profound national belonging. The power of recognition explains why marchers I interviewed had kept their identity card and medal from the march. Something beyond money was at stake; Sanae, a daughter in my household, and I both felt marchers' longing for it pervading our interviews. Sanae said, "They think we're with the state [*dawla*]." I disagreed, saying I had been clear about the nature of the study. She specified, "It's been thirty years—and they're still *waiting* for the state." Indeed. The point to emphasize again is the mass-mediated and mass political nature of this expectation.

## The People

> We serve you great nation
> Our blood for your glory,
> As time passes.
>
> To protect the homeland
> To pave the way to your glory,
> We serve you, the masses.
>
> We serve you dear Morocco,
> Protect you at any cost.
>
> We serve you my Great King,
> Your soldiers, with our arms aloft.
>
> —from Mohamed al-Bidawi's "The Nation's Call" (nida' al-watan)

Hassan II's televised and radio broadcast announcement of the march, and its subsequent use throughout the execution, constituted a "powerful media campaign for the national cause that enflamed the country" (Vermeren 2002, 70). That such a campaign was possible, as a simultaneous broadcast to different cities and rural regions, that is, a national address, was relatively novel in 1970s Morocco. In the decade preceding the Green March, and especially the first half of the 1970s, Morocco had witnessed a "veritable blast-off" (Jaïdi 2000, 64) in communicative technologies and production; registered TV sets increased from around 8,000 to around 450,000, spreading at the same time from urban Morocco to newly electrified areas of the countryside. This television infrastructure added to radio capacity already in place (which, given the low cost and high mobility of transistor sets, already numbered in the hundreds of thousands, if not millions).[8] The monarchy monopolized radio and televisual media—political parties relied on print media—particularly through Radio-Television Maroc (RTM), directed by the Ministry of the Interior as a political mouthpiece of the state (Jaïdi 2000, 59). The success of the Green March and the "primary role" of TV and radio further bolstered these infrastructures, as the march signaled to RTM officials the benefits of new, more powerful broadcasts (Akhchichine and Naji 1984, 213, 201). Tellingly, the march persisted as a theme in the state's subsequent media planning (Akhchichine and Naji 1984, 304).

The televised and radio-broadcast messages disseminated by the state in the announcement and buildup to the march, including Green March anthems commissioned by the state, reiterated themes of sacrifice for mass belonging, and of mass belonging as the condition for the king's recognition. Indeed, Hassan II's initial call to the nation specifically invoked a history of mutual recognition between the throne and "the People." If such a mode of address suggests intimacy, his notion of exchange emphasized the immediacy of spiritual fusion:

> My Dear People, you and the throne have exchanged, you have exchanged inspiration [*tabadaltum al-wahi*]. Your taking a firm stand has forever inspired the throne to rise up. And the feelings and judgments [*taqyimat*] of your kings have forever inspired you to action. Thus Dear People, each [of us] traces the path for the other, the path of dignity, victory, and the reassertion of Moroccan pride. And now once again we will exchange inspiration and dreams.

Hassan II's images of the people's exchanges with the 'Alawite sovereigns are of a spiritual unity; exchanging "inspiration" (*al-wahi*) evokes immaterial or immediate communication, even "suggestion" (*iha' thati,* autosuggestion) and electronic "transmission" (*wahin* as "radio transmitter"). That immateriality has, of course, a political message, a message of perfect communication merging the king with the collective will of the people as a unified rather than disparate body. But while Hassan II described the relationship as timeless and ongoing, he also invoked the specific historical ritual of connection between the People and 'Alawite monarchs—the Oath of Allegiance, *bay'a*—and its specific historical medium of connection, namely, writing. The oath in Morocco, he explained, was "unique among Muslim nations, [in being] never only oral, but always written," and marked by a "special stamp [*tab' khass*]." The mention of a written stamp (as opposed to "inspiration" or ephemeral orality) highlighted a medium that, as Hassan II then elaborated, brought tribal leaders into contact with princes and kings, hand in hand and face to face. Moreover, he said, the *bay'a* was extended to those "unable to read and write" the document itself, by virtue of an intermediary, the state notary. These are historical details, he said, but, "for those interested in further study, I can charge the Minister of Culture with providing a public lecture, and a series of articles on the subject."

The mention of the written seal invites listeners to imagine the established power of writing and hierarchy, of the seal and of social stratification. It evokes the power of the state notary who would mediate commoners' exchange. But it does so in a broadcast medium that supersedes and also circumvents it. Historically the seal of the sovereign, the *dahir*, granting recognition to tribal or Sufi or corporate leaders, was guarded carefully as a literal mark of distinction (Berque 1955). Its value accrued by its singular rarity and even cult status. Here, however, all members of Hassan II's audience could imagine participating in the elite tradition. Indeed, a few minutes later in the same speech, Hassan II specifically noted that marchers would receive their own mark of recognition:

> My Dear People . . . I have provided the means, and ordered governors in each province to open offices from tomorrow on to register men and women volunteers. I will be among the first to put my name on the record of volunteers. I will proudly avail myself of a Participant's Card [*wariqat nakhib*], and I will be proud to have a Volunteer Card [*bitaqa li-tatawa'*] for the march to recover the Sahara. This is the real crown, the real scepter, that will last for my children and my grandchildren: the stamp of nationalism [*sibghat al-wataniyya*]—no, I say, the stamp of God [*sibghat Allah*]! And whose stamp is better than God's?

My interviewees carried and showed me their identification cards (ID). Two other marchers I have met in Morocco have done the same. In one sense the ID or the medal responded to the call for an interview, that is, it marked one's participation. But this is very much the point: the ID *proved* something and in so doing held a power to compel recognition even from a stranger (and foreigner). It is this recognizability that matters, binding one's own face to a general system. It is not absurd then that Hassan II claimed that the ID, as the stamp of nationalism or of God, was "the real crown, the real scepter." It suggested a replication of the great written stamp, the "special seal" of the 'Alawite throne—as if each person, having responded to the king, received his or her own "special seal," and so held that contract with him. It is a striking, and utterly modern, image of royal recognition granted simultaneously to hundreds of thousands of individuals.

The price of this recognition is abstraction, as the ID (like the census), in the service of the nation, discerns not particular human beings but serial subjects whose recognition derives first from their incorporation into the mass. It is significant then that Hassan II's call to action emphasized numbers, enumerating quotas of marchers from each region (306,500), as well as the government officials, doctors, and functionaries needed to guide and care for them (43,500), the number of trucks (7,813) and liters of fuel (2,590) needed to transport them, the tonnage of food (17,000) and liters of water (63,000) needed to nourish them. This focus on scale invited marchers to think in terms of a mass collectivity, indeed to realize that collectivity in a physical act. This mode of enumeration and abstraction was celebrated in the Green March anthem, "The Nation's Call" ("nida' al-watan"), quoted above. Like other anthems broadcast on state television and radio in the wake of Hassan II's call, this one reiterated themes of mass national unity—of the people as a unified body of atomized individuals—under the king's command: "350,000 parts of your people [*atraf sha'bik*], oh My Lord/ Women and men from all parts of your Kingdom." Middle-class Moroccans have alerted me that Hassan II chose 350,000 marchers because the number equaled Morocco's annual birth rate (cf. Weiner 1979, 26). Each marcher was, in other words, expendable. Yet here it is celebrated. The repetition of "350,000" in the song evokes the massiveness of the event and, more particularly, the grandeur of the marchers as a *mass body,* a composite of similar and even interchangeable subjects, rather than diffuse and disconnected individuals: 350,000 "parts of your people."

The abstraction of a person into serial quantities would make little sense prior to modern census-taking (B. Anderson 2006, 168); it correlates not at all with the old sharifian social hierarchy and exchange where spatial proximity was social power, that is, where distance and proximity indexed social rank (Hammoudi 1997, 68–75). Potentially anyone can hear the call anywhere, and this very abstraction from particular personhood to "anyone" is the virtuous condition of national consciousness and belonging that "Our Master's Call" celebrated. To respond to that call meant identifying oneself not with one's social qualities (of name, family origin, age) but with its mass addressee, "the people"—that is to say by becoming a number—"one digit in an aggregable series of replicable" nationals (B. Anderson 2006, 169). The adoption by participants of this rhetoric of mass-mediated belonging, that is, the saturation of popular by official rhetoric, suggests that indeed volunteers desired this mode of identity and recognition—that the social and even psychological force of the march was inseparable from this mass-mediated identification.

Laroui's description of the march as a *moussem,* a sacred pilgrimage, is thus apt. For Moroccans who responded to the call did so by transcending ordinary social bonds for a national *communitas.* To be sure, this is hardly unique to Morocco. Indeed, Hassan II's call illustrates one of Benedict Anderson's arguments, drawing on Victor Turner (1967), that national consciousness emerged not only in simultaneous reception of messages but in shared conditions of liminality or "exodus" from prior social identity (B. Anderson 1994; B. Anderson 2006, chap. 4). James T. Siegel similarly has linked Indonesian nationalism to liminal conditions of pilgrimage and the broader collapse of social referents, permitting the temporary suspension of social differences and the "passage" to "the People" (2000b, 2000c).[9]

To compare nationalisms is not to suggest, however, that conditions of pilgrimage and liminality are generic. Hassan II's call struck a specific cultural nerve, the anticipation of recognition grounded, as Hammoudi argues, in sharifian ritual. Yet the material (literal) striking of that cultural nerve was forged by mass mediation: by mass communication and the discourse of "the people."

## "We Heard Our Master's Call. We Got Goosebumps."

The presence of mass media was reinforced as I asked volunteers how the announcement of the march "reached you" (*kif waslat lak . . .*). Most heard Hassan II's address on the state radio, listening with others, and some heard and saw it on television (RTM). One interviewee, Abdelhafid, described hearing it on TV and from the local officials (*muqaddams*) at a government office in Sefrou where he worked. Bahia, a woman from Fez who first said she had heard the announcement on television, later clarified that she had heard about it "from others who had seen it on TV." In a way that emphasized the feelings of direct connection, several interviewees described hearing about the march "from Sidna" and only clarified on my follow-up question that they meant "from the TV" or "from the radio."

Hearing the call generated for some a sense of excitement and risk. Abdelhafid explained:

> I first heard His Majesty's call—may God give him victory—I was doorkeeper at the *baladiyya* [local government office]. I felt courageous. I was the fourth or fifth to sign up.
> How did the call reach you?
> Out of love for "God, Country, and King [Allah, al-Watan, al-Malik]"
> I mean, how did you hear about the march?
> From the officials [*muqaddamin*] at the *baladiyya* and from the TV. I went directly to register. As soon as I heard His Majesty's call, I went.

Abdelhafid's response to my first question was telling; his receptivity to the call simply assumed the logistical means of hearing it—from officials and also from the television. The latter medium guaranteed this to be no local command, but "nida' Sidna"—a call originating with the king and addressed to the nation as one. This extraordinary element made responding a matter not of obedience, but of courage. There is no doubt that some marchers were ordered to march, for example, in the place of a local official's son. Yet my interviewees did not describe their experiences in this way. Indeed, responding to "our master's call" meant *defying* authority. For Abdelhafid courage meant the risk of *losing* his job at the local government office. His family, dependent on his employment, argued against his volunteering. "They said, 'If you go, you'll lose your job, your salary.' I said, 'Who's going to cut it—*Sidna*?'" Abdelhafid's brashness is unmistakable: responding to the king, he felt, gave him immunity from all other authority, including family and his superiors at the government office. Likewise, numerous women joined the march against patriarchal and parental authority (Weiner 1979, 31). Na'ima was sixteen and thus ineligible to march, but she defied her mother and brothers and fooled the local officials. She said nothing at home but dressed in a robe (*jellaba*) and high heels to register. Her mother was none the wiser, nor did Na'ima or her mother know that the brothers had also signed up. Na'ima and her siblings would later meet on the march, the national body providing the new medium of familial connection.

Such acts were not personal rebellion against authority in general, but rather rejections of one set of authorities for the command of the king and the nation. As Na'ima said, "I saw other people going, so I went too. It made me happy—glorifying *Sidna!*" To feel the immensity of the collective was thrilling for some: "When we heard the King's call, *we got goose bumps,*" said Mohamed S. from Fez. The presence of that collective is suggested by marchers' common description of their response to the call, like Mohamed S., in the first-person plural. Kamal spoke of seeing the speech on television, after which, he said, "We got up and volunteered with firm determination [*nudna bi kul hazm*] in the name of His Majesty. We participated with a feeling of happiness and joy! [*bi wahid al-frah wa bi wahid al-surur!*]." In Kamal's hometown of Sefrou this enthusiasm was not unique. He estimated that some six hundred people lined up at the town office to volunteer. Mohamed H., also in Sefrou, heard and went, like other people: "We heard about the march from the king. We went to the government office to register. We went [at once] like other people [*mshina bhalna bhal an-nas*]." Hussein described being out of school and jobless with his friends in Fez: "We were home and heard *nida' Sidna* on the radio. We all went to register. King Hassan was dear to us, so we went to obey our master's call [*talbiyyat nida' sidna*]. We volunteered all together, all enthusiastic, all one heart!" Moreover, Hussein said, laughing, "We didn't even know what the word *march* meant! Even if we didn't know what was happening, we were one heart!"

Obedience here does not equate to sheer coercion. Violence alone fails to explain the intimacy with the king my interviewees felt in receiving his call for volunteers. It explains neither the collective enthusiasm nor the specifically *national* feeling of belonging that marchers (and observers of the march) described. Rather, obedience entailed responding to "our master's call" and more specifically to entering the liminal space of "imagined community" (or imagined communitas). This imagined community was mass mediated, both by virtue of the technologies of the call and the discourse of the people and their "direct link" to the king. More speculatively, this community was liminal to the ordinary mediating structures of life and authority—of home and, for those who had it, employment—and perhaps even of the state officials themselves. Such a national discourse of immediacy is not simply eliding the structures of its own power (Mazzarella 2004), but rather highlighting their suspension: "a genuine experience of linkage *despite* social bonds" (Siegel 2000b, 282, emphasis mine). One seeks recognition not on the basis of who one is, but by virtue of a capacity to sacrifice it for the mass, to join the people.

In the Desert

Nearly three weeks passed between registration of volunteers and the beginnings of the movement. Volunteers were called suddenly by the town crier (*barrah*), some taking money with them and clothes, others not.[10] Marchers were loaded onto trucks and taken to Marrakech and from there to the border. In Tantan, Tarfaya, and Bettah, marchers made encampments, women in tents pitched in the middle of a circle of men's tents. Hassan II's plan included the division of groups by prefecture and then into sections of twenty-five people under the supervision of one leader chosen by the Ministry of the Interior. (Si Sbai, because he was literate, was such a leader.) Groups were given bulk rations of water, wheat, oil, and sardines to be distributed by group leaders.

The presence of the feared Interior Ministry as well as the separation of marchers by locale reiterates the monarchy's successful tactics (surveillance, divide and rule) for maintaining power. Marchers likewise described police beatings as necessary to keep order and as punishment of those who violated the communitas. Indeed these tactics did not hinder collective feeling or the occasional intermingling of regional groups. Rather, marchers described the elation and euphoria of collectivity: "There was a feeling of love (*wahid al-mhabba*) between people. . . . We were brothers and sisters," as Abdelqader, from Fez, put it. This unity felt particularly intense in moments of collective voice and vision, in some cases through religious symbols—"Everyone was chanting, 'La ilaha ila Allah! Muhammad rasul Allah!'"—including, on Hassan II's orders, hoisting the Qur'an as a gesture of nonaggression. In some cases people felt unified through drumming and singing pop music by Jil Jilala ("Laayoune, My Eyes" [laayoune 'ayouni]), whose song in honor of the march had received significant airtime on state radio (Weiner 1979, 32). In other moments, marchers chanted anthems broadcast prior to the march, such as "Masira Khadra":

> The valley, our Master [*Sidna*], is my valley.
> Safely we go and return.
> With us are God, the Prophet and Qur'an!

The content of the chants is critical, suggesting both a cultural/religious unity and a mass-mediated one (through pop music, anthems, and so on). But so too is the sheer power of chanting itself, what Jacques Berque described as "the imponderable elements" of nationalism: "mass enthusiasm, the incantation of Arabic words, the intoxicating effect of shouting, that collective hysteria which sometimes escapes all control, and yet that faith in its leaders, that exciting sense that someone has 'arisen' who will govern these forces and give them point" (Berque 1967, 82–83). The king's call stimulated and indeed governed these forces; the effect was at once to loosen ordinary social bonds and, in the same turn, to reaffirm the imagined links of the nation.

Hassan II continued to speak "directly" to the people (that is, technologically) throughout the next stages of the Green March. On November 6, 1975, broadcasting from Agadir on RTM, he urged people to cross the barbed-wire barriers bearing only red flags of the nation, green Qur'ans, and black-and-white portraits of the king. Without marchers' knowledge, the king had negotiated with Spain to permit the marchers to enter a band of the territory, but one which did not actually reach Laayoune. Marchers arrayed at the border, and the police placed loudspeakers on their Land Rovers to spread the sound. Marchers recalled the order to lower the flags and raise the Qur'an and, on a given command, to raise their flags. At two critical moments at least these speeches were definitive in moving people. Everyone said that the Spanish military-jet flyovers terrified them. They repeated the *shahada* (the Muslim declaration of faith). But a group of marchers I interviewed agreed that Sidna's speech calmed them, "We relaxed when the King spoke to us to say, 'You should not be scared. You are well protected.'" Evoking Hassan II's historical recall of the king's written "Special Stamp" and its dissemination, a marcher noted, "Very few people had radios. But those who did invited others to circle around, and translated [from classical Arabic to the vernacular] for the illiterate." The speech, one of the interviewees emphasized, "was live, from Agadir"—another feeling of connection with the monarch.

With the successful crossing into the Western Sahara participants witnessed "miracles" (*mu'jizat*). A full red moon rising in a dust storm reminded two men of King Mohammed V's apparitions in the moon reported by masses of Moroccans during his exile in 1953. For others General Franco's death was divine retribution. These miraculous moments occurred with the close of the Green March. Within another twenty-four hours, on November 8, King Hassan II addressed the marchers again from Agadir, via commanders' radios, to declare the Green March an unmitigated success and to call a halt to it and order the expectant marchers back to Tarfaya and their homes.

## Awaiting Further Recognition: Difference Returns

All was not well, however. The euphoria of the event was neither the only story nor the end of the story. For some the food and water rations given during the march were insufficient. Marchers left encampments for the nearby towns to trade what supplies and money they had for additional food. Stopping short of Laayoune was also a surprise. Na'ima said that she and her brother and "many people" wished to take the city as their just reward:

> There were many people who wanted to settle there. Wheat, oil, everything is cheap. Living there is cheap. Me too, I wanted to stay there because we were poor and my mother was working as our breadwinner but she couldn't take care of everything. We didn't have food. So my siblings and I, each of us decided to work to help her. We wanted to go there to find something, to live there and work there.

But, she continued, "there we found nothing." Many of my interviewees (twenty-three of the twenty-six) echoed Na'ima's comment, as well as her tone of defeat. "The king assured us that everything would be provided. But on the march the police were controlling who got what, who got water. There was wheat, oil, sardines, potatoes, but very little water" (Mohamed S.). At one point, he said, a man grew enraged by his group leader hoarding water "to *wash* himself with!" The man attacked the leader with a knife, only to be taken away by police. Na'ima noted that "Sidna gave us everything! Even cigarettes—though I was too young to smoke." But she added pointedly that police jealously guarded food, water, and supplies for themselves: "They were controlling everything [*msaytrin ala kul shi*]." According to Na'ima, there was clear favoritism, or as Mohamed S. said, "there were different classes [*kaynin darajat*]." The people of Fez in particular were "spoiled [*mdallalin*]," said Na'ima. They were given water preferentially, and women from Fez looked down on women from Sefrou. The key point for Mohamed S. and Na'ima was the unexpected injustice, one highlighted by the contrast with the communitas that they had experienced in accepting the king's call.

Notably, if the king's address to the people established a direct *national* connection, the breach of that connection was, as Mohamed S. and Na'ima emphasized, the fault of *state* authorities, including police and government officials in charge of logistics. Abdelqader said, "When the march ended, police took off [*hrab*] in their jeeps. A few trucks [that brought the marchers] started taking people back, but only three or four in a truck. We had to wait for two days before more trucks came." When the trucks finally brought them to Marrakech, marchers boarded trains for their home regions. Abdelqader lived within Fez, but marchers from the surrounding villages were offered no further transportation from the city train station. The government officials who had been so excited were nowhere: "We returned [to Fez] at one in the morning," Abdelqader said. "No rides—and no one there: no shaykh, no muqaddam, no caid, no khalifa."

In bringing up these serious injustices, marchers expressed anger. But as with Abdelqader's list of government functionaries, these were directed at representatives of the state, those well known for their mistreatment and humiliation of ordinary Moroccans. No one blamed or even mildly criticized Hassan II. His call was his promise. Shifting the blame to his state subordinates perhaps indexes the repression of political conversation that pervaded Morocco under Hassan II and continues to a lesser extent in Fez today. Yet this explanation still lacks force. People in Fez tend to fear and avoid the neighborhood *muqaddam*, the petty tyrant of the quarter. This fear indeed emerged during interviews, including with a group of marchers in a living room in the lower-middle-class neighborhood of 'Ayn Qadous. Although men and women spoke easily for the first hour, news of our interviews spread and more people came to speak or listen. As the small crowd grew out the door of the room and into the apartment foyer, so too did the risk of the muqaddam's appearance. A rumor of his arrival in fact began to circulate, and within a minute—seconds—my interlocutors dispersed. The state is most assuredly feared.

Abdelqader's listing of state officials—"no shaykh, no muqaddam, no caid, no khalifa"—implicated precisely that mediating chain of command which nida' Sidna had seemed at least temporarily to obliterate. If the king's call promised a direct connection, it was state functionaries—the social intermediaries—who broke the link, denying marchers the promised recognition and reward, by inserting themselves, even by their absence, between the monarch and his people. Mohamed H. complained, "We got back, and we got nothing, even though they said 'We'll call you.' We saw nothing from it." He had sacrificed for the nation, yet the state failed to reciprocate: "No one came to me. I didn't go to the government office [*baladiyya*] because no one there asked about us." Mohamed S. had criticized others' expectation of a material reward for heeding the call—"they have no conscience [*ma 'andhumsh damir*]"—yet he complained of the lack of recognition in similar terms: "No one even asked about us [*hatta shi wahid ma sawwal fina*]."

There were similar stories from nearly everyone I interviewed. Mohammed W. said that upon his return, "They gave us nothing [*ma 'atawna walu*]. We are needy people and we were promised many times to be supported and helped, but they gave us nothing. 'We will stand with you, we will help you, we will do things for you.' But we saw nothing from it." Two months after their return "they" gave marchers a party with tea and donuts! Mohamed mocked the absurdity of it. Risking his life for the nation and receiving . . . tea and donuts? "And the donuts were of very poor quality," he laughed with an edge, "Like rubber. *That's* how they welcomed us."

Disappointments arise of course from desire. Those desires rested on the possibility of direct exchange with, and recognition by, the exemplary center of the nation. The question is how such an expectation could be raised at all. Coercion does not fully explain the Green March or mass politics, and neither does the historical model of the monarch as master, his blessed recognition transmitted across a person-to-person hierarchy of known disciples. The Green March, in contrast, rested on mass politics and mass media, in which recognition would accrue to those anonymous individuals comprising the serial parts of the imagined community, "the people." Which is to say it was a distinctly *national* act, its conditions of possibility both technological and discursive: the national infrastructure of the call—the shimmering electronic connection with the monarch—and the discourse of "the people" as that imagined body worthy of the king's recognition. The peculiar power of the event rested on technologization of the ritual call: the transfer of tactile gift and blessings into distinctly modern mass-mediated connections.

## The Religious Field as National Domain

Coming in the wake of major political, economic, and ecological instability, persistent leftist and emerging Islamist critiques—and following near-lethal coup attempts in 1971 and 1972—the Green March permitted Hassan II's astonishing reassertion of political dominance and legitimacy. While in the political shadows Hassan II continued his violent liquidation of opponents, officially the march ushered in what regime and leftist parties (the *extrême gauche* excluded) branded as political "consensus" and provided the king with sufficient leverage for the subsequent decades of partial political and economic liberalization (Hammoudi 1997, 20; Weiner 1979; Vermeren 2002, 70–71; Z. Daoud 2007, 266). Mohammed Tozy, voicing a common (and pro-monarchy) sentiment within Morocco, describes the Green March not only as a reassertion of the throne's dominance of the "religious field" but also as a progressive step, the "democratic advent" of participatory politics in Morocco.[11] Certainly the march helps explain the nationalist longing behind the contemporary Western Saharan war.[12] Predictably enough, like the Throne Holiday, it now marks a national holiday with grand tributes in both government-aligned and party newspapers. Green March anthems have recently returned to the national stage, in state-sponsored festivals like Mawazine and on the satellite channel 2M's popular Studio 2M program.[13]

The legacy of this national call, however, is yet broader and deeper. Moroccan Islam rests in part on a system of relations bound to the central figure of the sharifian monarch as distributing center. The monarchy's national control of Islam's call gives continued sense of social order to many in Fez, not least those Muslim authorities who in staging smaller ritual calls of jinn exorcism and trance align themselves with its power.

Even beyond those ritual practices, the king seems in the popular imaginary to represent "the people," no matter how far they stand from him (Morris 2000). It is this power of recognition—still fully sought by those participants in the Green March—that assures a sense of unity as well as uniformity to a potentially fractious political field of differing and competing calls. I have argued for the specifically mass-mediated conditions of this sense of connection. From the nationalist movement to the present reform-minded Muslims, by assuming technological mediation, have articulated a view of the nation as spatially uniform and ideally transparent. In short, the monarch's capacity to reach a mass public via a centralizing call has remained a bulwark against the dangers of difference that emerge as contemporary urban Moroccans themselves are understood to be subjects of this communication. This very sense of social connectedness through communicative practice, however, means that uniformity and order rest on the control of ritual communications—the force of the call and its reception—among even marginal Moroccan Muslims and in the most private and hidden settings.

Not surprisingly then, the nationalization of the religious field presents a formidable challenge to those voicing differing calls. This is the case in the public and political domain whether actors voice their call in an Islamic idiom, as Islamic exorcists do, or in democratic and secular terms, as members of the reformist February 20th group do. This is so, even as these latter movements combine digital and "small media" (Sreberny-Mohammadi and Mohammadi 1994) with the broader reach of transnational satellite television news and religious programming. But it also affects the more everyday ritual practices of the call. In short, mass-mediation and effective nationalization of the call—the true consolidation of "Moroccan Islam"—has established certain norms of public ritual practice and communication that reflect the legacy of mass political reformism. In one sense, "conscious and conscientious" piety means that practitioners assume self-presence and self-awareness of their communications, as both caller and recipient of calls. In another sense, and closely related to this, practitioners largely associate the piety of calling and responding with public circulation itself, of transparent, uniform, and unified communication. And yet, it is *against* these norms that private and hidden rites take place and thus gather a seemingly antithetical power and authority.

# 4 Summoning in Secret

## *Mute Letters and Veiled Writing*

The occult "science" which enables the magician to call up jinn and make them do his bidding by invoking them by name and by writing down mysteriously arranged letters, figures, words, and numbers, is widespread in the East, but the Maghrebins are reputed the most learned and skillful in it.

—Edward Westermarck, *Ritual and Belief in Morocco*

A TELEVISION ADVERTISEMENT FOR Morocco's state-owned telecommunications network, Maroc Telecom, during the month of Ramadan, 1424, centered on the familiar Muslim scholar and authority figure, the fqih (Ar. *faqih*), in his local role as a Qur'anic schoolteacher. The advertisement opened with the fqih, plump and avuncular in white robe and red fez, strolling through a luminous nighttime suq, gathering wooden writing tablets and reed pens—those nostalgic technologies of premodern elementary education based on recitation and repetition—and then entering the little schoolroom where his bright and shiny pupils, boys and girls, await him, seated on mats in the old style. As he begins his lesson, one boy with a cell phone texts another; the second, receiving the message, turns to the first and winks—their secret communication confirmed. But the fqih at the front of the room catches the exchange and beckons the boys to show him this novel instrument. In classical education fuqaha' were strict disciplinarians who meted out beatings for inattention, but here he eyes the boys with pleasant curiosity, and all the children, obedient but familiar, now gather round him, sit in his lap and drape over his shoulders in affectionate intimacy. The fqih holds the cell phone, reading the screen with a smile. The commercial fades to an image of the cell phone resting atop the wooden board inscribed with ink—the displacement of the old technology by the new complete.

Since the early 2000s, Maroc Telecom has been Morocco's largest network by coverage and subscription and its advertisements emphasize both its national territorial coverage and, with familiar images, its cultural inclusivity. It extends and imagines the completion of a dream adopted with Moroccan nationalism, linking technology with community, and community with unity. Of course the sheer necessity for Maroc Telecom to advertise means that citizen-consumers remain to be summoned, and one can see in the discourse of the advertisements both the provoking and taming of desire for the network. The cell phone and the pleasures and the ease of digital communication are the centerpiece of the advertisement and object of desire—so easy a child can master it. But the fqih provides a vital cultural support for a world dominated by a new order and new tech-savvy generation in which the disciples initiate the master—where messages move laterally, rather than hierarchically. As a classical source of both the Qur'anic text and moral order he exposes the technology's new circuits of communication to authoritative oversight and thus transparent and controlled presence.[1]

This assertion of control reiterates a theoretical view of technology repeated in much scholarship on Islam and media, and in media studies of the Middle East and North Africa more generally, that technologized communications democratize authority and permit greater access to public communication. First, scholars argue, technologies of sound and print image, mass communications and mass education, have displaced both the exclusive religious literacy of traditional religious figures like the fqih and the state-controlled broadcast media. With the key exception of gender distinctions, hierarchy itself is viewed as weakened. Secondly, it is argued that this increasing contestation over this public authority, indeed the emergence of multiple overlapping publics, is played out in plain view, as a "politics of presence" in which previously marginal figures can negotiate a new kind of identity and self-image (Moors 2006). The refusal to accept religion's merely private relevance renders all debate public, and publicity itself, a sphere of regulation and discipline. The two points are strongly related, in asserting both a novel subjectivity and a novel social space for its performance. More to the point, although media studies and public sphere theories for Islam and the Middle East and North Africa have come a long way since their mid-1990s "infancy" (Eickelman and Anderson 1997, 43), they still assume that religious calls circulate horizontally and thus transparently, and indeed, that they gather their power by virtue of new acts of pious displays available to *anyone*. Yet these logics of transparency and sameness, as articulated in revivalist discourse, have their own logics of power and control by which human differences are ideally organized and controlled—forms of gender and class and consciousness in particular. Transparency in other words is not a fact of communication but a demand, one articulated by some explicitly as a call to the nation or the king, or to a more proper Islam to which Moroccans or Moroccan Muslims must respond to be considered "pious." These calls either do not recognize, or they seek to control and recuperate, popular desires for difference, desires for special and inexplicable powers or qualities that few can claim. Framed in this manner, these other desires are themselves understood as responses to power—inappropriate power—which is to say, as the effects of other calls that leave their objects unaware. Jinn cures are a privileged focus of these concerns, and even when historically prior, the practices are now refigured (in terms of normative transparency and modern piety) as foreign. Yet these curers also speak to real and urgent desires on the part of both practitioners and patients or clients, and they remain dominant or at least popular ideas among not only underclasses and old women, but also middle classes and young men. They form a powerful backdrop precisely for the very calls that seek to eradicate them, and as such deserve analysis.

In urban Morocco these (now) antithetical powers of communication, while concerning powers to give voice to and control the jinns as a potential and differentiating presence, do so in distinct ritual and media: in saint veneration and (mostly) women's spirit mediumship, which we examine in the next chapter, and in men's magical writing, which we examine in this chapter.

Curiously enough, magical writing is a power exercised (in secret) by the very figures of religious authority to which the Maroc Telecom advertisement pays homage, that is, the fqih. Fuqaha' are not only Qur'anic teachers—indeed they are rarely so today in Fez. Rather they are talismanic writers who, in the popular imagination, draw on exclusive powers of ancient and secret signs, in material inscriptions and secret amulets that people seek out and pay considerable sums for. These powers of writing are occasionally reinforced by a fqih's claim to baraka, but other fuqaha' do not make such claims. And whereas baraka's power is often the power to summon a crowd or public, the fqih's power, as Durkheim distinguished magic from religion ("there is no Church of magic"), rests on what circulates without provoking public notice or response (Durkheim 1995, 42). What seems above all to matter is that fuqaha' are masculine bearers of a force that controls jinns, and that circulates in inscriptions both hierarchical and occulted, rather than horizontal and transparent.

## "The Stranger"

The title of fqih derives from the classical Arabic *faqih,* a scholar of jurisprudence (*al-fiqh*), who elucidates the shari'a, the law or path common to all believers. In Morocco, however, there has been no institutionally granted title of faqih for a scholar of fiqh; religious scholars in general, with an *ijaza,* or diplôme from the state-accredited institutions, al-Qarawiyyin in Fez, Dar al-Hassaniyya in Rabat, al-Kutubiyya in Marrakech, bear the title *'alim* (pl. *'ulama'*). The word faqih is used occasionally in written discourse as a synonym for 'alim, and likewise in colloquial usage it suggests mastery of a field of knowledge or simply a master, similar to the term of respect, *ma'lim,* for a craftsman (or a Gnawa master). But the term *fqih,* the social roles to which it refers and the authority it signifies in urban Morocco, is colloquial, referring to historically modest scriptural authorities tasked with teaching and reciting the Qur'an, as well as some scribal and notarial duties. Fuqaha' are analogous to other local scriptural authorities in rural and urban Muslim societies—*fundis* with "legal learning," or *'ilim fakihi,* in Mayotte (Lambek 1993) and *malams* in Kano (O'brien 2001; see also Masquelier 2007, 49; Boddy 1989, 223; Holý 1991, 30–34; El-Tom 1985). As with these authorities, the historical position of fuqaha' rested on a structure of knowledge transmission based on the corporal and mnemonic reproduction of texts, on person-to-person learning, traceable through extensive chains of transmission (*isnad*). That is to say, they embody a structure of knowledge, the value and power of which historically derives from its exclusive storage in the person of the authority rather than in the general circulation of multiple copies.[2]

Prior to the spread of mass education in 1960s and 1970s Morocco, Qur'anic education, in the *msid* (the Moroccan equivalent of the eastern *kuttab*) attached to a mosque or *zawiya*, was public education, and by all accounts, fuqaha' as mnemonic bearers of the "Qur'anic presence" were central figures of scriptural and moral education. Curiously, however, this did not make the fqih a familiar, or entirely assimilated, religious figure. Rather, as Dale F. Eickelman's masterful study of premodern and early colonial Moroccan scholarship describes them, fuqaha' were "professional outsiders"—"strangers" in Georg Simmel's sense of being both "'near and far at the same time,'" who (along with Jewish traders) "constituted the only category of 'outsider' ordinarily present in rural society" (Eickelman 1985, 67–68; see Simmel 1950a, 407). This foreignness was of course exacerbated by the peripatetic habits of fuqaha', moving between urban centers and rural periphery, and from Sufi zawiya to zawiya where both person-to-person studies and access to scholarly libraries could advance one's learning. But Eickelman also rightly argues for their sacred "mnemonic possession" of the Qur'an as the source of foreignness. Bearing Qur'anic knowledge they served as "a concrete symbol of the link between the local community and the wider one of Islam" (Eickelman 1985, 67). To this mark of difference we should add another distinction, namely, the fqih's mastery of the empirical written trace in a primarily oral society. Indeed, as Geertz's foreword to Eickelman's study notes, the fqih's mnemonic archive disturbed apparently fundamental distinctions between orality and literacy across ethnographic worlds (Eickelman 1985, xiii). Rather like the stranger, and like Derrida's logic of the supplement suggests, writing was both inside and outside, a quality of the outside already established inside the society, but one brought out by the fqih's presence (Derrida 1976).

The writings of fuqaha' were scriptural, notarial, and secretarial, but also magical. Examining 1920s rural Morocco, Émile Laoust described the fqih as a "Master Jacques of the sacristy," his scriptural and more recondite tasks overlapping:

> He lumps together all the functions the numerous members of the village require. He is the muezzin who calls the prayer; imam who appears before the faithful whom he leads; hazzab who recites the Qur'an; school master who gives the Qur'anic lessons by his well-known methods; grand priest of the sacrifice, he slaughters the victims in certain solemn affairs; magician, his amulets pass as a cure-all; and, if he's from the Sous, his reputation for finding treasure is universally established. [As a] public notary, he records official acts, letters of repudiation, and by necessity all correspondence passes through his hands. He recites prayers on the deathbed; prepares and bathes the dead, reciting the final prayers upon the tomb. (E. Laoust 1924, 7–8)

If written sorcery was "beyond the pale for good Muslims" (Eickelman 1985, 67; cf. Berque 1955, 316–18, 329, 355; E. Laoust 1924, 12), fuqaha' were nonetheless well known for talismanic writing in an astonishing variety of forms. Westermarck's detailed descriptions include an array of practices of inscription and consumption, some Qur'anic, some magical—on bowls and diluted and drunk, or on papers or an egg—that fuqaha' still regularly practice in curing and manipulating jinns (Westermarck 1968 [1926]; cf. El-Tom 1985). Rather than sorcery, talismanic writing formed a field of knowledge, 'ilm ruhaniyya, spiritual science, combining the rigors of science ('ilm) with the blessing and trace of a healing divinity.[3] But it is worth noting the significant differences between this writing and the fqih's other textual, and explicitly recitational duties. For whereas these latter—the calls to prayer, for example—specifically generated a public, talismanic writing did not; rather it functioned, if not antisocially, certainly asocially, evading public presence. And as the former explicitly public duties of fuqaha' have waned, it is this writing that remains for them today as a fetish, crystallized within it all the strangeness and mystery of their prior authority.

## Spirit Problems, Spirit Powers

If fuqaha' were strange in the past, that strangeness was nonetheless accommodated to a world of differences in which expectations for mass subjectivity and mass society did not yet obtain. Their strangeness now comes in part from their difference *from* these conditions, and the publicly expressed expectation that mass schooling in Morocco, as it developed in the postindependence 1960s, would in fact lead to their disappearance. Which is to say, at least in the view of some urban Moroccans, they are in part strange today because they are obsolete. Their skills were not entirely useless; the increased need for Arabic-trained schoolteachers saw some fuqaha' recruited into accelerated teacher-training programs (*takwin al-mu'alimin*) (Boyle 2004; Spratt and Wagner 1984). But their positions in public schools were considerably less exalted. Now viewed as menial bureaucrats overseen by far younger men with wholly different educational values. Not surprisingly, rare depictions of fuqaha' in postindependence Morocco convey a sense of uselessness and malaise, weakness and disposability (Maher 1975, 82–83; Rabinow 1977, 101–2).[4]

Yet as their public profile diminished, their hidden skills remained in demand. In fact fuqaha' are plentiful in urban Morocco, including both Rabat and Fez where I sought them out for interviews and observations. To find them one can follow word of mouth. Casablanca-based fuqaha' occasionally advertise in new cheap weekly newspapers, and fuqaha' in Fez and Rabat print business cards (with their cell phone numbers, of course), but generally one follows the recommendations of family and family friends, as well as strangers one meets while waiting to see the fqih. Fatima, the mother in my household, recommended one fqih who had written her talismans more than two decades prior when she suspected her then two-year-old son was possessed—he habitually wandered outside the house and once all the way to a distant suburb toward Sefrou—but the fqih, known only as "the Algerian" had recently died. On Fatima's friend's recommendation I found another fqih with a bustling business—his office waiting area filled with clients waiting in plastic chairs—and so gleaned further recommendations from others.

Fuqaha' in Fez, in the narrow sense of jinn curer, are invariably men. In Rabat, in my experience, they tend to be older men, with Islamic exorcism the choice of practice for a younger generation (see Spadola 2004). In Fez medina, however, they tend to range in age from early forties to very old. Fassis critical of the practice attribute this fact to the high demand for magical writing among less educated Moroccans, in particular the rural immigrants (who do, in my experience, form a large body of the clientele). Some fuqaha title themselves "Sharif so-and-so" to reinforce the impression of bearing baraka. Again, Fassis attribute this to "traditional beliefs" of less educated Moroccans. But this does not seem to be essential to the practice (only in one case did this claim seem to reflect a true lineage or background), nor of course does this claim guarantee the efficacy of the cure.

The education of these fuqaha' suggested a departure from old channels indexing the postcolonial upheaval and transition in which they matured. All had memorized the Qur'an with a fqih, a feat requiring several years of study, yet only two had ever served as a Qur'anic teacher, and none did so now.[5] Three men with whom I spent the most time represented this diversity of origins. Ahmed, whom we shall meet in more detail, specifically avoided this approach, which his older brother had followed and found unsatisfactory. Instead he pursued advanced studies at the Qarawiyyin mosque university. Another, Abdeladhim, had simply found the classroom space and the daytime training too foreign and confusing. Aziz's training—despite others' insistence that he must have studied with a Sufi shaykh—claimed to have taught himself by reading works of *'ilm al-ruhani*, including al-Buni's *Shams al-Ma'arif*, available in reprint, and lesser-known works sold as photocopied manuscripts along the perimeter of the Qarawiyyin library in the medina.

What these men and other fuqaha' shared was a claim to write magically—secretly—in ways that master the jinns. Their offices or studies, where they saw clients or wrote their cures, were piled with small collections of books and loose-leaf papers and pervaded by the odors of saffron ink and various incenses—*jawi* (benzoin) and sandalwood. Aziz, suffering a degenerative muscular condition, crouched spiderlike on a cushion behind a wooden crate heaped with white slips of paper and ink jars, black and brown, and two reed styluses. Ahmed created his own workshop in a makeshift wooden-and-tarp shelter on his rooftop, with the same array of instruments, but more books and a locked chest for ruhani manuscripts he had collected from a Qadiriyya zawiya library to the south of Marrakech. Indeed all of the men required manuscripts, "old manuscripts," to learn the craft that distinguished them as true fuqaha' and not simply Qur'anic schoolteachers or reciters (referred to as *talibs*, or students) in Fez.

People seeking out fuqaha'—men and women, and parents on behalf of their children—complain of a range of ailments, including physical ailments—changes in consciousness, physical paralysis, fevers, sores. They also seek help for emotional and mental disturbances: feeling depressed or anxious, psychosis, or possession by jinns.

Other problems are social. For women, domestic violence or a husband's infidelities, infertility or lack of marital prospects. For men, sexual impotence, unemployment, or a sense of being blocked from a particular duty or aim. Women expect these problems to be interpreted as troubles with jinns, or troubles that the fqih's manipulation of jinns can resolve. Men complain of sorcery, assumed to be the work of another fqih, paid by one's wife or other close female and described by colloquial terms "prevention" (*tqaf*) or "binding" (*aqd*).

For physical ailments, clients also habitually state that they followed the "modern" and "technological" routes first, but without success. Some clients started an allopathic route, including pharmaceutical regimens, but then abandoned them as too expensive to maintain, or too unfamiliar. (People expected quicker results and were surprised that prescriptions would need to be refilled repeatedly.) Others simply received no suitable diagnosis. In these cases, medical sciences had acquired a status it could not in fact attain—to the benefit of alternative therapies of the fqih. More specifically, by raising and at least sometimes failing expectations of certitude, that is, total physiological revealability (apotheosized in Fassis' reference to undergoing visual scans [*duzt skanner*]), allopathic remedies unwittingly strengthened the case for the fqih's special capacities beyond ordinary and available knowledge.

To fuqaha' these matters—physical, mental, social—constituted "spiritual problems" (*mashakil ruhaniyya*) amenable precisely to their field of specialty, namely, "spiritual science" or "spiritual medicine" (*al-'ilm al-ruhani or al-tibb al-ruhani*). "Spiritual problems" should more appropriately be translated as "spirit problems." Rather than referring to human spirit "*ruh*," mashakil ruhaniyya describe unseen, unknown phenomena—namely, jinns—that are not only inexplicable to "modern science," but which their sufferers also view as immune to pious practice. Fuqaha' and clients attribute spiritual problems to forces outside the ailing person herself: a stepmother, or a wife using a sorcerer's manipulation of jinns or a jinn's own love and thus relentless jealousy. At the same time, they bring a set of problems (domestic violence, for example) that require external interventions.

Put otherwise, the problems people bring to fuqaha' are either problems with family, or problems that one's family connections and resources cannot resolve. The large majority of patients I met—unemployed and underemployed single and married men, single mother heads of household, many previously solid middle-class Fassis—lacked, if nothing else, the family connections to aspire to middle-class security. It makes sense that the problems for which Fassis seek out fuqaha' and the solutions themselves originate outside and remain unsolvable by medical means, or by the aid of one's (limited) social connections. Indeed, it is hard not to see the repetition of particular spirit problems—mental, emotional, and psychosocial—as an idiom for contemporary structural conditions in urban Morocco (and across Muslim postcolonies) that exceed the solutions offered by local social connections. The current "marriage crisis" (*azmat al-zawaj*) among Moroccan youth is tied to high unemployment. Young men require financial stability to marry; lacking that, young men, like the younger brothers in my household, stay at home with their parents if they can. As Rachel Newcomb has described as well, underclass women seeking help from new women's NGOs were doing so in the absence of other support networks. In Fez, women who are uprooted from village life and suffer domestic discord or violence, postdivorce unemployment, and poverty lack recourse to older kin-based resolutions—the capacity to leave an abusive spouse and return to a father's house, for example (Newcomb 2009). As much as NGOs and fuqaha' differ in their claims, they both treat conditions exacerbated by neoliberal capitalism. Which is to argue that the etiology of problems in the Unseen Unknown—the idiom of jinns and "spirit problems" that evade the patient's collective or pious response—can also express a vulnerability to global and distant, rather than wholly local, vectors. While Fassis continue to reinvent and adapt new solutions, naming such problems as spirit troubles (rather than, say, "neoliberalism" or "bad luck") also resolves the problem, or at least provides a measure of reassurance that *someone* with a different power can resolve it.

To go to a fqih means to go to a man of religious authority, but of a particular sort: someone who is an outsider—a mystery—and as such the bearer of some power that allows them exclusive access to equally foreign and mysterious jinn problems. In some cases this power derives from baraka, or seems to, but always with the expectation of a written cure as an exclusive power, and also a secret power defined by difference: from ordinary social life, family, or modern technologies, and most of all from transparent circulation. That the problems themselves evade oversight is made obvious by the claim that the "skanner" is insufficient. That the writing resists open display is supported by the discourse and practice of secrecy woven around it.

## Writing and Secrecy

This difference is emphasized by the techniques of the fuqaha' themselves, in the form of a writing that they master, and by which they control jinns. Fuqaha' write talismans (*jadwal; jadawil*) or seals (*khatim; khawatim*). Clients refer to these talismans as "writing" (*kitaba*). People say they go to a fqih so he will "write something [*tayktib shi haja*]" or "write some writing [*tayktib shi kitaba*]." The simplest talismans, for attracting a spouse or lover, a *mahabba* amulet, contain Qur'anic text, for example, the well-known Verse of the Throne (Ayat al-Kursi), or short verses, "God's Word is Truth and All is His [*qawluh al-haqq wa lahu al-mulk*]." Yet even elaborately inscribed Qur'anic talismans—words written at 90-degree angles at the corners of a small paper or within a grid of nine or sixteen squares—are but a fragment of the still more esoteric and potent talismanic writing of fuqaha'.[6] These latter talismans draw on more recondite elements of 'ilm ruhani—astrology ('ilm al-falak), letters ('ilm al-harf), and names ('ilm al-asma') and are geometrically and textually intricate, comprising fine matrices of individual characters, bounded by the names of archangels and surrounded by saffron or dark-inked lines of spiraling Arabic script.[7] They are also exchanged for a *futuh*, or obligatory gift, for at least MDH 20 (US $2.50) and usually far more.

What exactly these formulae constitute differs according to different fuqaha'. These designs are invisible, however, rendered so by their mode of circulation. In the first place, although patients come to see a fqih (tucked away in the shaded walls of Fez medina), they do not witness his writing of the talisman, for which they may return in several days. In the second place, and more important, fuqaha' enclose the written talisman as an amulet—that is, they fold and tie or tape it inside a "*hijab*," meaning "that which hides," a "screen" or "veil," the same term used for a woman's headscarf.[8] This veil over the writing, like any space separating the sacred from the profane, is meant to maintain its purity and potency, for, as fuqaha' explicitly state, writing that is unwrapped from the hijab will spoil (*yifsed*).

Other features of the writing itself emphasize its separation from the profane as a difference and even antagonism between vocal and written marks, between the freely circulating and the occult. One obvious feature of the Arabic of fuqaha' is the script's utter lack of dots. Westermarck notes that the fuqaha' from a century ago likewise avoided the dots, explaining that jinn live in the dots, or alternately, that the dots were the children of the jinn. The fuqaha' provided me with two different explanations: first, this is the oldest Arabic, the Arabic of the Qur'an before standardization of the folios and grammarians' *tashkil* or *dabt*, that is, before the introduction of voweling two hundred years after the Prophet; second, such voweling is meant to aid in the *recitation* of the Qur'an. My interlocutor, fqih Ahmed, described voweling with some contempt, citing a proverb, "Three things destroy writing: vowels, breath, and speech [Thalatha *yabtalna al-kitaba: al-dabt wa al-nufkh wa al- kalam*]." *Al-dabt* (from d-b-t), means to vowelize, to determine precisely the spelling and pronunciation of a word. The breath, Ahmed said, would harm the angels—Sky Kings—that circulate when one writes.[9] Speaking raised an opposing danger of the jinn's overhearing: a jinn would receive the alert and "steal the words," which is to say, steal the power, of the fqih. A ruhani bookseller near the Qarawiyyin later explained it to me by comparing the fqih to a person unlocking the door to his house: "The jinn sees him just as he holds out the key and attacks."

A further guard against speech appeared in the writing. Whether Syriac, hieroglyphic, or very old, these signs neither could be nor were meant to be pronounced. The talismanic signs are mute letters. They are unreadable, which is to say, unrecitable. These letters often occupy the separate boxes comprising a larger square; the writing, like those spiral texts Messick has described (1993), is often circular, or at perpendicular angles. The form of the presentation is essential; to recite it could only be to describe it: "First, there's a square, then inside that the word "*alayka.*'" Mere description is inadequate to the task of the fqih's writing, which is, in other words, nonphonetic. It cannot be transmitted by voice and thus maintains its difference from common circulation.

The orthographic specificity of the fqih's script and the taboo on unwrapping and exposing the hijab both align with the denunciation of speech, breath, and the diacritics that permit writing's vocalization. Invisible writing, as much as writing without vowels or even consonantal demarcation (that is, *al-dabt*), is incapable of translation into voice and thus is, of course, silent writing. That is to say, if unveiling the script renders it visible, voice and vocalization extend its reach and explicitly publicize it. Invisible, mute, material writing—silent writing that resists conversion to public voice—resists a general circulation. "Magical signs," so writes Friedrich Kittler, "exist to be copied under the midnight moon, not to be spoken out loud" (1990, 6).

Ensconced in the hijab, the knowledge and the power of writing is the fqih's alone, and neither is nor ever was meant to summon a general public. Given the historical logic of exclusivity, it makes sense that the fqih's writing resists exposure. But that close guardianship of the writing is also required by the task of controlling the jinns; what spoils the writing is its exposure to the very circulation it is meant to capture.

## Calling the Jinns, Mastering Difference

Among the cases of curing I followed with Aziz and Ahmed, one stands out as both telling and exceptional: telling, in its illustrating the expectations of fuqaha' in treating, or really, working with jinns; exceptional, in the vivid challenge the jinns posed to Ahmed, a challenge with high stakes for the fqih as much as the jinns themselves. As I learned about the patient and her jinns, a story which we shall continue in the next chapter, it seemed a very unfair fight.

I first met Ahmed during a curing session with Zuhur, a woman suffering physical marks and mental-emotional signs of jinn possession. In her early thirties, she had attended primary and secondary school with Sanae, a daughter in my household, but had stayed in closer touch with Fatima, who suggested we meet. Sanae, Fatima, and I visited in Zuhur's small apartment in the medina where she sat with her feet and ankles wrapped in gauze, covering apparently open sores that plagued her. Her three children, all under seven, huddled quietly behind her when we met. While she had once been employed sewing beads on women's slippers, now she was unemployed. Her husband sold cloth in Fez medina but did not own the business and made only a little money on commissions. Zuhur explained that she was eating one meal daily so her children could eat three.

Despite the costs, she had consulted several doctors to treat the sores. She was given blood tests, she said, for cancer, Hepatitis B and C, and HIV. Like others I spoke with she had received an MRI, "duzt skanner," which having confirmed nothing, convinced her that allopathic medicine had failed her, and so sought out spirit cures. Fuqaha' had diagnosed her as possessed by multiple jinns and given her talismanic writing, but without apparent resolution. But Zuhur acknowledged that as allopathic medicine failed her, she suspected that so too would another fqih. She certainly believed in the powers that an expert fqih could offer, hence she willingly sought out Ahmed for yet another diagnosis and treatment. Her problems were medical, but also socially and doctrinally complicated. Zuhur's ailment came, in part, from jinns, who were calling her into their service. They appeared in dreams that left her paralyzed and fearful. Her mother and grandmother were familiar with this problem—they too were possessed by jinns—and so pressed her to follow a particular course of action: sacrifice to the jinns, a trance ceremony in their honor. In short, her submission to jinns meant a submission to kin and ritual structures that made their apparition possible. The call of the medium was also the call of jinns.

Like others in Fez, including between Fatima and her daughters, there was a generational difference at play. Zuhur's role model for resisting the call of jinns (and older kin) was in fact her own sister who, inspired by Islamic revivalists, had taken up the veil and adhered strictly to her prayers. Zuhur insisted that she too was pious, a good Muslim (even if she did not pray or veil). She looked to the fqih to cut the connection to jinns that called her, thereby alleviating the demands of kin who in part mediated that call.

Although Ahmed wrote his talismans in the rooftop workshop, he was loath to bring Zuhur, and Sanae, Fatima, and me, into his home. Neighbors might have questioned the impropriety of it, but Ahmed explained that his wife's illness precluded it. Already weakened by diabetes, and in a state of nearly perpetual convalescence, she herself was too vulnerable to attack, should a jinn be exorcised from Zuhur and seek another body to possess. So the first session took place at Zuhur's friend Naʿima's house. And Ahmed, more vital than other fuqahaʾ (he had been a boxer and a fighter in Morocco's Liberation Army, and a proud participant in the Green March), sat in khakis and wool, eyes shiny, big hands folded, listening to Zuhur's account of her sores. As fuqahaʾ routinely do, Ahmed asked for her name and her mother's name. He wrote these names on a slip of paper and then, drawing on numerological science, quickly calculated the value of each letter. She was "sabti," or Saturday, meaning that her spirit troubles came from a Jewish jinn. The necessary action now, he said, was exorcism.

Ahmed urged us to make Zuhur comfortable resting on cushions, and taking her right hand in his, he pressed his thumbnail under hers and began to whisper in her ear. I could not hear him, nor could any of the observers. His recitation lasted only a few minutes, at which point Zuhur slumped to the floor and wailed. Her sadness seemed to me very deep, and the crying cathartic. Everyone scurried to support her with pillows, and Ahmed continued to whisper in her ear. Her crying quieted and she began to move her lips.

Ahmed said, "Al-salam ʿalaykum." Zuhur, or rather, whoever had now come to possess her, responded very weakly, "Wa ʿalaykum al-salam." Ahmed asked for her name, where she lived. The jinn who responded said her name was Aisha. She lived in a river under the bridge near the neighborhood of Mawlay ʿAbdallah in nearby Fez al-Jadid. Ahmed asked how long had she occupied this body, and to identify her faith. The response contradicted the fqih's assessment. "I am Muslim," Aisha said. Moreover, Aisha asserted, her presence was salutary not harmful: "I take care of her [Zuhur]. She is my daughter, and she loves me. I'm with her to protect her."

With that Aisha faded out and Zuhur fell limp. Ahmed whispered and pressed into Zuhur's thumbnail, and another voice arrived. Ahmed began to repeat the questions to identify the new jinn, but a door slammed and Fatima strode into the room chuckling. Zuhur abruptly sat up, blinking and disoriented. There was a brief pause, then Zuhur's friends began chatting energetically and lit cigarettes while Zuhur laid quietly on the floor. Na'ima's mother brought tea and cookies. Ahmed left with 300 dirhams (US$ 35), which he explained would pay for the treatment materials. The gesture was meant to head off any question of his own self-interest, but his fee immediately raised the point and would be a repeated theme throughout the treatment.

When we met again two days later Ahmed had prepared talismans for Zuhur. There were nine strips of paper—three sets of three—and a hijab. Ahmed explained that she must use them over the next three days, after which he would visit her again. Each day Zuhur was to soak one the sets of writings in water, then swab the water over her body. Likewise she was to soak the second set of writing in water and then drink it. The last set was for burning, which she should do at the day's end. He said that she was to wrap the hijab in plastic and wear it around her neck at night.

Three days later, our third meeting took place at my host mother, Fatima's house, as she insisted. "Zuhur loves my mother," Sanae explained, and so too apparently did Zuhur's friends. When Ahmed met us again, they were clearly enjoying the atmosphere with Fatima's plentiful supply of tea, cookies, and cigarettes. But Zuhur's sores were still open, and she wore gauze wrapped around both feet and hobbled slowly. She complained about the treatment. On the first day, immediately after holding the hijab in her hand she felt something pulling her hand away from her. She had worn it, in fact, only two days, during which time it burned the skin where it rested against her chest. She took this to mean that the jinn disapproved of the treatment, and she removed it the night before the third meeting.

Once again Ahmed pressed his thumbnail under Zuhur's and whispered in her ear. After a few minutes, a jinn began to growl in Zuhur's throat. Ahmed spoke.

A: Al-salam 'alaykum! Al-salam 'alaykum!

Z: IIIIIIIIIIIEEEEEEEEEEEHHHHHHHHHHHHHH!

A: Who are you? Mimun? Sabti? [that is, Jewish?] You're Mimun? Bismillah al-rah-man al-rahim [In the Name of God, the Merciful and Compassionate]. Speak! Who are you? Speak! Are you Mimun? We've come just to talk with you, just to visit you. Are you Mimun? Sabti? Well? Say "Al-salam alaykum."

Z: Alaykum saaaallllllllllmmm

A: Ah! Are you "shamlikhi"? Jewish? You're Jewish? Are you going to be truthful with us today Mimun or lie? Bismillah al-rahman al-rahim.

Z: Why did you write against me? ['alash dirti liyya al-kitaba]. So I would go away? Ehhhhh?

A: No, I just want to work with you.

Z: Ehhh?

A: So, answer me. Al-salam 'alaykum. You're shamlikhi? Go easy on the body [hawal ala al-juta] . . . be easy.

Here, as Ahmed had predicted, a Jewish jinn was possessing Zuhur. His tone of voice was urgent, but open—in a way that Islamic exorcists find wholly impious, a way of paying homage to the jinn and allowing the difference of its call to remain and even to take on social significance. This accusation reflects a truth, which in short order became apparent in Ahmed's continued engagement with Mimun, whom he only urged to "go easy" on the body. Mimun nevertheless rejected the engagement, focusing rather on the talismans Ahmed had written for Zuhur.

Z: So, why did you hang the writing around my neck?

A: Here I am, I'll take it away for you.

Z: And why that manuscript on the table?

A: You're staying with us now? Not going away?

Z: Why did you put the writing around my neck?

A: Talk to me, then.

Z: Why did you do the writing?

A: "You have your religion and I have mine" [that is, Qur'an 109:6]

Z: Why did you put the writing around my neck?

Ahmed's response—"You have your religion and I have mine"—deflected Mimun's question. Zuhur had sought out Ahmed precisely for his writing, the power of which rests on its capacity to take control of the jinn—to control their mysterious difference that the patient bears and suffers. The secrecy of the writing, the power of its circulation, must match that of the jinns; the writing is there to call them—to summon their difference and convert it into useful, if occult, communication. To maintain that power, the writing must be guarded against excess exposure. Such, of course, is the purpose of the hijab. The distinct power of the writing, its difference from ordinary speech, matches the difference of the jinns. The conflict between the fqih and the jinn over writing is thus a matter of the power to control difference by virtue of powerful communication.

Ahmed's interest, however, would soon be clarified as something more than just exorcism or curing. Everyone sat transfixed.

A: Will you speak truthfully or lie?

Z: Did you write to destroy me [*tahalkni*]?

A: I will make writing to destroy you and burn you.

Z: What do you have that can burn me? You can't control me.

A: I have what burns you—the Qur'an.

Z: The Qur'an? We have our Qur'an too.

A: You have the Torah.

Z: We have the Torah. We work with our Torah.

A: We have your Torah within our Qur'an. Mimun, go easy on the body!

Z: We didn't attack her; she brought it upon herself.

A: Today is Saturday. I just want to ask you some questions, then you go on your way.

Z: So ask. I'll go away. I have a lot of work to do.

A: I want to ask you about the madrassa at Zalyifa.

Ahmed's words as I reproduce them here sound threatening, but his tone was really more conciliatory, even pleading. Mimun was in charge, his tone accusing and then dismissive. Sanae, and Zuhur's friends too, later emphasized the jinn's power and the fqih's acquiescence, which was indeed obvious. All agreed that Mimun's power overwhelmed Ahmed's capacity to exorcise him. But Ahmed was really pursuing another aim. Ahmed's purpose became explicitly to harness Mimun's communicative power—his call—to send him afar to gather evidence of a secret treasure.

A: I want to ask you about the madrassa at Zalyifa.

Z: Why ask me?

A: In front of the classrooms: Is there something there or not? Yallah! Go there now and give me the news. Is there something made of gold there? Why doesn't the divining work? I've been there.

Z: Wait. I have to rouse my servant.

A: Ahh. You're the King [*nta-l-malik*].

Z: Yes, I'm Queen [*ana malika*].

A: Malika. No problem. Welcome. You're of the People of the Book. I work with you.

Now Zuhur began to groan and writhe. He tried to maintain her presence, shouting, "Leave the body alone! Don't possess her [*matsar'hash*]!" He then recited an *aya* from the Qur'an and asked God to be "kind to the possessed body [*irham hadhi-l-jutta*]." Zuhur calmed, and Ahmed continued to press Mimun, his tone desperate.

> A: Your servants—have they brought a response?
>
> Z: Wait. My servant is coming. He tells you there's something difficult there. . . . There's a guard there. [Speaking to the servant:] Tell him "Malik sent me. Malik says clear out."
>
> A: Mimun, I'm the one who gave the land for the school. I need to know if something's there. I'll work with you. I'll treat you kindly.
>
> Z: You have no choice but to treat me kindly! I'm King on my throne. You'll treat me with respect, as do the jinn and humankind! . . .

After a pause, Mimun acceded to the fqih's command.

> Z: It's there.
>
> A: Is it close to the classrooms, next to the teachers' residence, or is it far from there?
>
> Z: Wait, wait. Who did the divining there [*rama al-tarbi'*]?
>
> A: That was me. What's there? A box?
>
> Z: Three small casks [*khuwibat*].
>
> A: What's in them?
>
> Z: Golden broach, in the middle is a design of a rooster. There are two others, inscribed with a head. Wait . . . [long pause]
>
> A: Mimun. Speak, Mimun!

Ahmed's desperation was painful. Like Zuhur and Sanae, and so many people in Fez, he needed money. His practice of talismanic writing was explicitly self-interested; even without children, his wife's illness meant a financial strain. This was, of course, a matter of her survival, and his anxieties pervaded our conversations. Here he pleaded with Mimun, promising him, "This woman [Zuhur] will prepare everything you ask for." Which is to say, through her limp body he offered tribute to the jinn. But Mimun left, and in his place came Aisha. Her voice, soft and wilted, faded in and out. Zuhur sat up and slumped over as it came and went. Ahmed commanded her too to search the school at Zalyifa, but Aisha refused: "I'm sick . . . I'm sick. . . ." Ahmed was exasperated—"I can send a jinn to gather news of the war in Iraq, and this jinn can't tell me what's at Zalyifa?!" Zuhur's friends butted in to press Aisha with questions of their own: "What is the situation with my brother-in-law? Is he in serious trouble?" "Do I have a jinn?" Aisha responded: "Yes, the situation is serious with your brother-in-law and will take the hardest work now." "Yes, you have Black, and you have Aisha."

The women's excitement in speaking with Aisha only emphasized Ahmed's ineffectual presence. If his writing was meant to control the jinns, or to impress the patient and her cohort, it competed with the powers of communication the jinn herself offered—namely, a glimpse into the Unseen Unknown. This is precisely the power of spirit mediums in Fez, a power located most often in female bodies, but centered on the jinns themselves. It was this direction Zuhur herself seemed to be headed, for after this encounter Zuhur dropped the treatment. She kept the writing, but did not use it. Instead she began to prepare for the trance rites with a Gnawa group, which is to say, she began the necessary steps to become a spirit medium. Her rejection of the fqih's writing, discussed with her friends, centered in part on his avarice and self-interest—a quality he hardly hid from them in attempting to control rather than to exorcise Zuhur's jinns. No one mentioned his lack of baraka. The key reason came down to the jinns themselves demanding their sovereign due, which no writing could divert or expunge.

After this encounter Ahmed too seemed lost. When next we met we walked down Talaa Kabira in the medina; Ahmed pointed to stores once owned by Jews who had since left Morocco en masse in the 1960s. He said Morocco had lost something. He explained that Zuhur had not followed his treatment and therefore could not expect to heal. He asked me if the women were perhaps planning a trance ritual with Gnawa. I acknowledged that they were. He sighed. "She will have to repeat the trance rite year after year." We walked down Talaa Kabira, and Ahmed held my hand.

## Conclusions

The position of fuqaha' in urban Morocco is ambiguous, even among those who believe in their power. On the one hand, this reflects a sense of their being either good or evil: Fuqaha', as clients and others alike assert, can be *rabbani,* "Godly," or *shaytani,* "of Satan [Shaytan]." On the other hand, however, their ambiguity rests on a deeper condition of social effect without public appearance. For whether or not their writing is rubbani or shaytani, it is secret. This is the source of both its power and its danger, giving rise to the common criticism that fuqaha' are only self-interested. This is no doubt true in some cases, but it also reflects contemporary structural and social function of fuqaha'—or, more precisely, their apparent lack of one. Accusations of self-interest and antisocial behavior reflect his outsider status that, no longer summoning a public around him, appears excessive by virtue of being hidden.

For scholars of the Islam and media, drawn to an ideal of public sphere, knowledge and power in massified form are assumed to flow democratically, that is, equally, available to all. The persistence and prevalence of fuqaha' presents an important counterexample. It calls into question the presumed publicness (or even the counter-public but still discernable presence) of religious calls by signaling a power within but not fully controlled by the space of circulation. That the amulet is a refuge of difference appeals to clients as a power adequate to solving problems equally inscrutable and inaccessible by ordinary interventions.

# 5 Rites of Reception

THE EXORCISM RITES of the fqih, his talismanic writing and acts of summoning, had done nothing to quell Zuhur's pain, but rather provoked the jinns' ire. Her turn toward another solution was imminent, but seeing another fqih for more writing and more exorcism was out of the question. As Janice Boddy describes a Zar initiate's journey from a *faki*'s talismans to trance, Zuhur's turn away from the writing cures involved a turn toward a different set of techniques, a different ethical relation, and a different kind of subjectivity and social life (Boddy 1989, 222–24). She would submit to their call, accepting, as Aisha commanded her, the burden of spirit mediumship or "seeing" with the jinns. To become a seer meant acquiescing to Aisha's desires—for particular colors of cloth, varieties of incense, a sacrificed rooster, and most pressing, a *lila*, or nightlong trance ceremony of the Gnawa.

Sitting in Fatima and Abdelqader's house, drinking mint tea and eating Fatima's cookies with Sanae and me, Zuhur pointed to her bandaged leg. "Here, right here, you could see to the bone. Four days now I have no peace. Only when I trance [*jdeb*] will I relax." Sanae turned to me to emphasize the point. "She *must* trance. Aisha told her, '*Here's what I want: I want this, this, and this.*' At the lila, she'll trance, trance, trance! [*Jdeb! Jdeb! Jdeb!*]" There was much to do before the lila: Zuhur had to provide Aisha with henna in designs inscribed on her own hands, wrists, feet, and ankles. She needed to purchase and prepare incense and herbs (*bkhur*) and rosewater for the entire pantheon of jinns. She had to make Aisha bread without salt and buy her a pair of pants, a caftan of black with yellow, red, brown and blue spots, and a headscarf (because "my

Aisha is pious by nature"). She needed to provide dinner as well—a couscous and meat platter, cookies and coffee and tea—for the Gnawa musicians and guests.

The trance ceremony would after all be a highly social ritual, linking the call and command of the jinns to her broader circle of family—her mother and uncle, her husband and children—and friends, and their families. Zuhur's intimates were largely familiar with her travails—but also with jinns and trance. Some of them would also trance, while others would attend to the care of the ceremony, and others would attend as well-wishers. The trance rite would make possible the reproduction of these social relations, as it would reproduce, on a microsocial and political scale, the broader cultural world of popular Sufism and sharifian power. The trance rites themselves would be overseen by a Gnawa leader (muqaddam) with links to the royal palace—his grandfather, descendant of recent slaves of the ruling 'Alawite family, had lived there until independence. Her purchases of herbs and incense and rosewater would bring her into the marketplace surrounding the shrine of Moulay Idriss in the heart of the medina, where shopkeepers line the narrow street to provide pilgrims the essential offerings for prayer at the shrine (and easily portable souvenirs for Western and Asian tour groups). Zuhur's further initiation process would require a pilgrimage to other saints' tombs, with their accompanying shrines to the pantheon of jinns, the mluk, whom she would now serve as body and voice. And, as the spirits demanded, she would have to do so repeatedly, year after year after year. These repetitions would remake Zuhur in relation to the jinns' power, as a recipient of their command, but also interpellate her into the social, political, and ritual structure that mediated and extended their call.

Exclusive and secret powers of summoning and controlling jinns differentiate fuqaha' from other Muslims, and indeed from Muslim public authorities. Spirit mediums, or seers (fem. *shuwwafat*, sing. *shuwwafa;* masc. *shuwwawaf,* sing. *shuwwaf*), also soothe over the differences jinns make in urban Moroccan life in Fez. Their powers are also exclusive. Like fuqaha', they often see for clients or patients in secret, providing answers for problems originating only where God and jinns can see and know. But seers also differ from fuqaha'. This is based in part on gender. Most seers in Fez are women. Men who adopt the identity of a seer are often marginal in their sexual identity, in some cases seeking marriage with another man as their possessing jinns demand. The difference between seer and fqih is also a matter of education; whereas fuqaha' make explicit claims to scriptural power and knowledge, seers do not, or cannot. Rather, it is the jinn that speaks through them that makes them worth listening to, and their own satisfaction of the jinn's demands that maintains her status as their medium. These demands involve the veneration of particular saints with whom the jinns are affiliated, which is to say, their call is not countercultural but aligned very clearly and explicitly with the popular Sufi orders and the recognition of sharifian power in Morocco. Thus during the annual saints' festivals it is common to find seers lined up outside the shrine plying their trade, their ordinarily recondite practices now fully public and protected by the ostensible imprimatur of the saint.

The distinctions between fuqaha' and seers are of mediation and of the difference (the jinns) mediation brings out and controls. For fuqaha', scribal mediation; for seers, bodily mediation. These differences generate and reproduce specific kinds of gendered persons with different claims to power. Whereas fuqaha' claim their knowledge as their own, closely guarding it, a seer can only "lend her voice" to a foreign power that, while residing in her body, is most emphatically not her own (Siegel 2000a [1978]). She is not a master of jinns but their victim, her influence established on the fragile conditions that she admit unknowing and self-absence.[1] To be sure, seers' descriptions of trance suggest a spectrum of self-consciousness. It is the capacity to maintain a certain poise amidst trance, grounded in faithfully and regularly satisfying the jinns' demands, that distinguishes a skilled seer from a novice and makes the jinns' call for attention their own. The audience that forms, as my friend Mohammed expressed it, provides seers their version of an "ijaza" or "ithn"—a letter of credence—by which to establish themselves as bodily receivers of a voice worth hearing.

This audience is public in a particular way, made possible by personal invitation and intimacy with hosts of trance ceremonies and with seers themselves. Women are central, but it is not exclusively a women's public in the sense that Anne Meneley has described in Yemen (2007). More importantly the jinns' call to the seer, and the seer's extension of it in ritual does not imagine or address a national or transnational public—essential elements of new mass-market and mass-mediated Sufi and Trance "festivals." For all its connections to the broader sharifian culture, conventional practitioners of trance view the jinn's call as particular—not addressing all equally in the mode of broadcast, but striking whom it will, and thus distinguishing its recipients as the special bearers of a sovereign force. In this respect it shares the sense of exclusivity with the powers of fuqaha' and indeed suffers the same criticisms of secrecy and sorcery of which fuqaha' are the object. In a word, as much as seeing requires responsibility to jinns, it involves turning away from the mass-mediated call around which a national society is presumed to form, publically and transparently. It is thus antisocial and irresponsible even as it produces a form of particular sociality among kin and friends and clientele.

## The First Call

Zuhur's history with jinns was longer and richer than my intial impressions allowed. She explained that as a child she heard the music from Gnawa musicians, coming from the home of neighbors whom she did not know and did not talk to. Her mother feared that the music would draw her in: "She threatened the neighbors: 'By God, if you come for her, I'll kill you!'" One would think that her mother herself had nothing to do with Gnawa and their rituals. But when I asked Zuhur to describe her first episode of possession, she described herself at eight years old, in the care of her grandmother during a Gnawa trance ceremony (lila). Zuhur sat amidst the noise and smell of the ceremony, and during a pause she followed her grandmother as she accompanied the Gnawa leader, or *muqaddam*, to a faucet on the lowest floor of the house in near dark.

The muqaddam turned and, surprised to see Zuhur watching, shouted and struck her forehead with a bottle. She bled and "fell possessed" (*tqasat*). Her grandmother was livid: "Why did you hit her?! She's Aisha's daughter!" The muqaddam, Zuhur recalled, then healed the cut with the same knife used for the sacrifice. He pressed the knife to her wound and took it away, leaving no mark.

But since then a pain comes and goes at that spot.

During the past several years of sores and pain, she had also begun to see jinns in dreams, but also, terrifyingly, while she lay awake at night. Figures from Sufi orders' pantheon of jinns, the mluk al-jinn, threatened to hit her and to burn her legs. They demanded sexual intercourse, warning her not to sleep with her husband. The mluk had shouted at him, "*We* sleep with her, not you!" This was a prelude, however, to their demand for complete possession of her. In a recent dream all seven mluk called upon Zuhur to "gather up the platter [*hazz al-tabaq*]," that is, the seer's platter of trade tools—cards, seashells, herbal and mineral incenses, and colored cloth—and to "take up the pantheon [*hazz al-mijma'*]." That is, they commanded her submission to all seven and thus to become a seer in their service.

She was, in I. M. Lewis's words, undergoing "the first call of a dreaded sickness," one that indeed her grandmother had also received and accepted (Lewis 2003 [1971], 26). She did not understand the reason for the call. All she could think of were mistakes that perhaps her grandmother had committed, or she had committed, and for which she was now being held hostage. Her mother and her sister offered her advice on how to respond to the call. The two women's views however differed starkly in practice and doctrine—reflecting both her sister's turn toward revivalist Islam as well as the broader generational differences dividing conventionally gendered relations to jinns. Her mother advised her to pray to a local saint (Mawlay Bu Shta al-Khamar) whose baraka could provide succor at least by temporarily calming the jinns that tormented her. To Zuhur and her mother, however, this also meant paying homage to a jinn affiliated with this saint, so the visit to the shrine had only exacerbated the situation, further angering Aisha in particular:

> I left everything I had to do for Aisha and went to work for "the Ma'lim" [the jinn named Shamharush]. I left Aisha there high and dry [*khalit ha ariyana*]. I wore gray, the color of the Ma'lim. I made a sacrifice [*dabiha*]. As we walked in turns around the tomb two brothers entered and threw themselves at my feet. "Ya Aisha! You take my mind! You make me trance on glass! You break my legs!" I laughed. The muqaddam [of the shrine] yelled at them, but they held my legs. Later I slept, I saw sparkles, and my legs hurt in those places.

She visited another saint's tomb as well—Moulay Abdelqadir al-Jilali, a patron saint of the popular Jilala order, which also practices trance. This provided Zuhur more sustained relief, at least from night visitations if not the persistent sores on her legs. Her visit to the saint involved her own claims to piety: "I was crying. I said, 'God, I came to this saint [*salih*]. I'm a good person. I've suffered this illness. Help me out of this condition.' I said, 'I just can't become a seer [*shuwwafa*]. I'm a good woman, pure.'" In the same afternoon she described a dream in which a man and a woman came to her.

> They had seen Aisha and asked her where she was going. Aisha said, "I'm going to see to matters concerning Zuhur." The man and woman left Aisha to come to me. They brought me the *tabaq* and said, "Here is your livelihood [*rizq diyalik*]." I said, "No I don't want it. I don't want to do anything idolatrous [*shirk bi-l-Allah*]." They overturned the tabaq and left. From that day on I haven't dreamt of Lalla Aisha or of anyone from the *mijma'* [the pantheon of mluk].

Zuhur's younger sister advised the pious solution to refuse any exchange with the jinns whatsoever and to turn toward orthodox Islamic practices, which she alone in the family had already done. In Zuhur's description she had abandoned jinns and saint rites for revivalist Islamic piety and now dressed only in white, always wore the hijab, and prayed five times a day immediately as the call to prayer was voiced. Zuhur was sympathetic, and her own pleas to the saint reflected her desire to avoid the impieties forced upon a seer—jinns' inevitable demands for sacrifices in their name (rather than in God's name), for example. That she made this plea at a saint's tomb, however, would already open her to accusations of idolatry by revivalist Muslims (including her sister). Indeed from that perspective her claims to piety seem absurd if not outright hypocritical.

But it also reflects the kinds of hybrid forms and negotiations urban Muslim women make in Morocco between established rituals of saint and jinn veneration and a newer revivalist ethos, largely divided along generational lines. Thus in my household, Fatima and her daughters could both advise visiting a saint's tomb (for the good of my research in this case) but then differ in the details.

> FATIMA: At the door of the zawiya you stop and make sure you have the right intention. You say: "My Lord, and this Pious Saint [*wali salih*], if you give me X, Y, or Z—if you help me reach my goal (say, your book)—I will do a sacrifice for you.'"
>
> SANAE (interrupting): Mama! Don't—
>
> MOUNIA (interrupting): You *don't* say "My Lord and this pious saint"!
>
> FATIMA: Really?
>
> MOUNIA: Of course! That's idolatry [*shirk*]! You just say, "My Lord. . . ."

For the younger generation, addressing the saint alongside God is just understood to be idolatrous. In Moroccan reformist and revivalist discourse it is a critique of the saint treated as intermediary of God, regardless of one's intent. Moroccan criticisms have tended to be mild, however, or at least have precipitated less dramatic responses than the outright destruction of Sufi saint shrines by militant Islamic factions in Pakistan, Afghanistan, and postrevolution Tunisia and Libya. Nevertheless, the modern reformist ethos to which Sanae and Mounia implicitly subscribe, permitting the practice of visiting tombs, emphasizes that one turn to God directly. It is a question of one's orientation, the source of sacred power to which one turns, or rather returns, the orientation itself suggesting a prior summons.

## The Reception that Calls

Zuhur's sister had, at least for the time being, wholly supplanted one call for the other (see Masquelier 2001, 2009; Bernal 1994). This meant hearing the call to prayer, listening to its blunt and blaring signal over the microphones of the Fez mosques: to its electric echoes amidst the cobblestone. And it meant heeding the call of other revivalist Muslims, both in person in Fez and via the satellite channels that Fassis receive from the Middle East, Amr Khalid's new da'wa, as well as the Wahhabi-based arguments on *Iqraa*, the satellite channel from Saudi Arabia. These calls, so often described as *the* call to Islam, are of course *a* call of Islam. Not merely transmitted by particular technological media, the call is the call *of* that structure, made possible by it, and defining piety in terms, first of all, of *its* reception.

To say that this call is truer, that this practice is conscious practice, is to privilege a putatively direct call from God through television rather than from jinns through kin. It requires that one respond to a different source of power and thus become a different kind of person. It also privileges responsibility to a particular medium (or set of media); simultaneously, whether explicitly or not, it understands jinn rights and kin as another medium, one to be rejected and protected against. It is to bar oneself from the call of that medium. If both calls are bodily, if both calls appeal to the senses and cultivate receptive bodies, they do so with different aesthetics and norms of consciousness (Hirschkind 2006; Meyer 2011). Even as trance rights begin with conscious gestures, conscious movements of dance that attract the jinns (jedba), participants revel in the pleasures of noise and scent and accelerating movement, finally submitting fully to the power that the ritual has reproduced, that is to say, has once again summoned and unleashed. It is to give oneself over to and reproduce the ritual structure fully, without resistance.

## Jinns, Kinship, Friendship

This is not to ignore the particular people and human relationships that help to comprise and reproduce that ritual structure. Well before Zuhur was summoned to trance, so too was her grandmother. She speculated that her own possession by the jinns derived precisely from that lineage—as a debt unpaid and now inherited. Those accumulated debts reiterate the sense that the ritual of trance is the *response* to a prior command, and thus an act of responsibility, rather than an original act in itself. Even though Zuhur was responding to the jinns' call, that call, as command, was bound up with the people who preceded her and indeed who placed her in the position of suffering the call itself.

This assertion is not unique to urban Morocco or to these rituals of trance. In Hubert and Mauss's (1964) theory of sacrifice (sacrifices accompany the trance rites), so too is the act itself the response to a prior command, or contract, which the ritual practitioner is obliged to satisfy. According to Mauss and Hubert, sacrifice fulfills a contract with the source of all sacrality—that is, with the divine, and with respect to its singular law (Hubert and Mauss 1964, 100).[2] Sacrifice is not trance, of course, but the act is no less obligatory and no less aimed at the transformation of the condition of the practitioner herself (Hubert and Mauss 1964, 13). The sacrificial act for the jinns themselves—committed in the name of the jinn, rather than in the name of God—is repeatedly cited by Islamic revivalists as key proof of the whole ritual structures' idolatry.

From where does the sacred articulate its command? From the jinn? From the saint's tomb? Through whom is this command voiced? Through whom does one learn to hear and heed it? Others among Zuhur's community of friends—Na'ima, her friend Miriam, and their families—received the mluk al-jinns' calls through kin relations. Which is to say, the call of the jinns was also a call of kin through which it was articulated.

Zuhur and her mother were "close [*'indna qraba*]" with Miriam and her mother, who had indeed hosted Zuhur's initial exorcism rites. Miriam's mother was not herself a seer, but as Zuhur said, "she sees the jinns," and gave birth to Miriam's sister with the help of jinns at the tomb of Mawlay Idriss. I asked Na'ima how she learned of the jinn. "I didn't learn," she said. "This is a legacy from my kin: parents, grandparents, great-grandparents . . . [*wirati min judadi—jed, jed, jed . . .* ]." Her paternal grandmother is possessed by all of the mluk (*al-mluk kamilin*) and practices as a seer. Na'ima's younger brother is possessed by Aisha; her mother, by Mimun and Aisha. Na'ima's father, now dead, "wore Coffee-Brown"—the color of Bouhali, one of the pantheon of jinns. (When his sister went on the hajj, he said, "Bring me back a coffee-brown jellaba!") Na'ima's paternal aunt was also possessed by Aisha, and when she failed to comply with her commands, Na'ima's cousins suffered ill fortune—a lost job, a car accident. She went to a seer who told her that Aisha demanded a robe and long billowing pants of multiple colors, as well as a full application of henna dye on hands and wrists and ankles and feet. It cost her thousands of dirhams—a difficult sum for her—but she complied, and her children recovered.

Such are the sacrifices one must make to jinns, but also to one's family who understand and value the call. Far from the fqih's solitude—and far too from Zuhur's tales of suffering—bearing and satisfying the demands of the jinns generates a community. Giving voice to their call makes the internal struggle, as Vincent Crapanzano has argued of the related Hamadsha order, a publicly identifiable one, the marker of an identity (1973). Or as James Siegel has described women's dreams and possession rites in Sumatra, it converts a bodily, unconscious experience into a recognizable "set of signs" that one bears (2000a [1978]). Fundamentally, satisfying the ritual demands of the jinns puts the internal desire—even if it does not originate with one—into public circulation.

This state of community makes ambivalent subjects—indeed, it is hard to call the recipient of jinns a "subject" at all. In one sense, objectifying the jinns' call permits one to take hold of the call as one's own: the idiom in urban Morocco is of "having jinns." But "having" also bears traces of powerlessness—as in "having" an illness. Thus a very old woman, not from the family, but whom my household affectionately called *mrat ʿammi,* or "My Uncle's Wife," wore a bright-yellow hijab because she "has Mira," who demands it of her. Zuhur and her friends described themselves as "having" jinns: "I have Aisha [*ʿindi ʿaisha*]," Zuhur said. Naʿima said she "has" Bouhali; Miriam explained, "I have Malika and Mira." "Having a jinn" for Zuhur and friends meant indulging each one's particular desires and tastes, for alcohol, cigarettes, for example—but only insofar as those desires were themselves implanted in them from outside and were not the expression of will. The desires are typically stereotyped—Mira demands cigarettes; Bouhali demands alcohol; Aisha demands tables overflowing with every food and drink available.

A more objective view of trance and mediumship perceives a different kind of responsibility. Or more to the point, a different kind of receptivity. The seer's submission to the jinns' call generates its own kind of knowing, but in lending her voice and body to a foreign call, her claim to it, even to speak in its name, is lost. Even if the seer acquires attention and a crowd around her, it is not her voice to which the audience responds, but rather the jinn's. Hers is a power that presumes a state of powerlessness: a receptivity to a power that comes to presence at the expense of knowing. As Rosalind Morris writes, "To speak and not be the subject of speech, to know and not be the subject of knowledge: this is medium's predicament" (Morris 2000, 102). Not a subject, she is rather the object of the call, the recipient of the call, and her ritual a rite of reception.

That the call is transferred from generation to generation suggests the reproduction not only of a practice and an ethos, but particular social and subjective structures that, foreign to individual persons, exceed their control. The call of the jinns is not theirs alone, but the call of a social structure; it is a sovereign command that must be inherited and in being received can only be transferred. Possession itself is the mark of an inheritance that cannot stop, cannot be either fully assimilated or fully expressible: the legacy of a wound that one inherits, the very burden of which defies full comprehension.

## Trance Masters: The Ambivalence of the Margins

Here it is helpful to recall the larger cultural context for urban trance rites, whose historically marginal participants have included women of multiple classes (though of limited education) in domestic rites, as well as underclass men, and slaves and concubines. ʿIsawa groups that so concerned colonial-era nationalists do perform trance rites in homes in Fez; historically, however, Gnawa groups—themselves comprising slaves and concubines and their descendants—have played the more central role. As ʿIsawa members acknowledged to me, Gnawa have greater expertise with mluk al-jinn royalty, summoning not just one or a few of them, as ʿIsawa do, but the entire pantheon.[3]

The term *Gnawa,* as Chouki El Hamel has concluded, appeared by the seventeenth century in North African writings to refer to blacks in general from West Africa, regardless of ethnic origin (El Hamel 2013, chap. 8). More specifically in Morocco, the term referred to people of multiple ethnic backgrounds and concubines captured by North African slave traders from Malian and Hausa areas of what Arab geographers called *bilad al-sudan,* Lands of the Blacks. The Gnawa's rituals and past bear similarities to those of other trance practitioners of West African origin: the Bori of Niger and upper Nigeria (Levtzion and Pouwels 2000, 57; Tremearne 1914; Pâques 1991; Masquelier 2001); the Stambouli of Tunisia (Jankowsky 2010); and the Zar of Egypt and Northern Sudan (Boddy 1989; Westermarck 1968, 341–44).[4] Although trans-Saharan trade was established from as early as the ninth century, a large number of West African blacks in Morocco were reenslaved under 'Alawite Sultan Mawlay Isma'il (d. 1727), who consolidated and expanded Sharifian imperial power by forcibly recruiting a standing army on the model of the Ottoman armies, the *'Abid al-Bukhari* or "black army," as well as enslaving men and women to serve the households of the Sultan in Fez and Marrakech (El Hamel 2013, 155–65; cf. Ennaji 1999). By the early colonial period wealthy families of Fez commonly owned slaves and domestics, and women's participation in Gnawa rites widespread (Michaux-Bellaire 1910, 426; Le Tourneau 1962, 611). Well into the postcolonial period, as several Fassis attested, Gnawa performances were common, with the month of Sha'ban (preceding Ramadan) being a festive time of open doors and multiple Gnawa troupes moving from house to house.

For the undeniable violence of slavery in Morocco, the marginality of the Gnawa was also ambivalent. As Mohammed Ennaji points out, preindustrial-era slavery was a different, albeit oppressive, institution; like slaves and slave armies in the Middle East, the Gnawa's slavery meant proximity to power (Ennaji 1999). Like fuqaha', their foreignness of origin, language, and appearance has contributed to the popular view of their expertise with matters unseen and unknown, and specifically sovereign power. (In a reference to Fassi's reputedly light skin and thus aristocratic features, several Gnawa musicians repeated to me, "The only thing white about us is our teeth.") Gnawa's association with the monarchy is attenuated today but endures. Former slaves remained separate well into the colonial period, living in and around the Dar al-Makhzen, the al-Qasr al-Maliki or Royal Palace, in Fez al-Jadid, and receiving a monthly stipend until the exile of Mohammed V and the French appointment of Ben 'Arafa in 1953. Upon his return Mohammad V welcomed back Gnawa kin of the "Black Guard" as well as three teams of Gnawa musicians to live within his palaces, groups Hassan II was also purported to host in his Rabat Palace. Several Gnawa musicians in Fez made clear they had attended the king's daughter's heavily publicized wedding in 1986. Ba Boujmaa, the muqaddam for Zuhur's lila, was also proud participant in Hassan II's 1975 Green March, carrying a banner emblazoned in Arabic with "Gnawa" in white script. For Pierre-Alain Claisse, that relationship endures, with Gnawa masters functioning as the king's public mediators with the underclasses as "guardians of . . . the [sharifian] maraboutic tradition [who] embody the history of national unity" (Claisse 2003, 65).

If Claisse's assessment offers little practical description of that mediation, it is nonetheless the case that Gnawa practices, in mass-mediated form, today accrue new value as representations of Sufi nationalist version of Moroccan Islam. We shall examine examples in more detail in the next chapter, but suffice it to say that Fassi Gnawa, like Gnawa throughout Morocco, are aware of these transformations (Pacques 1991). Indeed, the Gnawa leader with whom I worked most closely—Boujmaa, the leader for Zuhur's lila—sought to capitalize on the transformation, taking opportunities to perform in the French cultural center in conjunction with the Sufi Festival and the Sufi-based Sacred Music Festival in Fez between 2003 and 2007 (on the margins of the festival, but drawing on its cachet and its tourist and local audience).

More significantly, Fassi Gnawa incorporated the new popularity of trance, and theatrical norms attending its mass mediation, into their public and private performances alike. Boujmaa and his troupe fully expected to perform for cameras. To my naïve surprise, during one lila, they suspended the ritual process—abruptly freezing during the gifting of milk and dates to honor the jinns (and spilling the milk)—to pose for my own camera. Over the course of several months in 2003 Boujmaa and his wife, who was the troupe's female leader (*muqaddama*, or "priestess"), also self-consciously salvaged and revived a Gnawa ceremony that had been neglected in Fez for at least forty years. The ritual itself, however, showed the signs of rust, for while he and his wife knew their choreographed steps, the other members of the troupe were considerably less confident in theirs; the lavish effort to sacrifice a young bull in particular wreaked havoc on the ceremonial props and players—the animal's arcing spurts of blood sullying a plastic throne and vinyl costumes. In general, Boujmaa's suggestions that he and I work together "to our mutual benefit" did not materialize.

It should be noted, however, that the opening of the market to new kinds of public performance provide far more opportunities for male Gnawa musicians than for female seers. For whereas Gnawa performers themselves do not fall into trance, but rather summon jinns to possess the ostensible audience (the women and men seers whom the jinns have initially called), women who do take mass-market stages (for example, Aisha, whom we shall meet in the next chapter) adopt an explicitly modernist posture of conscious performance rather than reception. They thus disavow any special power of seeing or being which the jinns presence would conventionally establish.

For Zuhur, already possessed, the initiation into "seeing" would mark a change in social status and an active confrontation with modernist distrust of utter submission to jinns—a distrust actively expressed in modernist criticisms of seers as secret charlatans on par with fuqaha'. That is to say, "having" a jinn is one thing, but dedicating one's life and body to their service is another. Being a seer means taking a distinct kind of community role, but also bearing the responsibility for others' spirit problems. Seers receive clients much as fuqaha' do, in small rooms in the medina, and like fuqaha' they diagnose the name and nature of the jinns at the root of the problem. They advise clients to take certain actions: to sacrifice a rooster or goat at a particular saint's tomb or spirit shrine, or within the home if the home is haunted. They recommend trance rites and provide contacts to the Gnawa or other Sufi practitioners who might best carry out their ritual. When necessary, seers prepare the cures on behalf of their patients, substituting their body for the victims in the process of trance, for example.

All of this provides seers a certain measure of prestige, as well as an income, modest, but substantially better than the small-time craft production and souvenir sales, cleaning and child care, street begging and sexual trade through which underclass women survive in the medina and other poor neighborhoods of Fez. At the same time, however, it makes seers the targets of criminal accusations of charlatanism (*sha'wada*), chicanery (*tkharwid*), and fraud (*nasab wa-l-ihtiyal*), as well as prostitution. When I began looking for seers to gather a sense of their practice and social position in fez, I found my access denied. "Because you are a man, they are afraid that you are police," Sanae explained to me. Calling on Sanae's assistance permitted increased access, although she would invariably enter the seer's room first to ask permission for me to enter. In several instances she returned with the seer's conditions for me to satisfy before gaining entry (I would have to sacrifice a cock). Others accepted my presence, though notably boasting that they did so because they "don't fear the police [*al-makhzen*]."

The term for police often used in Fez—*al-makhzen*, literally, "storehouse"—is an old term referring to the state more generally and the monarchy-controlled elite political, economic, and security apparatus in particular. The use amongst seers and ordinary Fassis is habitual rather than a critical comment on its continued power, despite the monarchy's claims to reform. But it is an important comment on the state nonetheless. It points up the distance between the centers of sharifian national culture and the marginal seers who link themselves to the center symbolically and practically. It points up the state's efforts to control or recuperate opaque spiritual communications amongst the masses. This at least helps explain why seers, so wary of police in their everyday ritual exchanges, openly practice around the tombs of popular saints Sidi Ben Hamdush and Sidi Ahmed Dghoughi during the national celebration of the prophet Mohammed's birth (mawlid) and underclass Sufi orders' pilgrimages; for there, as police patrol under Moroccan flags and banners lauding the generous sponsorship of the monarchy, the state is omnipresent, already encompassing the jinns' call.

At the same time, however, the practice of seeing is vulnerable to modern reformist critiques, and for reasons that mirror the legal problem of charlatanism—namely, the proliferating connections and social effects of the ritual practice. If the trance cure, as described above, involves the social circulation of a foreign command—the jinns' call—lodged within the body of the seer, this is precisely the source of its danger as well. That is to say, the public staging and reproduction of jinns' commands—on no matter how small a scale—is precisely what makes the rites a matter of concern and criticism for reform-minded Muslims who do not partake of the rites themselves. For critics unsympathetic or skeptical of the claims of possession at all, "jinn" is simply a foil for personal desires the possessed woman or man is too weak or impious to keep contained. This certainly was the view of my friends Mohammed and Najia. As Mohammed put it:

> They [women] talk and maybe they particularly like [the jinn] "Mira" because she smokes and it gives them an excuse to smoke. They like the parties. Or they will gossip and speak badly about others. "*She* said that. . . . [Mohammed adopts a conspiratorial voice and looks]. And *she* doesn't like it that. . . ." You will find families who talk a lot about the jinns—all the time—this and that all the time. Other families do not. But those who pass all their time talking about jinns will not fulfill the ritual obligations ['*ibadat*].

By this common view women disavow responsibility for smoking by ascribing the desire for it to Mira. The effect is excessive, or more specifically, excessive and destructive communication. The lack of self-control already invokes a plurality. It is not one woman but women. And then it is not just women, but families. Women and families involved in jinns do not merely talk occasionally, but do so "all the time," with the result being irresponsibility to God's call and ritual obligations. It is a particularly destructive, sickening, and repugnant kind of talk—gossip—what the prophet Muhammad decried as "eating your dead brother." Here the smoking seems hardly to matter, but it is certainly related, as one imagines the smoking too is excessive—repeated compulsively rather than as a simple pleasure. Like smoking, rites beget rites; the call is extended with each iteration potentially seducing and summoning others to it.[5]

If Mohammed could nonetheless imagine attending trance rites and accepted my invitation to the lila of Zuhur herself, he would do so with a particular posture of vigilance, to maintain a distance and immunity to a call that violated his own sense of responsibility and conscientious piety. Najia, for her part, declined the invitation, her own piety and sympathy far closer to Zuhur's sister's than to Zuhur's. To be sure, none of these women nor any reformist Muslim would claim utter freedom from responsibility or obedience, but rather the individual freedom to obey: the subject is responsible because she is conscious of what calls her, and of her own response.

As much as reformist views of jinn mediums, like fuqaha', tend to emphasize more their excess self-interest than their lack of self-control, the problem is that they summon others—who in turn lose self-control and self-awareness. The reformist concerns that the ritual medium can call reflects a broader question, certainly posed in everyday life in Fez, as to the source of control in the public affairs. Whether for example the state is present, or responsible, or simply neglectful. This point is reiterated in mass-mediated comments on seers, in which it is not ordinary people, but finally the state that must intervene to stop the circulation of the jinns' call. Thus a popular national journal's typical account of a medium—"Journey of a Female Charlatan ends in Prison"—could emphasize the stupidity of the clientele as much as the sinister intent of the practitioner herself. That story, serialized during Ramadan in 2003, was prefaced in each installment by this opening:

> Ghaliya, for those who do not know her, can heal impotence [*thqaf*], fight sorcery, attract a lover, open the doors to prosperity, expel bad luck, marry off old maids, and treat whatever other psychological and physical illnesses affect the deluded. It was she who trapped many in her web before she fell into the hands of the police. . . . Her house became a *qibla* [direction of Mecca] for all who sought a cure for magic. (*Al-Sabah*, Oct. 29, 2003, 14)

The newspaper invites its readers to view and assumes they do view Ghaliya—whose name echoes the Moroccan colloquial Arabic for "expensive"—as a type. "Those who don't know her," in fact, do know her because "her web" is the web of signs of a Moroccan seer and indeed of popular sharifian Islam generally. She treats all the cures that typical curers treat; her house is adorned with sheets of colored cloth and she adorns herself with the title "Sharifa"—meaning that she claims sharifian descent. It is a nickname, the paper asserts, that "she gave herself to add legitimacy to her work." But its very recognizability assures its success—which is to say, it implicates the broader system in which people believe in baraka and the special capacities it endows. Certainly she summons no shortage of clients. Her power to summon to that system is in fact the article's point: "the deluded" turn to her as one turn to the qibla—the direction of prayer, from which God's call emanates. She offers, and by extension, the culture offers, an alternative call toward which the deluded can and habitually do turn. Their lack of control and the connections it fosters finally require (as in al-Hajj's story in Chapter 1) the intervention of the police.

## Zuhur's Initiation

Stories of seers' ceremonies both critical and complementary often focus on the sheer excess of the provisions; especially where Aisha is concerned, the popular imagination conjures platters of meats and sweets and alcoholic drinks, to say nothing of the sacrificial offerings. As Boujmaa had assured me, there would be not one but numerous bulls and sheep sacrificed at his ritual revival. Zuhur's lila would be far more modest, a reflection perhaps of her limited means rather than desires. But this too would cost money: approximately 3000 dirhams (US\$ 300), which Zuhur could not afford alone. Sanae's mother Fatima, with whom I lived, began generously to delegate expenses. Fatima would host the event and pay for and prepare the platters of couscous and the multiple rounds of tea and coffee and cookies. I would pay 800 dirhams to the Gnawa ma'lim Boujmaa to lead the ceremony with four members of his troupe. Zuhur, with her mother's help, would pay for the henna preparation (both the henna and the artist), the clothing, and the bkhur.

Gathering at Fatima's for the baking and the sewing, Zuhur was cheerful, the atmosphere was bright, animated, festive. Fatima's friends came and went, in a whirl of warmth and wild stories supplied by Zuhur and friends, with much swearing to God: "I swear to God I saw it with my own eyes! Really and truly! [*bi-l-sah wa bi al-niyya*]." Lunches were served and eaten, glasses filled and refilled with tea, ashtrays in front of Zuhur and friends filled with snubbed-out Olympiques and black-market Marlboros.

Two days later, and one night before the lila, Sanae, Fatima, and I rode a taxi to Fez Jadid to meet Zuhur for the henna application. This took place at the home of Zuhur's sister-in-law, who was also the niece of a medina café owner I knew and associate of my friend Mohammed. The ten or so adults present (myself excepted) were women: Zuhur and her friends, the hostess, Fatima's closest friend and neighbor, and Sanae. Only Fatima knew the henna mistress (*mulat al-hanna*), a black, pretty, and fat woman who remained silent throughout. Sanae explained that Fatima knew who best to hire—a sign of the generational differences in ritual knowledge—and what to look for; the henna mistress "must be clean [*nqiyya*], wear nice clothes, and perfume, and must be pretty." The woman sat on a couch, applying the thick green henna paste with a plastic syringe, to Zuhur's hands, wrists, feet, and ankles. She worked steadily, laying decisive lines in long overlapping threads. No smudges and nothing erased.

The position in fact demanded more than artistic skill. This was the commencement of the lila, and already gifts were presented to the jinns. Throughout she placed small pieces of black benzoin on the brazier, or *mijmar*, wafting the smoke over Zuhur's henna. The hostess walked the mijmar around the room as well, bathing us in the scent. I commented that the henna was like the henna Moroccan brides wear; Sanae rejected the comparison: "This is a party for the mluk al-jinn [*hafla diyal mluk*], a lila of the mluk." She explained that the patterns on Zuhur's skin were for Lalla Aisha (dots), Lalla Malika (the arabesques).

Someone played recorded 'Isawa music on a small cassette deck. Zuhur's friend Miriam danced mildly. Zuhur slumped a bit, and everyone tensed in anticipation. Then she nodded side to side. A collective shiver and pause . . . but nothing more took place. Sanae explained that Zuhur had clearly wanted to jdeb, that she was not alone, that Lalla Aisha was with her. Surrounded by the lace patterns of the henna that seep into the skin, the henna rite marked the start of Aisha's presence.

## The Lila

The henna ceremony created an excitement and anticipation. It also brought women together in shared pleasure and ease. The presence of friends as well as family provoked conversations punctuated by laughter; except for the specific acts for the jinns themselves, there was little formality. The differences amongst them were reduced as Zuhur became the center of attention. This was most certainly a women's gathering and space of exchange beyond the demands of public exposure. The lila would offer a different atmosphere: including men, to be sure, but also more tense with a sense of potential danger.

In anticipation of the event the Gnawa ma'lim Boujma'a ordered that our house be cleaned from ground floor to roof and, especially, that all drains be cleared, cleaned, uncovered. All iron, all pictures, all mirrors were to be removed from the main room of the ground floor where the lila would take place. The space should be purified, like that of a mosque. But more particularly it should be hospital to the jinns who would come to occupy the space, summoned by the Gnawa's rhythms and the opening gestures of jedba or trance of the women and men possessed. When the Gnawa arrived— men in red and black, the red velvet hats that only occupants of the royal palace wear— I welcomed them in—"Marhaba bikum"—but was abruptly stopped by Sanae's father. "When the Gnawa enter our house, we do not say 'Welcome.' This is now the *Gnawa's* house, and we are *their* guests." The submission to a foreign power had begun, and it rendered us foreign to the very space we habitually considered our own.

Other guests began to arrive after the afternoon prayer taking seats at tables— segregated by gender. In a side salon, just the men and the five Gnawa musicians; on the other side, just the women. Fatima, Fatima's sister Na'ima, the housemaid, and another girl from the neighborhood brought around the first course, a round platter of couscous covered with squash, cabbage, carrots, and lamb. A second course of lemon chicken followed soon after: platters of chicken dotted with green olives, all bathed in caramelized onion and lemon peel. People reached in with pieces of bread and deft hands, slipping meat off the bone and gracefully into the mouth. Liters of Coca Cola and Lemon Fanta, silver pots of mint tea, and coffee in white plastic carafes all circulated and emptied.

The meal ended, the Gnawa left, and guests rinsed hands and teeth at the fountain between door and kitchen. A few drumbeats sounded outside, followed by women's ululations. The guests left the house to join the Gnawa circled up just beyond the gate separating our small quarter and narrow stone street from a moderately trafficked street leading to the main arteries of the medina. A river runs underneath the street, and ordinarily one can hear the rush of water. But two sets of drumbeats overwhelmed all ears, as sandalwood smoke settled in. The two men with drums stood at the edge of a circle; the three other Gnawa danced in jumps and bends, their iron castanets punctuating the steps with syncopated clacks. At that moment, two blind men, arm in arm, who had been stepping slowly and carefully along the edge of the narrow street came to a full and confused stop. They stood at a distance from the circle, frightened it seemed to me, by the sensory force. My friend Mohammed, vigilant, stepped out of the circle, took the men by their arms, and guided them past.

Boujmaa would later explain to me that the drumbeats were (sweeping his arms) the diffusion of a message: "Everyone hears the news [*al-akhbar*]. It is for the collectivity [*li-l-jam'*]." In one sense this harkens to Fez's older days, and the public presence of Gnawa during the festive days of Sha'ban. In another sense it recalls Gnawa's reverence for Bilal ibn Rabah, an early Meccan convert to Islam and the prophet Muhammad's first caller to prayer. It differentiates Gnawa from fqih certainly, but also from the seers themselves, whose voices cannot, or rather should not, carry indiscriminately. Still, it is an indiscriminate ritual communication that modernists criticize; Mohammed's concerns for the blind men were notable in part because no one else paid them mind. Not everyone receives the news or, more importantly, interprets the sound as an articulate message. For some, it is just noise.

The precolonial ethnographer Georges Salmon considered Gnawa in urban Morocco merely "street entertainers," and today Gnawa musicians themselves will castigate others whose practice consists of regular street performances (or busking), with hat in hand. Certainly in my experience, the Gnawa on the street were as often drunk as not. But in this instance the outdoor performance was brief, a prelude to the ceremonial opening of the door to the home—the site of the jinns' arrival—and thus the welcome for the jinns themselves.

The Gnawa splashed droplets of milk for the jinns in four directions as we turned back through the gate toward the door. Sanae and her aunt carried large white candles; Na'ima's brother and Mohammed hoisted a large brazier as the drumbeats changed. The Gnawa surrounded Zuhur, one of the musicians carrying the tray of milk and dates, one the tray of bkhur, and the others pounding the drums. Whoever had hands free, clapped. When we reached the door, the Gnawa sprinkled more milk at the threshold. The Gnawa, as the proper hosts, were now extending hospitality not only to the audience but also to the mluk al-jinns—the recipients of the offerings of milk and dates. As the lila began, the Gnawa welcomed the first of the mluk—al-Buwab, the Doorkeeper—with the Gnawa's multivalent refrain: Who will open the door? Later the closing of the door will mark the end of the lila: the last jinn is Aisha, also called Mulat al-Bab, Mistress of the Door.

Inside, the Gnawa surrounded Zuhur for a time and performed their own choreographed dance, feet slapping the cold stone floor, followed by a solo performance on the blue-yellow carpet. The Gnawa then took their seats on a set of cushions positioned as a small stage against one wall. Boujmaa sat in the middle, dressed in black gown with fine flower hem, a gold *taqiya,* or cap, and a long white scarf, his henna-laced, three-stringed *guenbri* in hand. The other men wore other colors—two red gowns, one green, and another, a crowd of green-blues. At their feet sat a brazier and several trays of milk and dates to welcome each of the mluk on arrival.

Mimun was welcomed: "Sidi Mimun, welcome. Mimun has come. Welcome Mimun." Zuhur, in a black caftan with a white headscarf, began her slow, moderate dance. Women's trance styles differ in Fez depending on their age and class. In lilas among the poorest Fassis I observed, the young women's gestures were chaotic, their bodies thrown to the floor. Older women I observed in trance—the grandmother in my own house, Boujmaa's wife, and another beautiful and very old woman for whom

Boujmaa's group played—had honed the skill of mediumship, and their gestures were stately and graceful. But, the style of trance also shifts with the arrival of different jinns, and even the beautiful old woman's gentle motions had turned to foot pounding and head bobbing and screaming in scratched bursts, "You led me astray! You led me astray! You led me astray!"

When the jinn Malika arrived, other women joined Zuhur and the tensions of the trance veered further beyond the mild trance that Mimun had induced. Zuhur maintained a steady trance, but Miriam's motions had grown wilder, her head jerking back and forth, and finally she screamed. Crying, she lurched toward a side room where several men sat, including Mohammed, and Zuhur's sister-in-law's uncle. He quickly made room for her on a section of the low couch that lined the walls and held her hand, reciting Qur'anic verse quietly in her ear. The lila paused for mint tea and coffee and for Fatima's cookies, which she had baked in a supplementary oven she brought out of storage for large parties. Miriam, now sitting upright, but dazed, said that the Gnawa's rhythm had been wrong. "That wasn't Malika's."

As the musicians reassembled, Boujmaa requested of Fatima's housekeeper to bring mint tea, dry coffee, and sugar to put on a tray. When the jinn Bouhali arrived he would be hungry and searching for food and drink. In the tall atrium of the Fassi house the atmosphere was festively ordinary again, a good Moroccan party. Zuhur's friend Na'ima fell into trance, but she was alone. Others chatted over the din, drinking from glasses they held at the rim and bottom to disperse the heat. They betrayed no sense of concern for what had passed with Miriam, nor what Bouhali might induce. Zuhur smoked a cigarette in the women's salon, and Na'ima swayed off the floor to join her. The musicians stood and filed out the front door, to drink tea and fill a long wooden pipe with *kif*, a finely cut mixture of marijuana and tobacco leaf.

Sanae and I joined them outside, and Boujmaa asked her who was sick—who had necessitated the ceremony. He was surprised, thinking that Zuhur was in fact already a seer and was performing the lila on someone else's behalf. "She's possessed. She's filled with the mluk," he said. Sanae explained the jinns' demand that she indeed become a seer. He explained that she would need to visit seven saints' tombs as well, beginning with Sidi Ali Bousarghine and ending with Mawlay Brahim, the Sultan of the Gnawa, to bless her platter of colors. "Will she need to repeat this every year?" Sanae asked him. "The conditions are between her and the mluk."

When we returned, I sat with the men. Sanae would later explain that I had missed important events among the women. Na'ima had looked around and said, "I want coffee!" Someone replied "Get it yourself," but then, as Sanae put it, she made "strange motions, chewing and rolling her head around, and speaking in the voice of a man." A woman had seized the moment to ask Bouhali about things hidden from their own view, passing her money hand over fist. Sanae continued, referring to the seer by both names, Na'ima and Bouhali:

There was a girl and her mother. I don't know them. He [Bouhali] said: "Look—that man you're going with—he's no good! We don't like him. He's not good and he's taking you on a dangerous path. Don't go with him." Her mother said, "You're right!" "Stay away from him, be patient. A man will come with a lot of bread and lead you to a good life." Her mother said, "Yes!" and gave Naʿima 100 dirhams.

This started a rush among the women to ask Bouhali, and Naʿima "began to see each person's problems." She told Sanae about herself, all of her friends. Everyone threw money, ten or twenty dirhams into Naʿima's lap. Sanae explained:

Aziza tried to give her money, but Bouhali said, "We don't want you, we want your sister." Aziza said, "My sister won't come to you." Bouhali said, "Now she's coming," and her sister got up and came as if someone came to her and brought her to the room. Bouhali told Aziza's sister, "You're the one who's the source of the problem." He gave her instructions: She has to do the henna, clothes, bread, and a sacrifice. [Bouhali continued] "You're still sitting! Get out of here! And don't say 'leave' in our faces. If you don't follow up and do what you must, not a single person among you sisters will open the door." All of them will stay with their problems. That was that, and Naʿima's mother gathered up the money.

Sanae's description—so similar to Zuhur's, or rather, the jinn Aisha's, last moments with Ahmed—captured the precipitous arrival and fleeting presence of the jinn, the sudden torrent of desires for knowledge, and the rapid closure of the exchange. One could not miss Sanae's fascination with the changes that came over Naʿima, and more so, the sense that hidden forces (which even though present remained mysterious) were at work, moving Aziza's sister and giving commands with an authority Naʿima could not herself claim. Nor could one miss the substance of the command to Aziza's sister: a summons to give the jinns their due. No reason given—just the call, and the threat of misfortune for her and her sister should she fail to accept it. So the call of the jinns reproduces itself in the ritual act, each act demanding another and another and summoning others anew to their service. No wonder Mohammed's wife Najia avoided the lila.

## Closure

The lila was readying for a climax with Aisha to close the door. The Gnawa began with another invocation; then with a single beat, wafting smoke of sandalwood and black benzoin from the brazier. Several of the women were already at the center, in the jedba, to beat the syncopations of the *qaraqib* and to repeat the calls to Aisha. "Welcome Aisha Sudaniyya." The floor was steadily more crowded with women, the jedba more sudden, and jolting, heads swept forward and back, long hair whipping, other women holding them upright with a scarf like reins wound around their waists. The drums in response now harder and louder, the metal clashes of qaraqib merging in a liquid stream of white noise. Next to me Naʿima's younger brother, a heavy boy with a thin moustache, lunged forward and hurled himself to his knees, head back and forth, shouting "Aisha! Aisha! Aisha!" His body flopped toward the Gnawa, up and down on his knees, and then onto the musicians, who pushed him back with their feet, the face of one in plain disgust. Now the lights went out, leaving only the glowing coals of the brazier. A sudden darkness, Lalla Aisha's wonderful terrible presence. Yelps and yowls in echo; a loud "Shh- shh- shh-" from nowhere. In the center of the floor, bodies now visible in outline, a light filtering in from the roof in the coldness of late Fez winter. Caught in the jedba, Zuhur on her way to receiving the call, raised her head, her breath streaming out in a pale cloud.

The social world of the lila dispersed quickly, a ritual amalgamation that for a time included Fatima and Sanae and then moved on its way. In the initial weeks following the lila, Zuhur described a continued struggle with the same ailment. But she had begun to see, and that mattered to her and her husband and children. It was, after all, a source of income. But she did not, as both Sanae and I noticed, seem happy about it. When I suggested that perhaps Zuhur did not want to be a seer, or at least felt ambivalent, Sanae shrugged, as if to say, so what? Why, after all, would Zuhur's interest matter where the jinns are concerned? Difference hurts.

What Sanae could dismiss in an instant, is nonetheless the pivotal point around which reformist criticisms of trance turn. In addressing and imagining a broader social world, Sufi and Islamic reformists alike imagine and seek to call—which is to say, to summon up—a conscious subject. Not a free subject certainly, but a responsible subject who can see herself within a field of similar subjects, a society defined by mass-mediated connections. The calls themselves differ: one to a new conscious rite of reception; the other to an exorcism of Moroccan culture. But each takes difference, and the difference communication makes, as the object of the call and the force to be controlled.

# 6 Trance-Nationalism, or, the Call of Moroccan Islam

Yasmine, twenty-four years old, and her boyfriend Aziz, both university students from Casablanca, display the tranquil assurance of children of the upper middle classes at the head of the country. "The King protects us. He won't let the Islamists impose their moral order," she says, dancing to Gnawa music, the genre imported to Morocco by descendants of African slaves.

—Hassane Zerrouky, "Les islamistes à l'assaut de Casablanca"

Following the May 16 terror attacks in Casablanca, the 2003 Moroccan summer of sacred music, dance, and cultural heritage festivals promised a return to normalcy. State-sponsored press and high-society magazines celebrated the Essaouira Festival of Gnawa and Trance Music in particular for demonstrating Morocco's "modernity" and rejection of "barbarism" (Alaoui 2003). The monarchy's main press organ *Le Matin* wrote:

> To those tempted by doubt [after May 16], the Festival . . . belies it. Morocco will always be haven and meeting place, faithful to its traditional blending of cultures and confessions. When each year, in a quasi-sacred ritual, almost 400,000 domestic and foreign visitors attend the Festival of Essaouira, Morocco vibrates in unison with the motley, colorful and rich trappings of its plural identity. (Alaoui 2003)

Writing in the same moment, *Maroc Hebdo International*, with a professional-class readership, invoked ritual unity as well. The closing band, Gnaoua Diffusion, "had the audience shouting in unison, the crowd in trance [*en transe*]: heads swaying and hands clapping" (Bernichi 2003, 30). "The Essaouira Gnawa and World Music Festival showed once again," *Maroc Hebdo* concluded, "that the Moroccan public is entirely capable of putting together large scale expositions. Not a single deplorable incident or act of violence" (Bernichi 2003, 30).

Here and habitually journalists invoked "trance" and "ritual" not as particular underclass Sufi rites—no bloody sheep or howling lunatics, no thrashing bodies either. The terms rather suggested a unified and docile group, indeed, a seamless public, its differences contained and controlled. Moreover, of course, a national public formed in response to a state-sponsored, national call. Still, colonial-era nationalists might have expressed some dismay—as current Islamists do—at the apparent reversal of trance's social and political significance. How might we account for the strange itinerary of once jinn-soaked trance rites—from the object of nationalist and reformist criticism to the very mark of middle-class youth belonging? By what discursive and material shifts could trance shift from the nadir to the apotheosis of Moroccan modernity?

The decades of the 1990s and 2000s, in which particular Sufi practices in Morocco witnessed new and continued rebranding as national and indeed nationalist practices, link these questions of trance to broader domestic and global markets for mass-mediated "culture" and cultural rituals. But the political and social significance of mass-mediated trance rites—their reemergence at a moment of political uncertainty and danger—brings us back more directly to guiding themes of Islam's calls in urban Morocco and the control of social margins and social difference. Under what technological as well as political conditions can Moroccan elites imagine a religiously uniform public? And with what political implications for the multiple calls of Islam staged and circulated in urban Morocco?

These questions address the current Sufi revivalist call as they do anti-Sufi calls signaled by Islamic exorcisms outlined in the next chapter. To acknowledge their differences rejects the premise of Islam's reducibility to one call. At the same time, however, despite political animosities, the two calls partake of modern reformist legacies and aspirations. Each practice seeks social unity, even orderly uniformity; more particularly, participants in both movements imagine a pious society as one in which social differences are reduced—domesticated or expelled altogether—by a broadcast or technologized call to consciousness and an attendant piety, which is to say a conscious and orderly response.

Here I trace this cultural shift through the story of "Aisha," an educated, upper-middle-class cultural activist and actress who stages innovative mass-mediated Gnawa performances as a "call" (*da'wa*) for Moroccans to return to their cultural and religious origins. That her work and her call are staged as trance performances, and in the character of a seer, is exceptional; ordinary seers perform domestically at risk of criminal accusation and contempt from cultural modernists and Islamists alike. Aisha is aware of this critique: her adopted persona as seer reflects an alternative response—a modernist, mass-mediated response—to her own difficult experiences with the jinns' call.

That Aisha publically eschews any claim to jinn possession or seeing in order to speak in the name of Gnawa culture illustrates norms of public performance similar to those required of women in other acts of cultural production, in new media of cultural performance (Najmabadi 1993). At the same time, and more generally, it illustrates a social hierarchy upon which the popularity of trance is premised. Few Moroccans in Fez (or in any city), and certainly fewer Moroccan women, draw upon Aisha's class resources as the daughter of a sharifian family. This is all to the point: the Moroccan Sufi revival, in advocating mass social order and subjectivity, defines these as responsibility to a uniform call. That call emanates from the state and from a sharifian cultural elite secure in the knowledge that it reflects their interests.

## Festivalizing Islam

In May 2003, days before the terrorist attacks, and leading up to celebration of the prophet Muhammad's birth, Sufi devotees from around Morocco made a pilgrimage to the tombs of popular saints Sidi Ali bin Hamdush and Sidi Ahmed Dghughi, near Meknes across a wheat plain from the holy city of Moulay Idriss. Several women in the extended family of my household, including Sanae, her mother Fatima, and her aunt Na'ima, were planning to attend and so was I.

Over the paved walkways leading to bin Hamdush's tomb enormous banners with royal insignia stretched and fluttered. Moroccan green and red flags and white banners with gold-colored crowns were surrounded by the national motto, a mixing of Islamic and sharifian authority, inscribed in Arabic: God, Country, King (Allah, al-Watan, al-Malik). Next to the tomb sat a row of women seers shaded by parasols with cards laid in piles. Gray-uniformed police walked in pairs, but took no note of the women—their practices here remaining within the control of the saint and the state. We stopped only briefly at the saint's tomb; the women pressed ahead to a battoir for the sacrifice of goats and chickens and next to it a mossy shrine dedicated to Aisha, whom according to legend Bin Hamdush brought back from the Sudan (Crapanzano 1973). There the sacrificial animals lay stiffening in the sun, while here in the dank shadows women lit candles and perched bottles of rose water along the stone wall of the shrine. Sanae and Na'ima lit candles—Na'ima, in her late forties, still seeking a husband—and then asked me to take their photograph, their arms around one another, smiling. A few minutes later, after watching the repeated goat sacrifices and congealed blood and flies, I set to wandering.

The tomb of Bin Hamdush rested on a mountainside of brown sandstone, prickly pear cactus, and dried grasses. The persistent drought in Morocco dried and silenced the air, and bodies in the early afternoon sun moved slowly, quietly. Near the tomb of the saint, I picked up the strains of a microphoned voice and followed the sound to a brilliantly whitewashed building next to a rosewater and candle vendor. Noting the open door, I walked the steps to an open room on the second story. There schoolchildren and adults sat in folding chairs, while several men in suits and ties stood at the front and one proclaimed the opening of this annual pilgrimage. I was kindly ushered to a seat, as an elegant and vibrant woman was introduced as Aisha, the Vice President of the Foundation for Moussems, the Environment, Heritage, and Continuity (mu'asasat al-mawasim, al-bi'a, al-turath, wa-l-tuwassul).

In comfortably elevated and well-educated Moroccan Arabic, Aisha explained the task of the foundation as da'wa, a call for reform (*al-islah*) for the public good of the nation. She cited a Qur'anic verse, "O men, We created you from a male and a female, and formed you into nations and tribes that you may recognize each other" (Qur'an 49:13), and continued:

> We should know our ancestors. Whether it is their clothes or their behavior, we should know the manners of our ancestors. It is a crime against humanity and against religion to lose that connection with those of noble intention [*shurafa' al-niyya*]. The Foundation helps us recognize the sacredness of this place [*qudsiyyat hadha al-makan*], and the supreme command of the nation [*qiyada 'uliya dyal al-watan*].

The Qur'anic verse is a favorite in Fassi Sufi discourse, often invoked in cosmopolitan largesse to explain and celebrate national and religious differences. Here Aisha interpreted it somewhat differently as a call for cultural continuity and knowledge under "supreme command of the nation." The logic of interconnection was the same, however, because the nation's command, in her view, assured connection of individuals as one, erasing or exorcizing any internal distance. "When we gather we think about connecting ourselves to one another [*tuwassul ba'dna ma' al-ba'd*] and connecting ourselves with the past. So there is no empty space among us, nor among the generations."

Aisha then thanked the audience "in the name of the Sidi Ali Festival [*mihrajan sidi ali*], in the name of the sacredness of this place, and this spiritual festival [*mihrajan ruhi*]; in the name of the president of the Foundation and his vice-president, in the name of the Cooperative of the Hamdushi Shurafa'." A man interrupted, reminding her to declare their efforts in the name of Crowned Prince Mawlay Hassan III, the newborn son of King Mohammed VI, which she did to the crowd's applause. She then called for God to bless the Hamdushi Shurafa' and King Mohammed VI (the crowd applauded again), and she looked toward the children in the audience.

> In the name of the Association for Mawsims, Environment, Heritage, and Continuity, and in the name of society as a whole [*al-mujtam' ka kul*], we would like to distribute some gifts to the children. This doesn't mean that one who receives a gift is better than the others. This never means that. It is only encouragement to concentrate on your studies. It is still early in the semester.

As Aisha passed out the gifts to several scrubbed and bright little children, a man in the corner began to recite the declaration of faith, "La Ilaha ila Allah, Muhammad rasul Allah," which others took up. Aisha, gesturing for the closing word, thanked everyone for joining together "as one" and reiterated the significance of unity (*wahda*): "Unity means cleanliness, because if the place isn't clean then we are not clean as people, as Arabs or as Amazigh. Each of us is responsible for the smallest piece of peel thrown on the ground. So even if one of us throws a peel on the ground, we are all responsible for that action." The national rather than local or genealogical definition of the event was marked in ways that one might take for granted. Aisha addressed the audience not as pious followers of bin Hamdush as a blessed font of baraka, but rather as members of a nation-state and of "society as a whole." But her message was ambivalent. On the one hand, sameness and unity, "connecting" with each other and the past, and "unity" through collective responsibility for "cleanliness" would eliminate all traces of difference: not a single peel or waste product of unity's fruits. On the other hand, the blessed distinction of shurafa': the audience owed gratitude to the Hamdushi lineage, whose saintly ancestor the festival honored—and the sharifian 'Alawite monarchy—who provided sponsorship and secured its participants. Even the student awards were ambivalent; the merit of some did not detract from the sameness of the group. Rather than a paradox, one could identify the interdependence of mass politics and hierarchy: unity, being the reduction or control of difference, would depend on the power embodied in the shurafa' along with the sharifian state. Only their greater and encompassing distinction could domesticate the differences among the masses attending the festival.

Massification of religious practice is, in other words, not antithetical to hierarchy. That the festival participants are indeed imagined as national, which is to say, as generalized Moroccans rather than as a particular kind of devotees, was best encapsulated by Aisha's reference to the celebration of Sidi Ali not, in the traditional term, as a moussem *(Ar. mawsim)*, but as a mihrajan, a "festival" or "exposition." Moussem is an old term and an old Sufi practice, centered on the pilgrimage to a specific saint and his tomb, or to a specific spirit and her shrine. Mihrajan has come into vogue only since the 1990s to name precisely those more touristic and market-friendly—or more cosmopolitan and corporate—gatherings such the Gnawa Festival in Essaouira and the Fez Sacred Music Festival and the Fez Sufi Culture Festival. If the moussem's point of reference is the saint's tomb, irreplaceable in its specificity, the mihrajan's is the global market and its endlessly repeating copies. (The motto of both Fez festivals is "Giving a Soul to Globalization.") To separate the two terms is increasingly difficult, indeed irrelevant. In 2003 the Moussem of Moulay Idriss in Fez became officially renamed the Mihrajan of Bab Boujeloud. Aisha's reference to Sidi Ali's moussem as "mihrajan Sidi Ali" reflects the nomenclature of the National Office of Tourism and the Ministry of Culture and Communication under which, rather than the Ministry of Pious Endowments and Islamic Affairs, the "festivals" are managed. It also reflected the shared desire to domesticate difference, in which the ministry frames the events.[1]

Aisha's participation in that newly festivalized moussem eventually prompted me to contact her for interviews, and her "call" to reform would remain central to our discussions. But her work with the Foundation for Moussems, Environment, Heritage, and Continuity was only part of the impetus for our connection. In the summer of 2003, during the ninth edition of Morocco's first commercial mihrajan, the Fez World Sacred Music Festival, I would see her again; here, in what she described as "trance theater," Aisha performed the story of a seer in a Gnawa lila ("Spectacle 'Dada la Gnaoua'") with the Gnawa master, Boujmaa and his troupe, who had led Zuhur's lila as well. Prompted by the convergence of trance and cultural politics, Aisha and I discussed her "sociocultural call" *(da'wa susiyu-thaqafiyya)*, including the performance of mass-mediated trance rites on Moroccan television and radio, and her recently released CD of Moroccan folklore, with an audio version of "Spectacle 'Dada la Gnaoua,'" titled "Hajjayat Dada Gnawiyya" (The Story of Dada Gnawiyya).

Aisha's "socio-cultural call" in the Fez Festival framed Gnawa trance as theater; rather than possessed by jinns, she was, of course, self-aware and self-possessed. It was on the basis of this distinction that she claimed—and received—the authority to speak in public in the name of Moroccan culture. Yet, as I grew more familiar with her and her political and personal story, it became clear that her work, like those of ordinary (or at least conventional) seers, in fact responded to the jinns' call. It also became clear that she conscientiously avoided any public suggestion of her own possession—and that exploring her story would have to respect the discretion she herself exercised on her own behalf. It was not so much that the two modes of personhood were unrelated; rather it was that her resolution of private anguish was public performance and that doing so meant adopting dominant reformist norms of mass-mediated, mass public performance. Aisha interpreted jinns as a fact of explicitly national culture and their call as the nation's call.

That she could consider such an interpretation stemmed, at least in part, from a lack of kinship or friendship ties, such as Zuhur's, that might permit her to respond to the jinns' call in a conventional way. This is not to suggest that Aisha resolved her first encounter with jinns with ease. In 1994 she was a communications student in university, with a "secular ['almani]" outlook: "I had an experience. I was leaving the hammam, with my sister. I felt as if someone had touched me. I had henna on my jellaba, and it seemed like it wasn't fresh, as if it were just beginning to harden. I went home and washed the jellaba and let the incident go. But it kept happening." Indeed the encounters with jinns intensified; preparing for a party she shook out a dress to wear. It had been covered with henna. She put on her jellaba, and it too was marked with henna. She began to see "dreams that would later happen, things that were confirmed," culminating in a dream in which all seven of the mluk al-jinn demanded that she hold a lila, make the sacrifice—in short, that she become their medium, a seer.

Aisha was perhaps familiar with henna application as a step in a shuwwafa's preparation for a lila; at least she grasped the nature of the jinns' demands. Nevertheless, she responded to the henna marks in a "secular" ('almani) and "scientific" ('ilmi) manner, as was appropriate to her present university cohort. "I studied a lot of this material as a researcher from a position of absolute secularism ['almaniyya]. I tried to do a psychological analysis, to find a scientific explanation." The appearance of henna coincided, however, with "depression [ikti'ab]" and a feeling of political and ideological isolation from her cohort. By this time she had "stopped praying with any conviction" and now feared herself "on the route of secularism, of unbelief [ilhad], in which there's only materiality [madi]."

Aisha's description of herself in crisis suggested heading in a direction—"the route of secularism"—having lost an apparent anchor of daily prayer and more general belief. But the jinns were pulling her in another direction. The henna marks, as traces—already applied, "beginning to harden"—suggested some prior encounter, an anterior commitment, a call from her origins. But her familial origins barred her response. Her lineage was sharifian—which in her view gave her "good relations with the jinns." No one in her family—not her mother or grandmother or her sisters—had participated in trance rites and certainly not of the Gnawa. Indeed her only prior experience with them derived from childhood memories of fearsome Gnawa passing in the street. If Zuhur and other women could turn to family to support her reception of the jinns' call, Aisha could not. Now married, her husband and her children alike disapproved of her attendance of lilas: "Even my children cried 'NO!'" By 2000 her husband divorced her and took her children.

These last developments might, of course, drive a person further into depression or even madness, and she experienced a period of tremendous uncertainty. She visited a seer who confirmed the problem: the mluk al-jinn were demanding that she become a seer. She did not want to pursue this, but she sought out Gnawa to perform a lila, and then another and another. This brought no relief and indeed brought her into contact with "shaytani" acts, things Satanic or evil—"candles," "shadow tricks"—that left her "terrified" and all the more isolated. But this period subsided. For Aisha the divorce and liberation from child care, as well as her continuous recourse to family wealth, provided her more personal and artistic freedom to dedicate herself to her "sociocultural call." Indeed, reaching out to a broader, national audience was precisely what she needed to resolve the crisis precipitated by the jinns, which ordinary trance rites could not cure.

By this time Aisha had already contributed to Moroccan media and politics. Studying communications she had practiced journalism and remained affiliated with the Maghreb Arabe Press association in Rabat. She likewise participated in national cinema, playing a supporting role in Mohammed Abderahman Tazi's *À la recherche du mari de ma femme*. She had also recently cofounded the Association for Mawsims, Environment, Heritage, and Continuity, through which I first encountered her. Her innovation was to bring performance arts and political action together as "cultural activism" and more specifically as a "sociocultural call." Her efforts would be multimedia and multigenre in scope, with an explicit aim of revitalizing Sufi culture in the moussems and, more specifically, Gnawa and other (in her words) "folk arts [*funun sha'biyya*]." A major part of this latter effort she described as "Trance Theater," and it was under this title that she performed her major showcase, "Spectacle 'Dada la Gnaoua,'" in live venues, such as the Fez Sacred Music Festival, an opening for the Rabat Museum of the Oudayas, and multiple stops in the Netherlands and Germany. But the piece was also more flexible, and she was able to reproduce its opening sequence in other forms, including her collection of Moroccan folklore, available in 2003 in CD form and broadcast on the Tangier radio station, MEDI-1.

For Aisha adopting this position as spokesperson—caller—for Moroccan national culture helped to resolve a crisis of possession that transcended her personal milieu, including her "secular" cohort and own family and friends. This very distance from the tradition was all to the point: Aisha came from a different class background. A member of a sharifian family, she was also well educated and well connected within elite cultural circles. Like other upper-middle-class and upper-class urban Moroccans, including Moroccan women, her distance from Gnawa trance as a cultural form, and her given social superiority to its conventional practitioners, gave her the cultural leverage to speak for it. That is to say, for all her uniqueness as a performer, Aisha embodied a larger cultural trend of upper-middle-class adoption of trance as national culture—a call to national belonging that her performances capitalized on and extended.

Trance's modern itinerary includes Moroccans' (or a class of Moroccans') continuation of colonial-era cultural representation—and more specifically, the domestication of technologized trance that evaded the first Moroccan nationalist reformers. That domestication, however, also demonstrates the success of a reformist piety—a bourgeois piety—enforcing public display as consciously (and conscientiously) national. Under conditions of national control, and more specifically, the control of a particular class within the nation, trance has become a rite of reception for a call not just of sovereign spirits or kin-based ritual media, but emanating from the mass media and the market.

## Reclaiming Technologized Trance

Aisha's explicitly national call to and through trance, including "Dada la Gnaoua" to which I shall return, demonstrates the rituals' common extraction (and extractability) from context, such as was begun with colonial film and photography, which Moroccan nationalists opposed. The state's strategic renewal of popular Sufism in the 1990s paralleled Morocco's efforts to capitalize on heritage, including the selection of the entire Fez medina as a UNESCO World Heritage Site, similarly based on colonial strategies of architectural preservation (Rabinow 1989; Wright 1991). Of the older rites, it is no longer 'Isawa but Gnawa music, the so-called Moroccan Blues,[2] which most readily adapted to the market, incorporating not only technologies but other genres with apparent ease. While such adaptations were the effect of widespread individual marketing initiatives (Pâques 1991; Becker 2002; Kapchan 2007), the conditions for circulation were also provided by state media, as by the mid-1980s Moroccan broadcasting authority, Radio-Télévision Marocaine (now the Société Nationale de Radiodiffusion et de Télévision), was regularly staging Gnawa and underclass Sufi performances alongside others captioned and catalogued as "Folk Arts" (*funun sh'abiyya*) and "Folkloric Dances" (*raqsa fulkluriyya*), but also as "National Songs" (*aghani wataniyya*) and "National Dances" (*raqsa wataniyya*), sometimes identified with a particular region. At the same time, and in larger concentration, the channel also broadcast historically aristocratic Fez-based Andalusi music and upscale Malhun recitals (sung poetry with orchestral accompaniment) as evening entertainment and programming filler. Indeed until the mid-1980s, these latter high- and middle-brow cultural arts appear with far greater frequency than the Gnawa-'Isawa or the Berber dances. But the 1980s also marked a turning point, as from 1984 through 1989 the ratio reversed and the station broadcast 487 performances of the Gnawa-'Isawa—mostly Gnawa—compared to 292 Andalusi and Malhun performances. This was only enhanced by the emergence in the mid-1990s of mihrajans, with televised reproductions of the Sacred World Music Festival of Fez first appearing in 1994, the Culture and Tourism Festival in Azmour in 1997, the National Festival of Folk Arts in 1999, 2001, and 2002, and the Gnawa Festival of Essaouira repeated yearly from 2001 onward.

This sampling speaks to a far broader dissemination of trance rites, which Pâques 1991, Becker 2002, and Kapchan 2007 have detailed with differing explanations. Writing on the Gnawa in southern Morocco, Pâques identifies the influence especially of televised performances in transforming Gnawa from a practice of cosmological knowledge to mere performance to please the "'fan'" (1991, 317). The presence of the camera in particular—including her own, having recorded two 16 mm films of the ceremonies without bringing their production to completion (Pâques 1991, 316)—permits the reproduction of rites previously achieved only in the medium of ritual itself and, in doing so, transforms them.

> Now [the Gnawa] pursue two dreams: to travel abroad, which no African can ignore, and to appear on the public stage like TV stars. One consequence is that, even while maintaining the content and rhythm of their performance, they carry out their dances facing the public rather than being turned toward their ma'lim. The quality of the dances and chants finds itself improved; the discipline of the staging more rigorous (except among the old Gnawa who remain entirely indifferent to the spectators). . . . The demand seems to be increasing: We are moving from a ritual to a spectacle. (Pâques 1991, 317)

Pâques's extraordinary image of the Gnawa from inward to outward facing, suggests also a departure from ritual specificity to mass mediation, from an identifiable audience of the ma'lim and other Gnawa specialists to an anonymous collective. If this initial shift permitted particular Gnawa to shine on the global stage, the proliferation of such venues on cassette, screen, and festival since Pâques's analysis has only intensified the possibilities. Subsequent decades have generated still greater malleability of performance, and greater transformation of audience, than Pâques might have imagined.

As Cynthia Becker (2002) convincingly shows, the popularity of the Gnawa prompted the adoption of the "Gnawa" name for purposes of national and global marketing. In southeastern Morocco in the late 1990s the Ismkhan, a "folkloric troop" of sub-Saharan slave origins, notes, "shed the unfamiliar term Ismkhan and renamed their group the Gnawa of Khamlia" (Becker 2002, 120) "The Ismkhan remain hopeful," she says, "that the popularity of Gnawa recording artists and the Gnawa Festival of Essaouira will attract both Moroccan and European tourists" (118). As anticipated, their healing ritual performances in 2001 and 2002 attracted record crowds. The shift in audience, as Becker notes, also entailed a ritual transformation with the group's ceremonial slave sale displaced by a generic "trance" performance: "While the healing ceremony still continues, their recreation of the slave market rarely occurs from year to year. Instead, Moroccan tourists crowd around the Ismkhan to be entertained by the popular hadra or 'trance dance.' Professional photographers are available to take pictures of Moroccan tourists posing near Ismkhan men" (Becker 2002, 120). Abstracted from a particular history, the ritual is no longer about slavery; its mass reproduction renders it—the story, the act—accessible to any (middle- to upper-class) Moroccan. Such transformations of trance rituals' meaning and function, in the 2000s as in the 1930s, are not merely witnessed by the camera but are rather its effect. The Ismkhan's renamed ritual anticipates their reproduction as images to be seen from afar, that is, on the national and global tourism market (Morris 2000). Indeed the camera's ubiquity is what blurs the line between performer and audience, caller and receiver: creating a stage for the technologized call to national culture, "trance" is a new rite of reception—the reception that calls to national belonging. The accessibility of trance as a popular practice is not limited to Morocco of course. As Deborah Kapchan has suggested, the circulation of live performances and reproductions of Gnawa especially have contributed to the spread of digital "trance culture" across Europe, the United States, as well as (as I emphasize here) within Morocco itself, with trance now a "transnational category of the sacred" (Kapchan 2007, 1), and popular Sufism of the 'Isawa and Hamadsha a European sign of Moroccan belonging (Zillinger 2008). But nor should this same dynamic in Morocco be overlooked.[3] That is to say, it is not *only* a transnational condition, but one shared within Morocco itself and part of the broader production of "Moroccan Islam." Indeed Becker's detailed description of a group willing to change its name for marketing purposes helps identify a more general condition of malleability in which Moroccans with still less "personal" or "familial" connection to the Gnawa—such as Aisha—find their resolution in the globalized marketplace of national culture.

In Fez and other cities it is young and more privileged Moroccans, the main demographic of the Gnawa Festival audience—rather than performers themselves who mark the trend. In an early interview with two older Gnawa, the three of us sat in silence (they holding their instruments) while a young man who accompanied them spoke for the better part of an hour about Gnawa culture and Gnawa knowledge (*tagnawit*). The old men were black; the young man was, like Aisha, very white-skinned—the mark of a Fassi past and viewed as a sign of class privilege. His expertise came from no familial or ethnic connection; rather, he had "discovered" himself to be Gnawi after listening to recordings while working in his father's fabric boutique in the medina. The point, it seemed to me, was clear: the more privileged could speak about the men as Gnawa, for they, at least initially, could not speak for themselves.

When I shared this story with Aisha, she pointed to the broad movement among Moroccans to recover and fulfill a sense of identity. "Many people," she said, are "discovering for the first time that they are Gnawa. They don't know it until they hear the music." She explained that Gnawa is deeply embedded in Morocco, unlike the distance that exists for people approaching Malhun music, that high-cultural specialty of Fez. "It's from childhood, and it's something that cannot be described by experts. There is something people *feel* but can't *express*—but it comes out in trance. It's a *feeling*."

The lack of expression (*ta'bir*) did not mean a lack of coherence. Her audiences, as evidenced by the videotapes she shared of her performances, clearly adopted the familiar gestures of trance, the swinging of the head and holding arms behind the back. In this sense their performances were entirely similar to the logic of conventional trance and spirit curing in other cultural contexts: a set of inchoate feelings, disturbing in being inside but inexpressible are resolved by the curers' coherent articulation in ritual (Lévi-Strauss 1963a, 1963b; cf. Siegel 2003, 2006). Curing or trance is the resolution of a difference that cannot be otherwise expressed—an identity, as Aisha described it, there, but called forth only by the music itself.

That the call is triggered by recorded and mass-produced music makes the feeling no less intimate, or perhaps authentic. Rather it permits the sense of intimacy with difference to pervade a larger audience and with novel significance—the democratizing, or massifying, of affect, perhaps (Hirschkind 2012). Indeed, in Aisha's view, her knowledge and embodiment of "authentic Gnawa heritage [*tagnawit*]" was superior to that of Boujmaa or others, certainly seers themselves, whom she considered unaware of the social and cultural, "symbolic" implications of the ritual (cf. Kapchan 2007, 214–15). For them, she said, the color black in ritual trance is "only for the mluk." It is "just black." For her, however, black is explicitly representational: it stands for the slavery in which Gnawa practices developed in Morocco. "We had slaves," she said. "And we don't talk about that." That is why she writes and performs "Dada la Gnaoua": Dada is the black nanny that privileged Fassi families kept; that is how "we"—an upper-class community—have a sense of Gnawa implanted since childhood. But that experience remains unspoken; if it is not taboo, it rests in oblivion. These inchoate traces of Gnawa's history are neither present nor absent, neither fully inside nor outside—at least until the call of the Gnawa music, or her sociocultural call, is heard. *Then* the difference that was there all along is recognized; then the traces can be assimilated, accepted, and fully known.

Representational mediation, of course, differs quite starkly from the transmission of the jinn that overcomes all conscious articulation. It also departs sharply from the logic of guarded difference and distinction that conventional trance rites mark. Here, suddenly, the call of difference is resolved into the sameness of a common identity available to anyone and everyone, or at least, to any *Moroccan*. As in Aisha's description of reform, given in her address at the "Festival" of Sidi Ali bin Hamdush, the recuperation or salvaging of difference is total. All that is required is a call.

The call of a national difference is not the same as the call of a jinn, or of kinship structures—no matter how invisible each is. The difference is one of medium, digital and broadcast, rather than kinship and ritual. The former precipitates a different loss than that of a seer's unconsciousness, just as it points to a different kind of "reception," a different kind of person receiving the call. It is a person defined by her place within a society addressed by a mass-mediated call, a society of similarly positioned subjects desirous to fully know and experience a national difference. These senses of desire and loss are the effect of technological mediation, its dominant representational logic engendering the discourse itself of lost origins or vanished pasts (Ivy 1995). Thus does the call imagine a social totality, standing "in the place of" a lost past that the call has awakened (Morris 2000). It is a call marked by multiplicity, of copies and stagings, for indeed the loss is implacable, engendered by the very repetitions of spiritual presence that would seek to heal it.

## Technologized Voice: To Recuperate Unity

This feeling, and its implantation in childhood, is the theme by which Aisha frames "Spectacle Dada la Gnaoua" for Moroccan audiences, the poetic introduction to which ("The Story of Dada Gnawiyya") I shall read here. Serving as an explanatory frame for the performance of Gnawa rites outside of their ritual function, the poem packages the lila for audiences with no firsthand or kin-based knowledge of the rituals. It is also the most widely reproduced part of her act, appearing on her folk-arts collection and in her Medi-I program. Which is to say, beyond singular performances, the piece is meant to guide Moroccans to a world they "know" from childhood, but which none-theless remains unknown—an internal difference Moroccans must come to know. Awakening to culture as a difference to be brought out in performance is the overall aim of Aisha's activism as a "call," in which, under Sufi sharifian class leadership and the Moroccan nation, all other internal differences can be dissolved.

Aisha begins her performances of Dada Gnawiyya dressed as a seer, in prepara-tion for a lila. But rather than dance to Gnawa music provided by the troupe she col-laborates with, she recites and sings an homage to Dada, her nanny of Gnawa descent, and presumably a ritual practitioner of trance as well.

[Singing]

A Rari ya Rari, teller of tales.
A Rari ya Rari, who draws children into sleep.

[Reciting]

A fairy tale from you, O Dada!
Which you tell once and again.
5   And the child who shuts his eyes, O Dada,
Ripens and falls into sleep.

The hum of the bamboo flute,
Tender in his head,

Brings dreams grand and colorful.
10   The children's little heads so heavy
Even the older, most attentive
Poor dear! He tires of resisting and so
Opens one eye and closes the other.

O Dada, tell again and again!
15   So the Storyteller, who fosters sleep for the kids,
Brings it on his fingertips.
And even the older, most attentive falls asleep,
The scent of sleeping children spreading and
Mingling with the words.

20   Tell more and more!
Behold! The Storyteller.
In length and width he has no limit,
He does not eat or drink,
And none sees him.
25   He watches over the children during the night.
For surely there is slumber
for every little head.

In sleeping each child will find
what he missed in daylight

30   And who disobeys his mother
Auntie Ghoula will spend all night,
Running atop his body.
Until Rari forgives him, lifts him out of sleep,
So he may return to sweet sleep.

35   Ya Allah! Tell again and again!
Oh Rari tell!
Oh Rari, whose tales foster sleep in the children
So the one who does no mischief
Will enjoy unending play
40   And a flapping wing will lift him up
So high above the others.

Dada's fairy tales
Were always in my head
That she told again and again
45   Oh Rari,
Whose tales foster sleep in the children
And help them grow both night and day.

So my life will grow longer,
With goodness of every kind and color,
50 And with no lack of children I will never die.

O Rari, Tell a tale
Dada was always in my ears
When I was just a little girl
Playing haba and mala
55 With the other children.
Joining the crowds to follow funerals and drum-beaters,
Then sneaking my way back,
To avoid a beating with the stick.
Playing with the zellij tiles
60 Talking to holes in the walls
Telling endless stories.

Until we started having secrets
And exchanging rumors [*hak wa ara akhbar*].
Ants never betray secrets,
65 Or mix meanings [*kaytbakik*]
[Oh it was] the most pleasant of companionships, Oh my!

O Rari do tell!
Where are you O Mommy [*mwima*] Dada?
Where is he whose tales foster the children's sleep
70 When the flowers on the cheeks flourish?

I slept in one time and woke up to another,
The place and the faces were the same
But my union [*'ashar*] with Dada
Was blown away by an old wind

75 We were girls and boys
One single handful, no difference made between us.
[Yet] the wind blew [it away]!
"Girls with girls. Boys with boys."
"Girls with girls. Boys with boys."
80 Space in between.
Trouble if the either should approach!
We were one single cut of meat.
What happened?

[Singing]
A Rari Ya Rari
85 Ya Rari A Rari

A Rari Ya Rari
Bringer of sleep to the children [*drari*].

The poem opens and closes with a lullaby. The inner stanzas contain at least two clearly distinct parts. In the first, the speech is didactic, relaying generalities about Rari, Dada, and their relationship to children, and the sleep or dreams that serve as their just reward for obedience or disobedience. If Dada "Gnawiyya" is one of the black sub-Saharan slaves and concubines and nannies, belonging to the royal family as well as the wealthy families in Fez under sharifian rule (Ennajji 1999; Michaux-Bellaire 1910), "Rari," perhaps a dialectal version of "Storyteller," or "Rawi," is not a historical figure, but rather more divine. He is masculine, all-seeing but unseen, limitless in size (evoking the Qur'anic reference to God's Throne "extend[ing] over heavens and the earth" [Qur'an 2:255]), and bestowed with a life-giving, regenerative power (46–47) and forgiveness (34). In addition to describing generalities, the narrator also adopts an imperative tone, commanding Dada to "tell more."

In the second part of the poem, there is a shift to the past tense. Here the tone is distinctly autobiographical, giving explicit voice to "I" as the narrator tells her own story, presumably that of the poet framing the Gnawa lila for the audience. In this latter section, the command to Dada is replaced by a more pleading call to Rari ("Oh Rari, do tell!") and indeed a loss of Dada. This feeling of loss provides the general frame of the performance as both a cultural and a personal recuperation of a childhood experience previously inchoate, and of a social unity—precisely the repetition and recuperation of cultural practices and belonging that Aisha's "sociocultural call" aims to awaken.

The arc of the poem then is a compound loss of Dada, her voice and her stories, as well as early childhood as a time of perfect social unity. But it speaks repeatedly of recuperation and return. The first instance is in sleep itself, induced by voice and sound that fully pervades the self: "The hum of the bamboo [flute]" is "tender in his head" (7–8), just as Dada's stories were "in" the children in several ways: "in his head," "in my head"—meaning also "in me [*fi rasi*]"—and "in my ears." The power of the voice is apparent in its diffusion in and with the listener, a diffusion that moreover mixes with the scent of the children sleeping (18–19). But, as voice mingles with an odor, we are reminded that, rather than unique properties of voice, what is valued here is total circulation or coverage. Indeed the sleep-inducing voice compels a recuperation or completion—even payback—for what the child "missed" or "what passed in the light of day" (29). Thus total coverage also permits a balancing of accounts, rewarding or punishing children: "Oh Rari, whose tales foster sleep in the children./ The one who does no mischief/Will enjoy unending play/And a flapping wing will lift him up/So high above the others" (37–41). But also: "[W]ho disobeys his mother/ Auntie Ghoula will spend all night/Running atop his body" (30–32). The point again is a completeness that can only, from a belated adult perspective presented at the end of the poem, be experienced as something far away and thus in need of recall and recuperation. Mediation, the call, is both the horrible condition and also the solution to life as Aisha's poetry and politics have it.

The second half of the poem indeed emphasizes that the condition of unity prior to loss is one of communicative bliss, in which there is no mediation apparent. The narrator recites, "Dada was always in my ears" (52). Dada/sound fosters cohesion and completion. With Dada "in" her, the girl plays with others, merges with crowds, and responds to the beating of drums. With Dada in her ears, the girl picks up such signals and indeed coheres with whatever she encounters. She may have broken rules in picking up the dream beats, but she escapes a beating, persisting in her play equally inside as outside the home: "Playing with the zellij tiles [an interior decoration]/Talking to holes in the walls/Telling endless stories" (59–61). Inside and outside are undifferentiated, or easily overcome. The girl's stories go through the walls, through their holes, perforating boundaries.

This condition of undifferentiation, of merging with people, is a kind of subjective condition that Aisha links to belonging in Morocco. But, again, unity and sameness is something lost. In its place there is material communication, and thus difference. "Until we started having secrets/and exchanging rumors [*hak wa ara akhbar*]. Ants never betray secrets/Or mix meanings [*kaytbakik*]. [It was] the most pleasant of companionships, Oh my!" (62–66). Secret words, like the veiled writing of the fqih's hijab, form with lines of demarcation, insides and outsides—the effect of which is distance and ambiguous companionship. It is space or distance that takes objective form, as in "It's just 'Take this' [*hak*] and 'Give me' [*ara*] news [*akhbar*]." "Hak" and "Ara" are said when handing somebody some thing, or asking for some object, a cigarette or the house keys. They are imperative but familiar in a way that lacks the etiquette or distance of high Arabic. The result in the poem is not warmth but vulgarity, a fall of the immaterial interior voice into mere object to pass. Again, at stake is the reemergence of difference itself: "We were girls and boys/One single handful, no difference made between us./[Yet] the wind blew [it away]!" (75–77). Or again, "We were one single cut of meat./What happened?" (82–83). But after, difference is the rule: "'Girls with girls. Boys with boys.'/'Girls with girls. Boys with boys.' Space in between./Trouble if the either should approach!" (78–81).

Here loss is understood as space, absence, but a material absence: a gendered difference tied to material separation—leaving only individuals to exchange with one another. The story appears as a real life. The loss is personal, autobiographical. The poem in fact links them together such that the autobiographical ("I") coincides with loss: if this is a tale of the accession to language in general, it also means that in telling one's own story one experiences distance from the past. But particularly given the poem's place within Aisha's cultural activism, the autobiographical gesture seems to me crucial. One gathers (at least I did) that she is remembering the Dada of her own childhood, and in our discussions, our consistent use of "we Moroccans" and "our culture" did nothing to dispel the impression. When I did ask about her childhood, she said that in fact she had no "Dada" and reiterated that she was discussing a cultural rather than strictly personal theme.

As Benedict Anderson has argued of modern autobiography and national consciousness, the genre naturalizes the personal identity as the effect of a simultaneous historical movement, that is to say, it emphasizes the subject's "progress towards and absorption into his historical role" (1998, 84). If Aisha is not recounting "history" on a grand scale, "culture" nevertheless plays a similar role, in which, as Anderson's thesis on nationalism argues, subjectivity takes a novel form of exchangeability. It does not matter that Aisha has neither Gnawa heritage "herself," nor that she "herself" did not have a Dada whom she missed. These things are available to her as a "Moroccan" and, more specifically, as a "Moroccan" of a certain upper-middle-class means who can speak for Dada, even adopt her position of storyteller.

Whereas ritual mediumship affirms the reception of the jinns' call as a source of distinction, Aisha's broadcast performances affirm and model a *general* Moroccan subject *receptive* to a shared call and thus capable of incorporation into mass society. In this instance, lacking a familial connection or ethnic origins in the Gnawa does not mean Aisha's relationship to them was inauthentic or even ahistorical; rather, this is a history mediated by the technological conditions of mass national society and thus one available to anyone. It is on the basis of this distinction—fostered by technological reproducibility—that Aisha could reframe the "enigma" of the Gnawa rites, not as a source of personal uniqueness (and potential enrichment), but rather as a mass "spectacle" (Benjamin 2008). When the call is technologically reproduced and detached from any particular legacies, persons of remarkable difference can be exchanged for each other as its recipients. Exchangeability comes because of shared call of origins, or more precisely, the call of origins *newly* shared—the source of which is technological reproduction.

It is a truism that origins are established only in their repetition, which is to say, in the absence of the origin as such. And national origins are those established in mass-mediated repetition and a mass consciousness necessitating the call. Consciousness of origins, and desire for their recuperation, at the same time it views them as distant, lost, present only as traces. Via a technologized call and serially receptive subject, we can imagine with Aisha their full recuperation, the erasure of difference, and return of a perfect unity—that society she described at the saint's festival, "no empty space among us, nor among the generations."

## Everybody Trance Now

Aisha's call need not succeed on its own, for as she asserted, she is not alone in discovering trance-nationalism. The popular dimensions of trance were demonstrated to me at the Moussem of Moulay Idriss Zerhoun in 2010, which I attended to see the procession of the 'Isawa, Hamadsha and Gnawa Sufi groups, advertised for weeks in advance in the shaded foyer of the saint's tomb. A shopkeeper acquaintance of mine in the town, Abdelhaq, had assured me that the event would bring "all of the teams, from all of Morocco," and so we met in town, his six-year-old son joining us dressed in a white jellaba with gold stitching and pointed yellow leather *balagha* slippers. The atmosphere was certainly electric; sipping tea on his rooftop we could hear crowds gathering in the town's central plaza, Sahat Mohammed VI, the former bus terminal, constructed for pedestrian life with royal funds. As we descended at dusk Abdelhaq commented on the ubiquity of thieves, but as we threaded through the crowds we encountered mostly loud, giggling, and self-absorbed teenaged boys and girls, pressed together in jeans and tight t-shirts and slicked hair and superfluous sunglasses. As Abdelhaq explained, they are Moroccans living abroad, returning for the summer. "People are coming from all over," he said.

Abdelhaq lead us to his family's spot, his wife and daughter, his sister and her children, on the front steps of a pharmacy, in white plastic chairs as the first group, a team of 'Isawa Sufis from Rabat, began to move, their name lettered in gold on black against the reddish glow of a silk carpet held on scaffolding and wheels. A group of women shurafa' of the 'Isawa lineage, dressed in the pleasant elegance of caftans, waved to the crowd. Behind them, forming a ring around the muqaddam, a group of lower-class adepts in plain robes bobbed their heads in trance. Further behind, two young shurafa', strapping men, rode on horseback, their wrap-around sunglasses matching the smooth curve of their haircuts. A line of metal barricades, and police of no fewer than three distinct types, seemed ready to keep order, separating spectators from spectacle.

The crowds, safely behind barricades, held cell phones aloft to photograph and film, and in my anticipation I felt the crowds' awe. Abdelhaq's sister vigorously pressed my left shoulder and pointed—"look, look, she's in trance [*katjdeb*]!" But the woman's dancing was rather mild and drew no attention from the crowd around her, who were, in any case, more focused on their phones. The first group passed, now performing and waving for crowds further along in the square. Now the second team of 'Isawa, lead by elegant women shurafa', followed by rougher adepts, moved into position. The crowd's interest had already shifted, however; this was visibly the last group to be marching, and whatever awe the first group inspired had suddenly dissipated. The youthful crowd was now far more interested in itself.

Several fashionable teenaged boys jumped the barricades and, circled up next to the 'Isawa adepts, performed the trance dance. They did so with cell phones aloft and pointed at themselves—not so much possessed as playing for their own cameras, enacting the YouTube-era imperative to "broadcast yourself." Several police moved in to put them back in place—but now other teenagers jumped the barricades as well. In a rush the barricades were being pushed aside and the teenaged crowd, exuberant and implacable in their collective self-absorption, spilled into the group of 'Isawa adepts and shurafa'. The poised 'Isawa women shurafa' looked terribly offended. The team leader, now wholly ignoring his trancing adepts, furiously pushed young men and women out of the way to maintain some coherence because the police had given up any attempt to maintain it.

The sacred had been breached—the old hierarchies and distinctions collapsed—the awe of the spectacle turned toward sheer fun. But the chaos was also controlled. The police really did not need to intervene; the mass-mediated subjects of the teenage crowd—that is, conscious of themselves as reproducible images (Morris 2000)—responded to norms of conscious and controlled trance. The participants, with their pleasures of self-broadcast, reflect the elite and upper-middle-class conditions of Aisha's call. For, despite her uniqueness as a performer, her project enacts the contemporary form of popular Sufi trance by which privileged mass consumers experience national belonging.

Trances' historical itinerary has followed the technologized call—the ritual reception and embodiment of jinns as difference displaced by the embodiment of state-sponsored and mass-market culture. Yet the call cannot be fully completed. It must be repeated. Indeed, the very fact of an elite and state-sponsored Sufi nationalist call—"spiritual security" bolstered by the state's physical and penal security apparatus—points to the always incomplete project of summoning and managing urban masses subjected to global economies and discourse. Nor is Sufi nationalism alone in calling. Islamists in Fez also call, and they do so with a competing discourse and practice of jinns and jinn curing. This too is a legacy of nationalist reformism, of technologized ritual, the modern mass-mediated conditions of communication, and novel demands for pious control.

# 7 "To Eliminate the Ghostly Element Between People"

## *The Call as Exorcism*

> Written kisses never arrive at their destination; the ghosts drink them up along the way. . . . In order to eliminate as far as possible the ghostly element between people and create natural communication, the peace of souls, [humanity] has invented the railway, the motorcar, the aeroplane.
>
> —Kafka, *Letters to Milena*

Let us return to the Islamic exorcisms with which I opened this book and to the cultural politics of communication and piety it embodies. I began with Islamic exorcisms, with one of Aisha in particular, because the practice vividly captures the social currents and political conflicts around the competing calls of Islam, from the dominant national influences of sharifian Sufism, to an opposing Islamist call. While this book has focused largely on dominant forms of Sufism, Islamic exorcism, grounded in the logics of globally circulating Islamic revivalism, shifts our perspective away from older popular Sufi authorities—the scholars and seers—of Fez, away from the struggling middle classes drawn to their informal economy and occult cures, and away from privileged middle classes who receive and transmit the nation's call in new mass-mediated trance rites. Instead, we see Fez and urban Morocco more broadly from the different marginal perspective of young, educated, and struggling men who neither benefit from sharifian logics, nor explicitly aspire to sharifian authority, small or large. Seeking a pious community grounded in (for them) pious norms of responsibility to God's call, they give voice to it through a practice of exorcism meant to cure not only individual bodies but also, explicitly, the body social and body politic.

From our vantage at this book's close, we can see this latter aim as the rejection of the dominant hierarchies of sharifian Sufism in Fez, that is, as a countercall to a counterpublic (Warner 2002; Hirschkind 2006). Given both the modern power of sharifianism and its revival in consolidating the "spiritual security" of the nation after May 16, 2003, we can grasp the political difficulty of posing such a call. At the same time, however, by revisiting Islamic exorcism now, we can also discern its contemporaneity with these politics of communication and piety, that is, its kinship with the reformist logics of the call that have been present in urban Morocco from the emergence of mass politics in the colonial era through today. These logics infuse Islamic exorcists' logical aims as both curers and callers.[1] They give sense to these callers' explicit critiques of older talismanic writing and trance rites, and Sufi nationalism's call as problems not only of doctrine but also of subjective and social order, and of order *as* controlled communication, as self-presence and social-presence precipitated by the staging of the call itself.

As I have argued, the reformist interpretation of piety as a function of communication, of subjectivity as receptivity to the proper call, is an effect of distinctly modern mass mediation. It arises from a technological imaginary bound up with the conditions of large-scale, indeed mass, communications, in which distances and anonymity—the copresence of strangers—are the given conditions of community (B. Anderson 2006; cf. Warner 2002). The promise of mass-mediated communications as the realization of community, however, generates its own conflicts. From the earliest nationalist efforts to the present, this imaginary has refigured prior or opposing ritual practices as themselves communicative acts and more precisely as competing calls generating divergent subjects. Islamic exorcists, for all their oppositional logic, share with Sufi nationalists and the state a mass-mediated desire for uniform or orderly practice within a field of the call defined by national "society." Like nationalist attempts to eliminate opposing calls, including those of Islamism, so too does the practice of Islamic exorcism betray structural and spectral anxieties of circulation. Specifically, Islamic exorcists grasp opposing forms of ritual practice—talismanic writing and trance examined in this book—indeed, jinns themselves, as uncontrolled communication, as an excess to be seized, presented, and expunged.

On the one hand, Islamic exorcists' fantasy of a uniform social space of piety and communication fits what Charles Hirschkind (2006) has described as Cairene callers' image of an "ethical soundscape." Islamic exorcisms involve some of the same ritual and technologies he has described there, including cassettes and pious listening. On the other hand, practices of Islamic exorcism both as cure and call dramatize a persistent sense of this soundscape's vulnerability—a soundscape in tatters and lacking all ethical certitude, a public sphere perforated and dark. From my first encounters to my last with Islamic exorcists, the discourse centered on what was not there but produced social effects nonetheless: a lack of Islamic comportment in Moroccan society, the public's lack of consciousness of Islamic traditions, the regular perpetration of sorcery, the constant call to trance, all promoted by an immoral but nonetheless nationally accepted and celebrated system of traditional practices and beliefs.

These elements of the discourse were not marginal but rather are symptomatic of the technological imagination in its local rendering. In conjuring and exorcizing jinns, ruqya in fact stages the exposure and elimination of secret and hidden communications and their material, if invisible, effects. Yet this is not simply about jinns. More to the point, it is not only about Islam in Morocco or even Islamic exorcisms, which are, after all, only part of a larger social and political vision of Islamic piety and social life. Framing differences of subjects as the effect of uncontrolled calls and responses to calls tells us something crucial about the call to Islam, indeed about the discourse and practice of the technologized call in modernity in general. For such technologized calls to and for communicative control not only attempt to discipline subjects. Each staging of the technologized call tries to discipline the medium of the call itself: to exorcise the distance, and thus potential differences, that mass mediation has made possible and indeed necessary to the formation of political community. Technological communications, to cite Kafka, have expanded the dimensions of "society" and introduced a "ghostly element between people," that each staging of the call itself attempts to exorcise.

Modern reformist movements, not only in the Muslim world, have performed different kinds of exorcisms—with varying scales of violence—and always accompanied by a call to order and consciousness of difference itself. Yet, as in ruqya, the problem of difference remains. Or, more precisely, the technologized call produces difference as a remainder of communication itself—material traces of difference and distance—the fantasy of uniformity as total receptivity refiguring other ritual media as obstacles and points of resistance to perfect transmission.

## Exorcism as Technologized Call: Mass-Mediated Authority

Islamic exorcism, *ruqya shar'iyya*, is popular across the urban Muslim world, and in Muslim immigrant communities in Europe (Eneborg 2012; Kruk 2005; O'Brien 2001). It draws on a vast mass-market literature, available in every Islamic bookstore I have entered in urban Morocco (and Egypt), as well as in burgeoning online venues, with instructional materials, videos of live exorcisms, and discussion boards requiring username and password. Although Moroccans in Fez and Rabat (and in Europe) practice it, it is not a particularly Moroccan tradition—neither embedded in local practices nor self-described as such; indeed, its practitioners value its foreignness from Moroccan culture as a sign of its Islamic legitimacy and universal relevance. Islamic exorcism is rather, by all measures, a global phenomenon and part of a global Islamic reformist ethos if not a coherent revivalist movement.

Practitioners trace its arrival in Morocco to the broader intersection of these global forces during the 1980s, with the growth of Saudi-financed Islamic training and media in Morocco. Islamic exorcism was adopted in Fez in the late 1980s by a small circle of five young men, all born in the 1960s. Indeed the practice was youth-driven; its growth marked a generational rupture both with established local Islamic institutions, the Qarawiyyin and Sufi zawiyas in Fez, and with older modes of education and practice, the mnemonic and scribal authority of fuqaha'. Only one of the five had memorized the Qur'an (his father was a fqih)—indeed he is the only raqi out of all whom I met in Fez, who had memorized the entire Qur'an via old methods. The others were recipients or products of the state's expanding mass-educational system whose literacy permitted their access to university training as well as conservative religious studies in Saudi Arabia and Pakistan. Finishing secondary school in Fez, one of the men pursued a degree in engineering at Université Fes-Saiss, while another graduated with a degree from Université Hassan II, Institut d'Agronomie in Casablanca, both fields that Gonzalez-Quijano (1998) has identified with new Islamist intelligentsia.

The circle of first adopters was likewise the beneficiary of Saudi and Wahhabi largesse in Morocco, developing the practice among peers in the novel urban social institution of Islamic "associations" (*jam'iyyat*) funded at the invitation of Hassan II during the 1980s (Basbous 2002). At Jam'iyyat Fez Jadid two of the five men, brothers born in Fez, were inclined to the practice after encountering Shaykh Sanhaji, a teacher of Qur'anic memorization and jurisprudence at the Qarawiyyin, who worked part-time at the association and accepted requests to treat clients. Tellingly, however, Sanhaji, whose education and expertise were grounded in those of fuqaha', had only provided the initial impetus for ruqya. For fully learning and adopting the broader ethos of ruqya, Sanhaji's knowledge (*'ilm*) was, in the words of one the first exorcists, "insufficient."

For these two brothers, learning the technical details of the practice required consuming specific instructional literature—mass-market manuals, pamphlets, and cassettes imported from Wahhabi sources in Saudi Arabia, Kuwait, and Egypt and passed via photocopy among practitioners in Fez, as on university campuses elsewhere in Morocco (see Eickelman 2003's reference to a well-known curing manual). It also meant joining a new network based in the new Islamic associations. Rejecting Sanhaji, the two left Jam'iyyat Fez Jadid for Jam'iyyat al-Imam Malik, where they joined with two other men familiar with the practice from conservative religious studies in Pakistan and Saudi Arabia, and with a fifth man who had adopted ruqya practice on the basis of his own reading and interest.

In the early 1990s the five men now began to hold public outreach programs (*nad-wat*) and meetings (*tajammu'at*) in Fez to teach ruqya and attendant Islamic morals and comportment, as the ruqya literature recommends. They would continue to do so through the 1990s and early 2000s, by which time these first ruqya practitioners, now in their later forties, represented the old guard in Fez. During the early 2000s numerous younger men were adopting the practice. In Fez, as in Rabat, those adopting ruqya after the initial wave were young Islamists, mass educated, and aspiring to middle-class success. Like the older men, they were learning the practice outside of older institutional frameworks, through mass-market literature and media that, at least between friends if not in larger peer circles, they shared and discussed. For the first raqiyyin and the new younger practitioners alike, the logic of ruqya was shaped by a particular social nexus of mass education and media—a logic of more horizontal communication at the very least. This coincided furthermore, in my experience, with their marginality to the cultural elite—there was no discussion of being shurafa' or of celebrating Morocco's Sufi heritage. Nor did exorcists claim access to employment opportunities that wealthy or upper-middle-class family connections in Fez could secure. On the contrary, the topic of livelihood infused the discussion with a mild but unmistakably bitter tone. For Ahmed, the Agronomie graduate, there had simply been no available jobs. Ruqya practice—he claimed to have exorcised more than three thousand patients—had filled the void. Although he did not demand money, he said, his grateful patients offered *sadaqa* (charity), thus permitting him to survive in this informal sector. Mohammed, in his early twenties, was living in Fez with an uncle and a cousin—all three sharing one room. He struggled to survive on a tiny salary of part-time woodworking. For these men, as for others, Islamic exorcism offered a mode of recognition for their labors in the absence of other channels. Learning ruqya was an act of entrepreneurial courage; with little investment and no credentials, one could learn and practice.

To be sure, the state's repression of Islamists following the May 16 bombings in Casablanca shifted the ground for those considering the practice. As the experiences of men at the Islamic bookstore suggest, appearing in the dress of an Islamist rendered one suspect. Indeed any association with Islamists rendered one suspect; herbalists in the medina refused sales of incense and herbal cures to Islamists. But this swift fall from favor is tied to broader social, religious, and political implications of Islamic exorcism. The adoption of new curing techniques gleaned through mass-market media rather than local institutions and rituals techniques accompanied a deeper shift in religious sentiment and commitment: becoming "multazim" or "engagé"—bound and obliged to Islam. It meant not only ignoring but also actively rejecting local curing techniques, including trance rites and talismanic writing. Indeed, it meant rejecting the authority of the fqih's knowledge, the training, and the logic of exclusive power, as well as the social hierarchy it embodied. Islamic exorcists, following the precepts out-lined in the ruqya literature, adamantly rejected talismanic writing—in any form—as sorcery. It did not matter whether it involved Qur'anic verse or not. Rather, in a rever-sal of the writings' secrecy and withdrawal from public circulation, exorcists recited the Qur'an aloud.

Such recitational practice did not in fact require memorizing the entire Qur'an, but rather memorizing particular chapters and "healing verses," available on mass-produced cassettes and CDs and marketed specifically as "ruqya" instructional cas-settes. When necessary, for example, when overcome by exhaustion during a lengthy exorcism, the curer could simply play the cassette instead. Young exorcists in Fez, like Mohammed and Abdellah, both in their early twenties, worked together to learn ruqya, studying from cassettes to memorize Qur'anic verses. Mohammed's initial interest in Islam had been sparked in secondary school, in "Islamic Formation" (*tar-biyya islamiyya*), which he enjoyed immensely and at which he excelled. His interest had waned, he said, when discussions turned to the details of Islamic banking, or, indeed, any detailed rules of legal interpretation. What he enjoyed were discussions of morality, "what was right and what was wrong." Ruqya, when he later heard about the practice from the uncle with whom he lived in Fez, piqued his interest as a matter of morality. As a child he had witnessed an act of sorcery, or at least the traces of a substance which his aunt was certain signaled an attack on the household, and had found it fascinating, if frightening. Now, seeking out ruqya techniques, he bought al-Buni's *Shams al-Marif al-Kubra,* a text to which fuqaha' refer. But Mohammed did not understand it, noting only that "it had a lot of talismans [*jadawil*]." His friend Abdellah explained that talismans meant that *Shams al-Maarif* was "sorcery . . . a very bad book," and recommended a mass-market handbook, published in Cairo and available in Fez in numerous editions, *Wiqayat al-insan min al-jinn wa al-shaytan* (Protecting humankind from jinns and Satan) (Bali, 2009 [1989]). He then purchased cassettes of ruqya verses of the Qur'an, and sat alone, listening, reciting, rewinding, and repeating. Abdellah further "coached" (*darribahu*) Mohammed, advising him on technique and bringing him to several exorcisms, just as Mohammed, having memorized more of the Qur'an, also coached Abdellah in his recitations.

Islamic exorcists like Mohammed and Abdellah were similar to other young men I met in Fez, including the sons of my household through whom I met them, who criticized older Moroccans' practices, including their parents', as impious and ignorant. To write or use an amulet or to participate in trance or make a sacrifice to jinns is impious. But it is also a social act, an act of "sorcery" that in Mohammed's words, "hurts people [*darar bil-nass*]: first it hurts the human soul [*al-that al-insan-iyya*], it hurts religion, hurts children; it hurts families, and hurts the entire society [*mujtam' ka kul*]."

The totality of society, or society as a totality, is a given in ruqya, and the imagined context for discrediting non-Islamic practices. The specifics of this discrediting are yet more telling. Distrustful of the practices of talismanic writing hijabs, and to 'ilm ruhani in general, they viewed the fqih's exclusive claims to the letter and to knowledge as indefensible supports of sorcery and idolatry. For Mohammed, the problem was its lack of clear communicability.

> You don't know what he's saying: He uses Satanic methods. [The fqih's] identity isn't revealed [*al-huwiya diyalhu ma katbansh*]. He takes hold of the person like this [thumb to thumb] and he mutters for him [*kaytimtim lahu*]. You're sitting next to him and you don't know what he says: Is it the Qur'an, Hadith? Is it a prayer [*du'wa*]? Is it names of the jinn, in Syriac [*siriyaniyya*] or Hebrew? Names outside the Qur'an? . . . I read only the Qur'an, and I read it aloud—till I'm red in the face [*bi wujhi ahmar*].

The description of inaudible "muttering" accurately describes the rituals of fuqaha', their guarding of secrets. In contrast, Mohammed recites the Qur'an and, he emphasizes, reads it "aloud" till the effort shows on his face. The corollary to this is the use of the microphone to enhance the Qur'anic sound and intensify its public reach. In contrast, like veiled writing, muttering hides itself even in the intimacy of a face-to-face encounter: "You're sitting next to him and you don't know what he says." Another exorcist considered such communications suspect because they established exclusive relationships between the fqih and the jinn.

An older exorcist, the son of a fqih, described for me his confrontation, as a young man, with his father. He was proud that his father had taught many people the Qur'an but found his talismanic writing dismaying: "You pray with your heart, and you recite with your tongue. Why then do you write with your hand?" The father responded cautiously, only saying to the young man, "This is difficult for you to understand." The answer was unsatisfactory, which the father acknowledged. The young exorcist remained troubled for several years, taking only minimal comfort in his father's mitigation of secrecy: at least he wrote his talismans on open paper, never hidden in a hijab. When finally he forgave his father, he did so only by accepting that the older man had not tried to teach *him* the practice. His father had refused to repeat the call; the circulation of magical writing would cease with the new generation.

Such social differences between parent and child speak to the changing values accruing to once authoritative and wholly respected religious figures. The differences are grounded in the changing contours of training, but also of media—from the ritual, mnemonic, and scribal reproduction by the fqih to the technological reproduction of the Qur'an and religious knowledge on the mass market. They speak to the changing sources of power to which curers, like other religious authorities, lay claim to domesticate the differences that jinns make in individual bodies and minds. That exorcists claim recourse to the Qur'an and the Qur'an alone distinguishes them, to be sure, from fuqaha' who seek out and use old "spirit science" manuscripts, who write the names of angels or Assyrian letters on the inner sheet of a hidden amulet, rather than the pure verses of the Qur'an. Yet exorcists' absolute rejection of writing cures—even those containing Qur'anic verse and Qur'anic verse alone—mark a departure from older forms and logics of pious authority embedded in Morocco as in other Muslim societies with a history of talismanic writing. It is not, in other words, only about the Qur'an as the source of power and social control, but also about the mode of its dissemination.

The subtle but significant differences between old and new forms of Qur'anic curing (that distinguish the fqih and Islamic exorcist from trance masters) speak precisely to these transformations in the logics of authority, and the kinds of personhood to which authorities lay claim. For, as exorcists seek to cure by reciting the Qur'an rather than writing it, they stage the call of the Qur'an in a particular way—privileging a kind of authoritative mediator or caller—to overcome the difference jinns make in subjects and society. Rather than keeping the message secret, Islamic exorcists broadcast the message—for anyone and everyone to hear.

The use of audiocassettes to memorize Qur'anic verses, along with the video recording and dissemination of the exorcisms signal the logic of general circulation that distinguishes the ritual act of Islamic exorcism as explicitly "legitimate" or "shari'i." That this shift parallels the technological reproduction of the message signals what Walter Benjamin has described precisely as a transformation in the power of the art object—and the observing subject—under mass-media and mass-market conditions (Benjamin 2008). For Benjamin, cult objects reproducible only by hand—or, for Benedict Anderson, religious scripts—gathered value precisely by their exclusive and unique presence in a particular place and time (B. Anderson 2006, chap. 1). In marked contrast, technologically reproducible objects—the industrial photograph, cinema, or print languages—gathered value by virtue of their ubiquity, their capacity to be anywhere, anytime. As Benjamin (and Anderson) make clear, this transformation is not merely a matter of the objects of reproduction, but of the subjects who receive and consume them. For whereas the former value of a unique object depended on an exclusive caste of persons to approach it, experience its uniqueness, difference, and distance at close range, now the masses are rendered equivalent by their consumption of the object—in the form of a copy—simultaneously.

Inasmuch as talismanic writing bears the traces of cult value for the fqih's clients, so too do Islamic exorcists oppose it on the grounds of its exclusivity. Conversely, Islamic exorcism privileges a generalized and transparent communication as the counterpoise to the exclusivity and secrecy of written cures. If the social institutions and cult value of "mnemonic possession" and exclusive literacy do not provide the logic for new Islamic curers, its subsumption by conditions of mass-market and technological reproducibility does. Seen in this light, memorizing only specific parts of the Qur'an to become expert in Islamic exorcism reflects not the continuity and authority of older recitation techniques in Fez and urban Morocco, but rather their ongoing displacement by technologically reproducible voice. Such displacement means that nationally televised Qur'anic recitation competitions in Morocco (like horse racing in Europe after the establishment of train travel) refigure the now unnecessary as ultra-specialized cultural preservation for leisure or entertainment (Schivelbusch 1986, 13). This only partly explains the aim of Qur'anic recitation in exorcism, however. Most important, in the age of generalized (or presumably generalized) literacy, secrecy of the mark rather than its clarity, exclusivity of writing rather than its open dispersal, is itself sorcerous.

Where then does authority reside, if not in the fqih's now-sorcerous writing, or in the orderly hierarchy of persons closer or farther from its production? Rather than exclusive skills as the central quality, or a quality of person that comes with exclusive training, exorcists emphasize the moral quality of the practitioner. For Islamic exorcists, certain basic skills are necessary: the memorization of a set of Qur'anic chapters or verses. Beyond that, however, the practice demands neither exclusive skills nor inherited status—not secret knowledge, not extensive training, and certainly not baraka. To the contrary it requires moral and pious rectitude: self-control and self-discipline. This quality of person is accessible to anyone who learns how to carry out the basic pillars of the Muslim faith: how to declare one's faith; how to properly wash and purify oneself; how to pray all five prayers; how to give zakat, and how to fast the month of Ramadan. And of course, how to make the pilgrimage—though this is an unlikely dream for young exorcists. The point made to me, repeatedly and emphatically, is that one's piety is not defined by social position, but by individual moral commitment, becoming engaged and staying the course.

To be sure many Muslims in Fez speak of the necessity of "faith" (*iman*) and proper "intent" (*niyya*) in living piously, but the discourse of Islamic exorcism centered on individual qualities of faith while discussions among fuqaha' did not. How to understand the repeated emphasis on strong faith (*iman qawi*) rather than exclusive skill? The cultivation of faith, patience (*sabr*), and a range of emotional qualities of piety is thematic among Islamic revivalist across the Muslim world. As Mahmood and Hirschkind have described it, the movements emphasize Foucauldian or simply practical self-fashioning. It is also crucial, however, to emphasize the historical specificity of self-discipline—a once recondite and limited practice amongst Sufis, for example, now assumed to the responsibility of anyone and everyone (Hirschkind 2006, chap. 2). Emphasizing moral qualities available to anyone—if they choose freely to embody them—is the corollary of commoditized and mass-mediated dissemination of God's call. It is a way of conceiving of differences between individuals when these have been endemically refigured as serial repetitions of an abstract subject rather than embedded within given and absolutely particular social relations. The emphasis on embodiment is not simply the continuation of an Islamic tradition, nor is it opposed to capitalism or secular modes of public life. Rather it is a demand placed on the body to communicate as a self-contained node within a broader network.

To put it otherwise, once all subjects are equally, or potentially equally conscious, communicative, and receptive, once social differences—the old hierarchies limiting access to the sacred—do not delimit or differentiate amongst subjects, all that is left is self-control. Privileging moral conduct and self-control in the absence of defining and delimiting social structures is to make a virtue of a lonely necessity. It is a response to a crisis of social reproduction entirely familiar to Muslims living under modern and neoliberal conditions. But it is also the logical fantasy of the technologization of Islam's calls: addressed to no one in particular, anyone could heed it. Those who obey, obey freely, consciously, conscientiously. Those who do not respond to a different call.

## Desiring Presence/Expelling Difference

Islamic exorcists' self-conception, their differentiation from fuqaha', suggests their mass-market and mass-mediated consciousness. Practitioners' definitions of the ailments and the cures sought, from individual cures to the larger call to Islam, do as well. Whereas curers, fuqaha', seers, and Sufi trance specialists view a jinn's call and disruption of individual bodies and minds as a fact of life, to be domesticated and soothed by the powers of writing or by propitiatory gifts, Islamic exorcists view jinn possession as a personal failing—the result of a lack of self-control. To be sure, they also view the problem as social: the effect of a jinn-soaked Moroccan culture of trance and sorcery. But this makes self-control all the more essential, as a response to overwhelming material and social forces. The terms used by exorcists emphasize the loss of self-control, the "addiction" of the individual to the practices of jinns. Indeed, the position and view regarding jinn possession is similar to discussions in the United States around drug use and prevention, in which individuals (at least in my youth) were exhorted to "Just say No!" The point in both cases is that morality, rather than a structural change, is needed; both cases assume a solitary individual as the locus of social control.

Islamic exorcists are, of course, adamant that jinns exist—that they are "real" and "exist" despite their invisibility. Their taxonomy of ailments differs however, and they are particularly skeptical of curers who attribute every disturbance to jinns. Islamic exorcists do not speak of "spirit troubles" and refuse the local terminology that is so recognizable from seers and fuqaha'. To the contrary, raqiyyin situate their diagnoses alongside biomedical discourses and take pride in stating that very few cases of mental or physical disturbance can in fact be attributed to jinn possession or *al-mass*. Thus, to the surprise of some clients, Islamic exorcists will recite on a patient for a period of minutes to hours and then, satisfied that no reaction is forthcoming, explain that they really need to seek psychiatric or neurological medical help (*tibb 'udwi*). As the mother of one incredulous patient said to me, "Have you ever seen a fqih say you *don't* have a jinn?!"

Yet even where jinn possession is not acute, exorcists will discern jinns' deleterious effects and advise caution to patients and their families. In ruqya lexicon, jinn possession can be initial—the jinn readying itself to attack—or it may be partial—limited to a limb or a section of the body. Here raqiyyin emphasize that possession is solicited or rejected by the victim him or herself, by their clothing and appearance, by their comportment, by the material décor in their homes. Wearing makeup or maintaining a state of ritual impurity attracts jinns; modest clothing, prayer, and ritual cleanliness serve as "self-fortifying" or "immunizing" (*tahsin*) acts to keep jinns at bay. "The jinns can't stand to see a woman in a veil [*hijab*]," an exorcist explained to me. "They can't stand to see Qur'anic verses displayed in a frame in the room. They can't stand to see the prayer rug folded on the couch." So too, states of emotional upset offer direct openings to jinns: heedlessness (*ghafla*), extreme fear (*khawf shadid*), extreme anger (*ghadab shadid*), and lust (*shahwa*). Women are usually described in Morocco, as in other Muslim societies, as the more emotionally volatile (Peletz 1996; Siegel 2000b [1969]), but exorcists notably speak in the same terms to men and women. The point is the same: self-control guards against possession, and developing self-control comes through orientation toward proper Islam. Islamic exorcists and the ruqya literature they draw on refer to the advocacy of proper Islam as "exorcism in stages" (*sar' bi-l-marahil*), and a critical element of the practice as da'wa. In my experience, curers included the patient's family (those available) in the process of the exorcism. In one exorcism I observed with Mohammed and Abdellah, the latter urged the patient, a teenaged boy they diagnosed with "initial possession [*al-mass al-ta'if*]," to take up prayer both "dedicated [*bi-l-haq*] and punctual." Abdellah reminded him several times that it was his duty to pray and that he was alone "responsible [*mas'ul*—answerable] for [him]self" and for his duties. They left him with several cassettes of Qur'anic recitation to play to create his own safe bubble. Similarly, seeing a young woman whose mother had previously sought psychiatric help and talismanic writing, Mohammed urged proper Islamic comportment. Speaking to her mother—the girl sat, with her head down—he explained that "she has to wear the veil, cover her hands well, and stay purified always. She has to read the Qur'an, one *hizb* [60th of the Qur'an] in the morning, one *hizb* at night, and recite supernumerary prayers in the morning and night"—she must enact a punctual, indeed immediate, response to the call-to-prayer: "She must pray five times daily—at the proper time. She must not miss it by a minute. The moment of the call, she does the ablutions, and prays." The mother, weary but receptive, nodded her head. It was not clear whether she could convince the girl to take up the practice.

But the logic of the effort is unmistakable. Adopting the veil or prayer recenters the subject as responsible to the call—to the call to Islam and the call to prayer. This is a subjective condition, but one premised on communication and consciousness—of bringing in and incorporating what comes from outside. Like listening to Qur'anic recitation on cassettes, as Charles Hirschkind has shown in exquisite detail, heeding the call is understood as cultivating a pious selfhood—and pious selfhood is understood as the effect of the call: that is, both preparation for piety, and an act of piety in its own right. The accumulation of individual practitioners heeding the technological call of the Qur'an could, for Islamic exorcists as much as for Cairene callers, promise to generate a seamless space of piety, interior to both the individual subject and society. But we should examine the distinct mode of sociality imagined here, for although this is ostensibly a social practice—of opening to an outside at the very least—ruqya curers strikingly emphasize isolated practice. This virtuous isolation reflects the conditions of raqiyyin themselves, unmoored, outside in the Sufi cultural system, lacking the kinship connections of upper-middle-class Fassis and their celebration of Sufi nationalism. More crucially, however, this isolation is recommended by the endemic impiety of national Sufi practices. For the lone Muslim, listening to cassettes or responding to the azzan is immune to the call of other collectives, other rituals, in Morocco. In other words, the desire for an ethical soundscape or uniform space of piety presumes the presence of other calls, indeed, fears the very conditions of circulation that make the pious call possible.

For raqiyyin, trance rites too, like the fqih's withholding and hiding in talismanic writing, presents a problem of communication, in this case an excess of connections. The trance rites certainly violate doctrine—the improper mixing of sexes, sacrifice in the name of a jinn rather than God—but the main problem is that connections proliferate, without proper oversight of either an exterior authority or oneself as subject. Of women performing trance rites, Mohammed argued, "They are obliged to follow the jinn, to satisfy their conditions, to become seers or sorcerers." Whereas the jinns in trance rites are grasped as a sovereign and ultimately controlling force, provided that one submits to them, raqiyyin view them as demonic, evil. "You understand," Mohammed said, that the Islamic curer is "at war with Iblis [the Devil]": "All jinns belong to one group [*fasila wahida*]: That group is of Shaytan [Satan]. Why? Because from the beginning he was a jinn, a jinn that oversaw twenty-eight nations [*umma*] on Earth. So the jinn *wants* to take you off the proper path [*kharij al-tariq*]; take even the most straight-forward, undeviating Muslim [*shi wahid mustaqim*], the jinn makes him zig-zag [Fr. *zigue-zaguer*]." The problem with jinns is their decentering Muslims, even the most pious. Tellingly, this is grasped as a failure of communication, a derivation, a zig-zag, from the Straight Path and direct connection. To allow jinns to take one over was like taking drugs. Muslims in trance are addicts. Mohammed continued, "For the woman, trance means she becomes permanently possessed [*mamluka*]. Every year, she has to do the trance rites again. She's obliged. If she doesn't do it, she has *problems*. She simply *cannot go without it*. In this way, she enters regularly into idolatry [*shirk*]." This is not simply an individual problem, but like much modernist discourse concerning drugs, in abandoning the inner center, the subject, irresponsible for him- or herself, blends into a collective. Mohammed further emphasized that a collectivity around trance finds sanctuary in private homes, at night. "The Gnawa or other Sufi orders come in and do the ritual night [*lila*] for her. There will be a black chicken, or a black goat, or a black cow, or a black sheep. There will, inevitably, be women doing trance [*hadra*]. They'll trance with their hair showing. They'll throw milk in certain spots [for the jinns]."

Mohammed's description of obligation was accurate. Women do trance with hair exposed, and they throw milk to the jinns. From his perspective, of course, receptivity to their sovereign commands generates irresponsibility, rather than pious subjectivity. The young exorcist further explained that such rites take place in public:

> There are even public festivals [*mawasim*] for the jinns. Did you know that? You go there, and you buy a calf for six hundred or seven hundred thousand francs [US$ 600–700], you'll take it and lay it in the shrine, and beg for help. What is really happening? Someone at the site of the sacrifice gathers the meat, someone else buys it for *30 or 40 million francs*. He takes the meat and sells it to the butcher. The extra money goes into a collection [*sanduq*]. Now come all the people named "Aisha" and they divide the money. As I said, those women are obliged to follow the jinn, to satisfy their conditions, to become seers or sorcerers.

Mohammed refers to the conventional festival for sharifian saints, the jinn shrines nearby. Although in his thinking the ritual is public, its operation involves, significantly, secrecy and the movement of money out of public view. Mohammed had nothing to say about the saints themselves, but like colonial-era nationalists' critique, the problem the ritual presents is the sheer volume of connections and the formation of a mass collective on its basis—a series of identical bodies all named Aisha. The current form of the tradition is partly the result of falsity; significantly enough its very publicity, conceals the true process. But this falsity in fact contributes to the ritual process. It produces an excess value, that is, "extra money," which permits and pushes the ritual to repeat and repeat again, indeed to fragment and proliferate into new seers and sorcerers. The excess comes at the expense of ordinary people's conscious awareness of the communicative process. What is needed is something to freeze or expose the movement of exchanges in order to bring people to awareness.

## The Call as Exorcism

Why have varied reform movements been accompanied by, or required, a call? Why has the technologized call become the exemplary act of religious authority in modern Muslim societies? To call means, first of all, to invite, incite, or command a response. Prior to any message as such, the call defines piety as *responsibility*—to one call rather than another. The call is a communicative force—not message but medium—that intervenes upon the subject and the social, demanding the self-presence of the respondent even at the expense of attention or connections paid elsewhere.

The images of the possessed reiterate overwhelming communications—forces of circulation that cause deviation, loss of consciousness, unawareness: mindless repetition. To the contrary, images of the responsible Muslim emphasize immediacy. Recalling Mohammed's recommendation (really, voiced more as command) to the young woman and her mother, proper comportment means responding to the call to prayer—at once. Any deviation within the space of the call—the space opened by the call—is foreclosed by the technological immediacy of its sending, but also by the pious norms of listening and responding. One is always accessible to the call, always on-call.

We should note here the emphasis on continuous practices. The young woman Mohammed spoke to was also advised to sleep on her right side. One must be on call, however, because one is already constantly and continuously summoned by the jinns themselves. More than any other Qur'anic verse, exorcists take pleasure in reciting chapter 7, verse 27: "They see you, Satan and his Tribe, from where you do not see them." The other, the foreign, is not located in a particular place, but rather dispersed across the landscape, as a continuous and unseen gaze. To be social is to be continuously public, which now means continuous visibility.

The call of exorcism presents itself as the call to discipline all calls, all differences, all *différance*: to overcome all vulnerability to communications. Because, of course, Islamic exorcism views Moroccan Islam as comprising illegitimate calls—of baraka and jinns, Sufis and the state. To generate a fully receptive and conscious subject is to exorcise all the other competing calls: to reduce all difference to a uniform presence and order—or, more precisely, to define uniform presence and order, as orientation toward a *particular* call.

Exorcism videos stage this presence and attempt to do so at a distance. They are thus a telling artifact of Islamic exorcism and of the technologized call more generally. Video exorcisms demonstrate presence—the summoning and controlling of distant unseen and outside forces into the singular body of the possessed. They do so, in a seeming paradox, at the very moment they participate in the reproduction of mass social belonging, in the reproduction of a mass public defined in terms of jinns and jinn rites. Videos are not, then, extra elements of the practice, separate from exorcism's greater logic. Rather ruqya is built on the presumption of community as necessitating a technological call, that is to say, as distinctly mass mediated. Rather like Sufi nationalism, or Moroccan nationalist reformism, Islamic exorcism assumes a technologized society. "Jinns" name that condition of mass-mediated society to which one is connected without the benefit of sight, and ruqya names an effort to control the connections and, most crucially, the differences that such mass-mediated communications open and enhance. Like modern nationalist reformism, such efforts desire and demand *presence* that would overcome differences and in which difference is defined as a subjective condition with social consequences: a lack of control of communication, but not a lack as such; rather an excess, a material/immaterial excess of communication that new forms of mediation have created. Such practice seeks to reduce difference through presence and exposure. This is made possible by technological mediation (live exorcism videos), and by social and self-control—and by the call that defines these latter as effects of the former.

## Aisha Exposed and Expelled

Aisha's exorcism with which I opened this book anticipated such a context—mass mediated, sold as part of its daʿwa efforts—for the jamʿiyya saw fit to record it. In the video, the exorcism comes as the culmination of an outreach event, like those others the jamʿiyya held and recorded until its closure following the Casablanca attacks. Exorcism videos are now available more online than off. But in the early 2000s they were circulating largely on video and audiocassette in Fez. The genre itself derived from the mass-market literature available in Islamic bookstores, specifically, a genre of book, "Interview with a Jinn," the most famous examples published in Cairo and Jeddah (Karam 1990; M. Daoud 1992), with numerous more recent works published in Morocco, each with pages of evidentiary photographs, with the eyes of the possessed covered in a black bar. The books and videos follow a typical pattern of summoning the jinn to presence in the body of the possessed and then questioning or interrogating the jinn under threat of torture (taʿdib) or burning (harq), both with Qur'anic recitation, to reveal its name, origin, and religion. The jinns are often foreign to wherever the book or video is based, or if local, then of a different religion—Jewish or Christian. In the latter case the videos close with the jinn's forced conversion to Islam and then expulsion.

Aisha's exorcism itself is part of a longer videotaped panel of lectures on sorcery, jinns and the Qur'an by the bookstore owner, and on mental illness, by a psychiatrist who offers the counterargument that possession can be explained scientifically as emotional or neurological disorders. The exorcism is clearly meant as a demonstration and corroboration of the Islamic curers' claims, but it is preceded by the examination of another young boy whom an Islamic curer dismisses as not possessed at all, but suffering a "medical illness" (*mard tibbi*). The boy is walked off stage, and one of the curers explains to the audience that 90 percent of ailments are physical illness and only 10 percent are from possession (*mass*).

The second case brought forth, however, confirms the reality of that small percentage. The curers ask a man, in his mid thirties, with a mustache, wearing a comfortable sweatshirt, for his history, and he responds, "I went out one night. I was all right, but somebody . . . and I was struck [*madrub*]." The curer asks, "Do you smoke hashish?" "No—I've never smoked in my life. Sometimes I see only fire in front of me." The psychiatrist interjects that this could be depression (*ikti'ab*). The man responds, "I feel. I feel. I feel strange, like someone's always with me." Now one of the curers quickly admonishes him: "No, you shouldn't say that. That's just the environment you're in. You mustn't let that overwhelm you. No you shouldn't say 'I have . . .' or 'I'm possessed by a jinn.' That's the Unseen Unknown [*alam al-ghayb*]." The point is clear: if saying one is possessed is a way of usurping God's unique knowledge, it is a common cultural norm. It is not only a jinn but the man's environment that has seeped into and overwhelmed him.

The Islamic curer then takes hold of the man, his right hand spanning temple to temple and covering the man's eyes; it is a different gesture from the fqih's thumbnail to thumbnail, face-to-face approach. Here the eyes of the possessed are shielded, as if to suggest the condition of blindness the jinns establish: "They see you from where you do not see them" (Qur'an 12:27). "Pass me the microphone," the man says, "and I'll recite on him." He begins the *Fatiha*, the Qur'an's opening chapter. He repeats it, at double speed. The style is clearly drawing on a technological aesthetic, as if the recitation were on a fast-forward reel. The client, under the influence of this repetition, his eyes buried in the curer's palm, begins to tremble. His mouth gapes open, then closes, then gapes. His shoulders wriggle. The curer repeats the *Fatiha*, again, still faster, as if urging the jinn to respond. At this point the mouth gapes and emits a loud squawk. The curer begins the Surat al-Baqara. The verse, "God has power over all [*Allah ala kuli shay qadir*]," echoes through the amplification system, and the trembling man's squawks are now full-fledged screams.

CURER: What is your name!

JINN: ghghghgaaaaaaak!

C: *What is your name!*

The possessed man hunches over the table, mouth pressed open. The curer clutches his head and covers his eyes. The jinn chokes out the name "Aisha."

C: Aisha who? Aisha Kahla? Aisha Gnawiyya? Aisha Sudaniyya?

J: Aaaa—Aisha S-s-sudaniyya

C: Where do you live? Where do you live?

J: In the square.

C: Which square?

J: On Talaa. [One of two main routes through Fez medina]

C: Talaa? Which Talaa? Talaa Saghira, or Talaa Kabira?

J: Saghiiiiiiiiiira.

C: Why did you hurt this man?

J: He was walking. . . . He was walking . . .

C: Why did you hurt this man?

J: He was walking . . . and he tripped me up [*khalat alaya*].

C: Who's to blame for that [*skhun huwa al-zalim*], huh? He can't see you—*you* can see him. *You* should get out of the street.

The phrase is meant to put the jinn in her place—it is clear she does not belong and more so that she is not worthy of belonging. The curer slaps the man: Slap. Slap. Slap.

J: I'm to blame! I'm to blame!

C: What's your religion?

J: J-j-j-ewish . . .

At this revelation the audience gasps. Someone off-camera shouts, "God damn you!" The head of the panel gestures to the audience to stay in their seats. The second curer steps in, asking Aisha, "Do you believe in the Prophet?" to which she replies in a small whiny voice, "I don't knooooow him." After reminding her that "Hell awaits for the lost [*khasirin*]," he asks Aisha how old she is. She replies, "Three hundred fifty years old." There is another gasp from the audience.

The men then tell Aisha that she should convert to Islam, to which she replies, "My ancestors won't let me." The second curer turns to the first, "Recite the Qur'an on him [the possessed man]." The first recites the Jinns Verse, in which a group of jinns proclaims itself to have "really heard" God's command. The possessed man's paroxysms reach an apex, and Aisha speaks again: "My ancestors are stabbing me with knives!" The second curer shouts, "You lie! Why are you pretending to be afraid? Have you ever seen a frightened jinn? Don't these words burn you? Whose words are these? *God's* Words!"

CURER ONE: I'll find out if he's lying with the Sorcery Verse [*ayat al-sihr*].

CURER TWO: Recite the Qur'an on him.

CURER ONE: Pass me the mic.

With each recitation of the Qur'an, the possessed man struggles and shakes, his eyes hidden by the curer's hand, his mouth agape, screaming and dripping long tendrils of saliva. The jinn is alternately presented as a powerful foe ("Have you ever seen a frightened jinn?"), and a wholly pathetic liar that the Qur'anic sound chastens and "burns." With each recitation the men are more triumphant, and Aisha more submissive. Finally she promises to accept Islam, and the men press her—bully her is more accurate—through the *shahada* (the Muslim declaration of faith) syllable by syllable. With that Aisha swears to "leave the man and his family at peace." Her presence recedes, and the man comes to.

From here the program continues only briefly, as the possessed man, now apparently cured, steps to the microphone and attests that he did not know where he was, which is to say, the episode of possession was real. One of the exorcists reminds the audience: "Sorcerers and charlatans have their houses in the medina; we have our house too. Come to *us* to learn the Qur'an and ruqya." The video closes with a printed message noting that whoever wants "to acquire a copy of this cassette" should call the jam'iyya. The jam'iyya's address and phone number is then listed, with the name of the neighborhood of Sidi Boujida modified, following the style of the Islamists themselves, to the abrupt "Boujida." Neither the saint nor the spirit is worthy of veneration.

## Conclusions

Ruqya and its videos aim to call or recall Muslims to consciousness, while defining consciousness in terms of communication itself—as the response to a particular kind of message in a particular kind of medium. That consciousness is threatened always by communications that send subjects afar, both from themselves and others. Exorcism eliminates the jinns as both absence and difference; it removes this ambiguity to make it fully present and thus accountable. The distance and difference of otherness would succumb to the sameness of the homogeneous "Islamic" society.

Like an act of ethnic cleansing, the exorcism takes difference as a danger. On the one hand, jinns are different—in all curing rites they stand for difference. But how that difference is handled, with what centralizing and stabilizing force, defines different political and social positions in urban Morocco, as well as different visions and versions of person and society. Jinns can be sovereign forces to be controlled by secret knowledge or soothed by propitiatory gifts; they can be cultural forces stabilized by Sufi hierarchy, and public forms of pious consciousness. Or they can be evil and demonic forces of a mass-mediated culture, forces that overwhelm subjects who are not otherwise conscientious and self-controlled. Here, Aisha's difference is utterly recognizable; yet it is this cultural recognizability that makes her dangerous. For here she stands for forces that seem culturally pervasive, forces that differentiate people as conscious or unconscious, legitimate or illegitimate, curers or sorcerers; the exorcism consists in controlling those forces of difference. She is converted to Islam as a prelude to her final eradication.

What is being eliminated here is difference itself, and crucially, not only in the content of the ritual, the dramatis persona, but by the act of summoning her. From afar, Aisha is brought close. From out there (to which we are blind) to here, now. This is a disciplining, even punishing act, and the Qur'anic voice itself, amplified and modulated in a technological aesthetic, is demonstrated as its medium—a force that eliminates the distance as the elimination of difference.

Ruqya has taken root in Fez among those who assume mass mediation as the condition social life in Morocco. The practice seeks and even assumes publicity and revelation—the immediacy of the mysterious—as a virtue, in a way that renders older practices foreign to its exhibitionary demands. Yet the practice demonstrates, or symptomatizes, a condition in which exhibition itself becomes a cure to the very distance and difference mass-mediated social life requires. It seeks to cure by closing or covering, as Samuel Weber (1996) has suggested of television, what technologization opens up. For this reason, "jinns" to raqiyyin are not what they are to fuqaha'. They are neither sovereign spirits nor amoral disruptions. Here jinns—wholly demonized—give a body to that "ghostly element between people," which as Kafka described it, mechanical communications were meant to erase but which at the same time opened up.

In this sense, like all calls to action and consciousness, ruqya must generate the public it seeks to address, or summon it into being. Indeed if in this case exorcism is a call, I have argued more broadly that technologized calls engage in a similar kind of exorcism. This formula to be sure risks reducing the breadth of da'wa to negation, thus eliding participants' tremendous efforts of social construction and reconstruction. But like other modernist calls to consciousness, the modern call to Islam—with its promises of large-scale unity and "imagined community"—have defined society in terms of proper communications, and virtue as responsibility to a general, mass-mediated call. In so doing, difference—redefined from colonial-era nationalism onward as an impediment to unity—has been recast as a difference of communication. The call to Islam is an exorcism of precisely such differences that have emerged after the fact, like 350-year-old jinns, as recalcitrant and uncontrolled connections.

# Epilogue

"The enemy," those who respond to something from beyond the frontier of communication . . .

—James T. Siegel, *Fetish, Recognition, Revolution*

THE PERIOD IN which I carried out this ethnographic study was pivotal in Mohammed VI's consolidation of control over the religious field. In the terms repeatedly offered in the decade following May 16, 2003, the king recuperated and enforced the "the spiritual security of the nation" (Arif 2008; cf. Kaitouni 2010). In practice "spiritual security" meant the state's reassertion of control over the calls of Islam—the domestication of Sufi practice, and the repression of Islamist dissent. Put otherwise, security has meant controlling the messages and media that might provoke responses among masses now deemed the site of potential threats to the national body as a whole.

The 2003 terrorist attacks did not, of course, invent the discourse of control; the monarchism that colonial-era nationalists developed as a strategic call to mass consciousness itself built on cultural history and colonial strategy. In turn it provided the ritual infrastructure for further monarchist calls in the postindependence era of Mohammed V and the postcolonial era of Hassan II. Hassan II's domination of the call of Islam—namely, his control of its media and his lethal repression of opposing voices—was pivotal to his sustained rule. Extension and domination of radio and television in the early 1970s permitted Hassan II's staging the most spectacular call to action in Morocco's history, the 1975 Green March, evoked by Mohammed VI immediately following the 2003 bombing.

The Moroccan state's control of broadcast media from independence through the 1980s, and the subsequent competition in the 1990s and 2000s from other communication technologies, from small media to satellite channels to social media, is a textbook example of current public-sphere theories of Islam and media in the Muslim world.

In this rapidly maturing field, Muslim politics constituted a contest over Muslim publics and, more specifically, the public mediation of sacred symbols. Diversification of technological media is framed as the democratization of the authority to establish public presence—a democratization of the capacity to call and in so doing establish oneself *as* the voice of the public (Mah 2000). Initial treatments of this process were markedly optimistic, often reiterating the same modernist fantasies of a universal network (Schivelbusch 1986; Mattelart 1996). Media theorists of "print Islam" and "sound Islam" envisioned egalitarian Muslim public spheres both global and local defined by the capacity of ostensibly "anyone" to claim authority (Robinson 1993; Eickelman 1985). More importantly, such a collapse of hierarchy would lead not to disorder but rather, in Eickelman and Piscatori's words, to "overlapping circles of communication, solidarity, and . . . bonds of identity and trust" (Eickelman and Piscatori 2004, xiii; cf. Eickelman and Salvatore 2002, 99).

Recent assessments by these and other theorists have been rather more cautious, emphasizing differences in power as well as in the impossibility of finally controlling circulation itself (Eickelman and Salvatore 2004; Moors 2006). Islamic exorcism is a case in point. To be sure, the proliferation of Islamic calls in the 1980s and 1990s, of which Islamic exorcisms were a part, demonstrate small media challenges both to the older exclusive scribal and oral-communications media and to state-controlled broadcast media. But the practice of Islamic exorcism and the experiences of its practitioners also demonstrate the uncertainty such technological communications can evoke at the moment they make a total and transparent space of communication imaginable. Inasmuch as exorcism signals a claim to the call available ostensibly to "anyone," of communication detached from hierarchy, it precipitates different fears of communication, and fear of difference as communication. But while most optimistic assessments of Islam's "democratization"—more accurately, its "massification"—have now been moderated, popular discourse surrounding more recent Arab uprisings renewed the claims.

The protests that emerged in Tunisia in late 2010 and quickly spread across the Middle East and North Africa marked a significant political rupture. In Tunisia, Egypt, and Libya authoritarian figures collapsed; in Syria another may fall, but only following protracted civil and sectarian war. Protests have been violently muted in Bahrain, Yemen, and Algeria. In Iran, where protests erupted in 2009, international sanctions may yet disrupt government control. In Morocco the state has at once violently stifled protests and arrested participants and also provided some measure of constitutional reform. Participants and observers alike in these protests and revolutions have argued over the extent to which so-called social media, namely, Facebook and Twitter, precipitated the uprisings or made them possible. As in discussions of Islam and democratized media, initial enthusiasm for "Twitter revolutions" gave way to more careful acknowledgment that these technologies fitted together with other media—other social structures of communicative possibility, such as labor unions and political parties, as well as satellite television outlets. At the same time, the more sobering fact occurred to many that technologized calls to political action, while powerful means of mobilization, unleash forces, including violence, that may evade their control. They do not build governing institutions and infrastructures; nor do they guarantee unity, whether sociopolitical or religious. Communitas passes—difference remains.

What remains striking, however, and remains in process in Morocco is precisely this idiom and logic of the call upon which political mobilization is premised—that is, the contemporary condition in which, while technologically connected, subjects must nonetheless be *summoned* into a self-present and self-conscious collective. The age of the technologized call is one that presumes fragmentation even as it promises unity— that seeks both to open and fill potential pathways of consciousness and community. In this regard the return of the discourse of "the People" is striking: the very audible slogan, "The People Demand the Fall of the Regime! [*al-sha'b yurid isqat al-nizam!*]"— shouted first in Tunisia and then repeated, thanks to media, everywhere—sought to revive an agentive mass body largely muted since the decline of twentieth-century revolutionary and anticolonial nationalisms.

Communications were indeed unleashed, but with what response? In Morocco social media protests summoned regular but disappointingly small crowds; in post-revolutionary Egypt, participants acknowledge the collapse of solidarity, with many liberals supporting state repression of Islamists. One need not play Cassandra to ask, What of this return or revenge of ostensibly surpassed differences? Is this the perversion of a properly unified people? Or was difference ever—will difference ever be— fully exorcised? Indeed, does the call itself risk promoting the very differences it seeks to eliminate?

One might expect some sympathy in Fez for the pro-democracy activists, mobilizing as the February 20th movement (named for the date of their first political call to demonstrate), who organized publicly in multiple cities beginning in 2011. My contacts with Fassis are limited, for the moment, to Skype and brief visits, but I have been surprised by the converse—the distrust of their call, and their intentions. Sanae and her family dismiss the protestors as "crazy [*humaq*]" and "glue-sniffers." According to Mohammed, medina folk were against them and in favor of the monarchy: "The king is doing a good job; it is his administration who are corrupt. He cannot solve the country's problems overnight." Furthermore, he said, "People in the medina are saying, 'Why should we listen to 'February 20th'? They can't even take care of themselves, so how will they take care of the country?'" A Fulbright scholar confirmed the sentiment, describing her older Moroccan interlocutors as dismissing the February 20th movement as immature youth needing "a good smacking."

A July 2011 vote for Morocco's new constitution, quickly proposed by the king, became a referendum on the monarchy itself. The lead-up to the vote witnessed competing demonstrations, that is to say, competing calls to action, across varied technological platforms. The February 20th movement posted Facebook and Twitter calls (*nida'at*), as well as disturbing video of police brutality against peaceful protesters. Such videos, including a series of statements by Moroccans explaining "Why I am going to demonstrate on Feb 20th" (and translated into English), and another from a Moroccan in New York City lamenting his native country's social inequalities and pervasive humiliation, attracted broad attention, both supportive and critical.[1] In countercalls Moroccan state television showed documentaries praising the monarchy in comparison to others. (A political cartoon in the national press showed a television arguing with a Facebook logo.) In Fez the local neighborhood head (*muqaddam*) canvassed door to door to recruit a show of support. My household members Sanae and her father Abdelqader described the recruitment to me as obligatory, rather than voluntary, but they were supportive of the tactic nonetheless as a necessary one for "maintaining order" (*hafz 'ala al-nizam*). My friend Mohammed also made a point of attending, he said, of his "own accord." In Casablanca elite and middle-class Moroccans joined a march organized by a leader of the Qadiriyya-Boutchichiyya Sufi order (and attended by numerous members), in "sincere support for the call [*l'appel*] of His Majesty King Mohammed VI" ("Marche de soutien à Casablanca," *Le Matin*, June 6, 2011, 1). Gnawa performers were also enlisted or chose to voice support for the throne. In the lead-up to the referendum vote, a group of Gnawa *ma'lims* toured the United States; the New York-based Gnawa master Hassan Hakmoun posted several YouTube videos denouncing the February 20th movement.

Not surprisingly, pro- and antimonarchy groups dismissed the competing call of the other. February 20th supporters named the pro-monarchy demonstrators as paid "thugs," a charge my interlocutors in Fez denied. Pro-monarchy voices smeared the February 20th movement by the simple repetition of images, posting (perhaps) doctored photographs of those who appeared in the "Why I am going to demonstrate" video posing in a church. The assertion was made that those behind the movement were MRAs—a dehumanizing acronym for Moroccans Residing Abroad—and thus not sufficiently Moroccan.

More broadly, the state and other pro-monarchy voices raised the specter of an alliance between February 20th and militant Islam. Echoes of May 16th sounded with a new terrorist bombing in April 14, 2011, this time in a popular café in Marrakech. Moreover, pro-monarchy sources continually characterized the pro-democracy advocates as a toxic mix of "extreme left and Islamism" (Karam and Fiévet 2011). This accusation was grounded in part in a real, if temporary, alliance between the banned Islamist political party al-'Adl wa-l-Ihsan and February 20th activists. But the putative risks of their political alliance gathered purchase among my interlocuters in Fez. Mohammed further explained to me the broader mood among his largely poor and lower-middle-class medina compatriots: "Every time February 20th calls, extremists from al-'Adl wa al-Ihsan come out. The people don't want it. They don't want the situation that would arise. Morocco has too many factions. They would fight for their share. We always have Algeria in mind. Or Iraq."

Whether pictured in a church, or dismissed as "MRAs" and thus insufficiently Moroccan, the February 20th movement's call was foreign and different, and it invoked difference as socially and politically uncontrollable violence. To respond to it was to respond to something, as James Siegel describes it, "from beyond the frontier of communication" (Siegel 1997, 226)—not a problem of an identifiable origin, but of uncontrolled dissemination. The performative power that February 20th might provoke would resist even the callers' recuperation. Difference is a problem awaiting a medium, a problem the call itself brings out.

This possibility of the call in Morocco echoes across other scenes of technological modernity, in which difference is figured as a problem of communication: the iterability of the call, even between origin and reception, is the necessary condition of communication—and also of its perversion. The call reemerged as a political theme in Muslim societies contemporaneously with mass-mediated life and with the forms of "media fallout" (Mcluhan 2001, 305) this entailed. The call continues to sound in encounters between old and new religious mediations: as some Muslims reinterpret established forms of person, politics, and receptivity as divisive, they look to technologized calls to discipline society and subjects as subjects *of* communication, *of* the call. The call is at once dangerous and fantastical, promising to some the overcoming of difference by a yet more powerful, encompassing, and disciplining medium.

Yet the call itself cannot so much eliminate difference as continually refigure difference as foreign and even ghostly intrusions: an old and non-Muslim spirit in a Muslim body, a militant and foreign Islam in the Sufi heart of Fez. So the technologized call, modernity itself, takes the form of an exorcism, expelling the ghostly spaces that pervasive mediation opens, the differences that communication makes.

# Notes

## Introduction

1. The best-known and most studied Muslim association for da'wa is the transnational Tablighi Jama'at—"tabligh," meaning "communication" of God's message. It has been used synonymously with "da'wa" only in the twentieth century (Masud 2000, xxi). National Islamic political parties and their publications foregrounding da'wa include the Algerian "People of the Call," the Iraqi "Party of the Call," and the Egyptian Muslim Brotherhood's party newspaper (al-Da'wa). "The call" is equally thematic in state-sponsored and private religious media: from the Nation of Islam's *Final Call,* to radio broadcasts in Iran (*The Call of Islam Radio*) and Saudi Arabia (*Nida' al-Islam*), to Egyptian satellite television preachers ("The New Callers" [du'a al-judud]), to the Moroccan state-sponsored Islamic journal (*Da'wat al-Haq*). On Muslim da'wa organizations more broadly, see Masud 2000 and Racius 2004.

2. In some ways Mahmood's emphasis on Muslim embodiment has worked against this interpretation. Mahmood's work, while drawing on theories of performative enactment, emphasizes piety as submission to and reproduction of Islamic norms. It is also clear that part of the practice entails refusing to enact and reproduce the norms of "secular" Egyptian society. Islamic da'wa acts to oppose this all-encompassing call and therefore indeed involves efforts to disrupt dominant structures. In denying ritual as a signifying practice and eliding revivalists' disruption of other dominant (that is, secular Egyptian) practices of signification, she effectively idealizes the interior effects of practice at the expense of its significance as communicative act, whether the subject intends it to be or not. See Hafez 2011 and P. Anderson 2011, for critiques of Mahmood's de-emphasis of social and cultural conditions.

3. For some Cairene callers, it seems secular culture and capitalism summons; in South Asia and Nigeria, Christian proselytizers summon (Masud 2000; Larkin 2008, 2012); in Niger, Sudan, and Morocco, spirits summon otherwise pious Muslims into states of irresponsibility and idolatrous ritual expenditure (Soares 2007; Masquelier 2009). Indeed, in Niger and Nigeria, the predominant reformist movement *izala*—Jam'at izalat al-bida' wa iqamat al-sunna—explicitly aims to "remove" Sufi innovations (*izalat al-bida'*) as the basis for reestablishing proper Islam (*iqamat al-sunna*).

4. According to the modernist Al-Azhar University scholar Mahmud Shaltut, "Thanks to radio broadcasting it became possible for the ritual practices of the people, their contractual affairs, and the customs and traditions to which they adhere to be in accord with God's principles" (Messick 1996, 310).

5. For media scholars with this expansive view of media, including scholars of religion and media, see Morris 2000; and the collections of DeVries and Weber 2001; Meyer and Moors 2006; and Behrend, Dreschke, and Zillinger 2013. Of these, Rosalind C. Morris's (2000) pioneering work on spirit mediumship and mass mediation in Thailand, in particular, has sparked an expanding critical discussion of intersections of corporeal ritual media and its technological extensions. Following Morris, such conjunctures are "increasingly taken as the starting point by scholars of religion to think about religious mediation in the age of globalization, mass media, and the circulation of so-called small media" (Zillinger 2010, 224). See also Mazzarella 2004.

6. The traditional biographies of Muhammad record his first revelation as Qur'an 96, which begins:

In the Name of God, the Merciful and Compassionate

Recite! Recite! In the name of your Lord who created
Created humankind from a blood clot.
Recite, for your Lord is the most kind,
Who taught by the pen,
Taught humankind what it did not know. (Qur'an 96:1–5)

7. On a small scale, classical Islamic jurists, like Christian clergy, took the sound of the call (or church bells) and the distance it traveled as a simple delineation of community. To hear the call from the mosque defined the pious Muslim as physically present and thus literally responsible to Islamic duty and community. Baber Johansen cites the nineteenth-century Damascene faqih Ibn Abidin's list of nine Hanafi definitions: "7. the distance at which the voice of the Muezzin can be heard; 8. the distance at which a voice can be heard" (Johansen 1999, 93–94n6). On a large scale, the domain of the Muslim umma (the *dar al-Islam*) is defined by the political limits imposed on God's call to humankind.

8. The power and authority of one medium or another classically focused on the relationship between writing and voice, with the latter figured as a medium of ostensible presence and subjective and collective coherence (Meeker 1979; Siegel 1979; Messick 1993).

9. The "call of conscience" is collective, even if, as Heidegger proposes, it "comes from me and yet from beyond me and over me" (1996, 320). As his autonomic formula suggests, Heidegger negates the medium by which the source of the call would aporetically be (recognizably) singular (Weber 2001, 128; cf. Ronell 1989, 79–80). "Recognition," writes James T. Siegel, "is the end of singularity" (Siegel 2006, 206). In broader terms, the call is a moment of the sacred's (singularity's) "auto-immu-nization" (Derrida 2002). For Derrida, it seems, maintaining secrecy in responding to the call is the asymptomatic limit to both recognizing and maintaining the singularity of the other (Derrida 1995).

10. Jenny White's helpful definition of Islamists emphasizes these national dimensions of Muslim politics, along with other key points addressed in this book, including the mobilization of Muslims as conscientious practitioners of the faith. Islamists, she writes, are "Muslims who, rather than accept and inherited Muslim tradition, have developed their own self-conscious vision of Islam, which is then brought to bear on social and political events within a particular national context" (White 2002, 23).

## Chapter 1: Competing Calls in Urban Morocco

1. Vincent Cornell (1998) and Scott Kugle (2006) have rightly faulted Clifford Geertz's (1968) reduction of premodern Moroccan sainthood to one charismatic martial figure.

2. In his two-volume opus *Ritual and Belief in Morocco*, Finnish ethnographer Edward Wes-termarck defines baraka as miraculous and transmissable "holiness" residing in a range of sacred objects and bodies—stones, caves, plants, springs, animals, and above all, saints—and closely tied to jinns. "It is not in every case easy or even possible to decide," he writes "whether the miracle-working power of which something is supposed to be possessed may be called baraka or not." Indeed, baraka "implies not only beneficial energy but also an element of danger [. . .] in many cases personified in the shape of *jnun* [jinns]" (Westermarck 1968, I, 35, 146).

3. For Furnivall, plural societies comprised relatively separate ethno-national groups meeting primarily through economic structures (that is, in the market), rather than through social ones. I distinguish Furnivall's thinking from Carleton Coon's raciological theory (1958) of Middle Eastern and North African "mosaic" societies, the contours of which were, to his thinking, quasi biologi-cal and unchanging. (For analysis of Coon's work in relation to Middle Eastern and North African scholarship, see Slyomovics 2013; and Shami and Naguib 2013.)

4. An excerpt (in English) of Mohammed VI's address to the Tijaniyya order and its support-ers is available at http://www.tijani.org/news/tijani-conference-2007/. For an analysis of Mohammed

VI's similar address to the September 2004 Sidi Shiker (or Shakir) International Sufi meeting in Marrakech, also delivered by the minister of pious endowments and Islamic affairs, Ahmed Tawfiq, see Ghoulaichi 2005.

5. Other festivals include Le Boulevard, a Moroccan hip-hop festival, the Agadir "Festival of Tolerance," and a third festival, "Mawazine," that is held annually in Rabat since 2000, which in the past several years included Elton John—whose very presence, Moroccan Islamists argued, constituted a dangerous call to same-sex desire. On the political uses of new festivals in Morocco, see Boum 2012; and Boubia 2012.

6. The major addresses were given in the days following the attacks, then on July 30, 2003, celebrating the Holiday of the Throne, an annual holiday established by nationalists in 1933, discussed below in Chapter 2.

7. For legal changes to terrorism laws, and for details on extrajudicial treatment of Islamist suspects, see Fédération internationale des droits de l'Homme (International Federation for Human Rights), "Morocco Human Rights abuses in the fight against terrorism," Report 379/2, July 2004.

8. The Qur'anic references to jinns: 6:100, 112, 128, 130; 7:38, 179; 11:119; 15:27; 17:88; 18:50; 27:17, 39; 32:13; 34:12, 14, 41; 37:158; 41:25, 29; 46:18, 29–32; 51:56; 55:15, 33, 39, 56, 74; 72 (Surat al-Jinn): 1–15; 114:6. To Iblis: 2:34; 7:11–18; 15:31–44; 17:61–65; 18:50; 20:116–23; 38:71–85. To Shaytan: 2:14, 36, 102, 168, 208, 256, 257, 268, 275; 3:36, 155, 175; 4:38, 60, 76, 83, 117–20; 5:60, 90–91; 6:43, 68, 71, 112, 121, 142; 7:20, 22, 27, 30, 175, 200–201; 8:11, 48; 12:5, 42, 100; 14:22; 15:17; 16:36, 63, 98–100; 17:27, 53, 64; 18:63; 19:44, 45, 68, 83; 20:120; 22:3, 52–3; 23:97; 24:21; 25:29; 26:95, 210, 221; 27:24; 28:15; 29:38; 31:21; 34:20; 35:6; 36:60; 37:7; 38:37, 41; 41:36; 43:36, 62; 47:25; 58:10, 19; 59:16; 67:5; 81:25; 114:4.

9. Mluk al-jinn, those "Possessors among the Jinns" are understood as "Kings of the Jinn" by some in Fez. Chlyeh (2000), however, considers the translation of "mluk" as "kings" to derive from researchers' confusion between Moroccan dialect and classical Arabic. See below, Chapter 4, note 9.

10. Hints of globalization appear with Crapanzano's discussions with a poor and marginal Moroccan, Tuhami, who describes Aisha in comparative national terms, emphasizing the nations with which he is most familiar: "'There are . . . also Lalla Aisha Franzawiyya [French Aisha], and Lalla Aisha Inglissiyya [English Aisha].' . . . He went on to name a Lalla Aisha for each country he could think of; he named Lalla Aisha Amerikaniyya [American Aisha] with embarrassment." The series of Aishas evokes what Benedict Anderson has called "the spectre of comparisons," the technological reproducibility, and thus abstraction and exchangeability, of subjects that grounds nationalism in the global age. The specter of comparisons permits a comparison of specters (Crapanzano 1980, 100; B. Anderson 1998).

11. Stefania Pandolfo's excellent studies of jinns and psychiatry in Morocco extensively pursue the notion of jinn as a psychic disruption. For Pandolfo the disruption is partly historical, an effect of colonialism and competing discourses of traditional therapy and possession. In other words, possession is not only, as I suggest here, elicited by ritual but also an effect of the multiplication of discourses itself (Pandolfo 1997, 2000, 2008).

12. See also Al-Ghazali (d. 1111) for a classical criticism of "servile imitation," mindless repetition, and inattention in Muslim worship (Al-Ghazali 1983, 34–39, 40–43).

13. Anne Meneley (2007) demonstrates that women's homosocial exchanges in Yemen changed over the course of generation, specifically showing the influence of Islamic revivalists ("Islahis" or "reformists") in changing women's behavior among women. Whereas older women viewed the domestic sphere as a women's public place for relaxed exposure to other women, including sheer clothing, younger women maintained their ostensibly public appearances, including their hijab. Meneley rightly interprets this as a transformation of women's norms, especially of hospitality, in a homosocial public sphere. One may also emphasize the collapse of public/private boundaries in the mass-mediated and mass-market culture she outlines—of veiled Barbie dolls—and a novel

awareness of, indeed vigilance toward, constant visibility adopted by younger women accustomed to such mediations of self.

14. Like the broader discussions this ethics involves the bodily sensorium so vital to Muslim politics (Hirschkind 2006; Mahmood 2005). Here Muslims foreground a discourse and practice of conscious bodily control in addition to enacting, as Hirschkind details, a preconscious conditioning (cf. Starrett 1995). It does not articulate a distinctly "Islamic" ethics as opposed to "Western," but rather a broader modernism, marking the dominance of mass-mediated communication in the religious imaginary of at least middle-class urban Moroccans. This helps explain the logic of Islamic modernists in expanding the duty of voicing the call to Islam to every Muslim, rather than just the leader, or one class (Mahmood 2005, 61).

15. Put otherwise, to embody jinns is to be summoned by communicative systems that—national, global, and relentlessly technological—defy individual oversight and thus privilege "transparency." See, for example, disruptions of spirits, sorcery, the occult linked to the traumatic effects of capitalism (Ong 1987, 1988); national politics (Siegel 2006; Ivy 1995; Geschiere 1997); colonialism and novel medical discourses (Boddy 1989; Pandolfo 1997, 2000, 2008; Taussig 1986); mass mediation of communication and exchange (Morris 2000; Behrend, Dreschke, and Zillinger 2013); and combinations thereof (Comaroff and Comaroff 1999, 2000, 2003; Morris 2000; Siegel 2003, 2006). On transparency, see West and Sanders 2003; and Morris 2000.

16. New generic reformist norms of "modern" public comportment across the Muslim world are often directed at women—"function[ing] as mechanisms for disciplining participants and installing a new sense of self, one directed toward self-control even if employing the language of freedom" (Moors 2006, 120). They also involve underclasses more broadly, as Lara Deeb has shown in the reform of Shi'i mourning rituals in Lebanon. Just as reform-minded Muslims from Lebanon to Niger, to Palestine, Mali, and Iran criticize "traditional" women as those "not-yet" self-aware enough to perform modern selfhood, so too are conventional jinn rites, whether too secret or too visible, invoking new anxieties and new demands for pious behavior appropriate to a subject "imagined as a citizen with a public presence" (Najmabadi 1993, 489).

17. Mittermaier's beautiful reading of dream interpretation and national politics and media emphasizes this element of the dream's power: "Although state officials, orthodox scholars, reformists, and rationalists try to banish dreams into the private sphere, dreams, like rumors, have a habit of spilling over. . . . Banned from national television and eyed with suspicion by al-Azhar and the Egyptian state, the dream emerged in other media" (Mittermaier 2011, 53, see also 201–31).

## Chapter 2: Nationalizing the Call

1. John Pemberton has pointed out that Mitchell's argument regarding Egyptian adoption of European "order" neglects older conceptions of "order." This essential point calls our attention to the ways that older conceptions of order, and older institutional structures, now appeared in their obsolescence not merely to hinder but also to summon potentially modern subjects away from the new order (Pemberton, personal communication).

2. Abdellah Hammoudi notes in passing, but does not analyze, the historical coincidence of these two nationalist themes—the critique and "decline" of the Sufi orders and the "creation and implantation" of the Throne Holiday (Hammoudi 1997, 19).

3. Sidi Mohammed's condemnation does not appear in Protectorate records as an official decree (*dahir*). The author notes that such an official law would be preferable. Other nationalist sources celebrate the prohibition, as it signals a symbolic alliance between the sultan and the nationalists (Rachik 2003, 82).

4. The sultan Mawlay Sulayman's (d. 1822) efforts were discontinued upon his death (El Mansour 1990).

5. Allal al-Fassi had briefly and clandestinely published *Umm al-Banin*, a small broadsheet with limited circulation (Souriau-Hoebrechts 1975, 86). Others wrote occasional articles on Moroccan educational and religious reform in the salafi journals *al-Shihab* and *al-Najah* in Algeria, *al-Manar* in Egypt, and, more rarely, in the Casablanca-based communist paper *Le Cri Marocain* (Halstead 1967, 125). The Berber Dahir saw the nationalists' print publishing expand in scope and volume, an indication of this being the sharp increase in books, pamphlets, and periodicals banned in the French Protectorate zone (Ladreit de Lacharrière 1932, 516). Nationalist Mekki Naciri published several works in Cairo, where an Egyptian-Moroccan Muslim coalition formed; in Europe, articles signed by the Comité d'Action Marocaine and criticizing the Dahir appeared in Shakib Arslan's *La Nation arabe* (Abun-Nasr 1963, 95). A number of longer essays were published as well; Mohammed Hassan al-Wazzani likely authored the *Tempête sur le Maroc: où, les erreurs d'une "politique berbère"* (Barbari 1931).

6. The association of these orders with the upper classes was durable, with even reformist critiques of Tijaniyya failing to dissuade some in the aristocratic class from affiliating with them (Abun-Nasr 1965)

7. Edmond Doutté observed the frissa in western Algeria, in terms that matched the Fassi rites:

In the middle of the path a generous devotee throws a goat with its throat slit, but left as is, without being skinned or gutted. At once, fifteen or twenty *khouan* [brothers, members of the Sufi order] drop to all fours and throw themselves on the body of the animal, pushing each other. With nails and teeth they rip open, tear out, and eat the bloody entrails. The intestines split open, excrement sprays over the innards, a nauseating odor spreads. Nothing stops them—worked-up, bloody-bearded, using their teeth to tear up the excrement-slathered meat. Skin, liver, heart, lungs, trachea, intestines, everything is devoured in the blink of an eye. It's the most horrible hunt imaginable. After a visit to the marabout [the tomb of the saint] at Ain al-Hout, the return is carried out in the same manner. The group stops in front of the house of the descendants of the marabout [the saint]; the flags are tilted and waved to the right and left as a sign of respect. A new victim will be offered up to the repugnant and sacred hunger of the Aïssâoua; but, not wishing to watch the disgusting spectacle again, I left the scene beforehand to return to Tlemcen. (1908, 483–84; cf. Doutté 1900)

8. Vincent Crapanzano cites a Moroccan proverb repeated among the Hamadsha order that emphasizes this distinction: "If the child of the saint falls into ecstasy, the followers of the saint will fall out of ecstasy" (Crapanzano 1973, 74).

9. More generally, the Protectorate sought to maintain the social structures of power, with the first Resident-General Marechal Lyautey famously demanding "that ranks and hierarchies [be] preserved and respected, that people and things stay in their established places, that the natural leaders command, and that others obey" (cited in Wright 1991, 89). For the first decade of the Protectorate at least, Lyautey's vision was successfully implemented (Rivet 1984, 107).

10. For an overview of the benefits of religious rites to the burgeoning tourism industry, see "Le Tourisme au Maroc: Les fêtes de tradition musulmane au Maroc" (*Bulletin économique du Maroc* 5[20]: [1938]: 124–25). On crowd control, see the description of celebrations of the Prophet's birth (*mouloud*, Ar. *Mawlid*), an occasion for underclass Sufi processions and trance rites, in 1934: "The festival of the 'Mouloud' took place in Tangier, from June 30 to July 3 [1934], with a particular flair, thanks to the concerted effort of the International Zone administration and tourist organizations. . . . The celebrations themselves, which attracted more than 10,000 natives from the French and Spanish zones, were quite lively, but all took place rather tranquilly" (*l'Afrique Française* 44 [7]: [July 1934]: 441).

11. The foremost authority on the 'Isawa order, René Brûnel commented, "The renown of this sect could not be greater. . . . Aissaoua, rivals of the 'Cinghaliens,' gave paying exhibitions in

Paris during the grand exposition of 1867. Since that period, the hadras [trance ceremonies] of the Aissaoua of Algeria, Tunisia and Syria have become the most commonly staged spectacles" (Brûnel 1926, xi).

12. This awareness of a global view among Moroccans extended to a concern with an already established Middle Eastern Arabs' dim view of Muslims from the Far West (*al-maghrib al-aqsa*) as magicians and sorcerers, based, in nationalist Said Hajji's words, on some "charlatan claiming to summon jinns at every moment": "The perception hurts when we realize that [this view] has a bearing on their judgment of us all. Yet the Moroccan intellectual himself... should have a guilty conscience, realizing he has done nothing to promote a better image of his country, its prestigious history and flourishing civilization" (Hajji 1934, 6).

13. He does so without suggesting a particular authority to undertake the task. Similarly, al-Sqalli's Qur'anic citation suggests that these Sufi participants need guidance to foster such a transformation. This guidance is expressed as God's, which is perhaps to note that al-Sqalli is not proposing a precise strategy for recuperating the communicative value of trance.

14. Nor indeed could emotional resonance be guaranteed for any of the novel terms central to Moroccan nationalist discourse in both French and Arabic: "the Moroccan People" (*al-sha'b al-maghribi*); "the Moroccan Society" (*al-mujtam' al-maghribi*); and "the Moroccan Nation" (*al-watan al-maghribi*). See B. Anderson 2006, on Javanese notions of sociality predating "society" as a homogeneous body.

15. The francophone readership was rather limited in early 1930s Fez. Nevertheless, Robert Rézette observed that *L'Action du Peuple* converted novel political terms into signs capable of a new generation's collective articulation—"a collection of slogans rather than coherent doctrines, but in which all the youth of the moment recognized their aspirations" (Rézette 1955, 75). Echoing Rézette's observation, Roger Le Tourneau, historian of Fez and director of the Collège Musulman de Fès, noted the newspaper's electrifying effect among previously disinterested students in 1933: "The success of the nationalist press has had effects on vocabulary: Love of the People [*l'amour du peuple*] is a widely sounded theme, giving rise to lyrical innovations. It was a perfectly unknown theme before the past several years, as the matter of the people had barely worried the Fassi bourgeoisie" (cited in "L'évolution de la jeunesse et les problèmes scolaires," *Renseignements Coloniaux: Bulletin du Comité de l'Afrique Française* 48[3]: [1938]: 29–31). Thus, not surprisingly, colonial functionaries keenly (obsessively) noted the emergence of novel terms and tactics among the urban youth, holding the French-language *L'Action du Peuple* and *Maghreb* in particular (rather than *Majallat al-Maghrib*) chiefly responsible for inspiring nationalist "troublemakers" (*trublions*), as well as for the larger transformation of colonial resistance from the outlying tribes to the urban sphere (Ladreit de Lacharrière 1932, 523–27; Ladreit de Lacharrière 1934, 266–67; Mohendis 1935, 91–92).

16. Regarding the notion of an integrated national state, Paul Pascon writes, "Only quite recently, during this century, has the theory of rural peasants' necessary integration with modern history taken shape" (1980, 16).

17. The 'Alawite dynasty, like other traditions of sacred kingship, had indeed used stagings of the sultan for demonstrations of sovereign power, with protocols of proximity, speech, and gesture positing the sultan at the center of a descending hierarchy of religious, tribal, and political notables. In Hammoudi's descriptions, this political theological staging comprised exchange of the notables' obedience and gifts for the sovereign's blessing (baraka) and patronage, a process marked by suppliants' pious fear of the sovereign and acceptance of the latter's absolute distance and difference from his subjects. Thus, Hammoudi points to the irreducible *distance* between the sultan and audience—in the ritualized shade of the parasol over the sovereign, his elevation on a horse, and in his silence: "In parades and ceremonies the person of the sultan is exposed to the public; but invisible barriers, in addition to the guards and courtiers, separate him from the rest of the world, just as taboos separate

sacred beings and untouchables. He speaks little and most often through the caid of the mechwar or the chief of stables, who convey his greetings to people" (1997, 74). We should note that "people" here does not equate to "the People," the latter a term of mass address.

18. Nationalists would rearticulate this criticism in the press upon their reappearance in 1937 (under a new journal title), with descriptions of notables from Meknes sent by "the Muslim population of that city" to the sultan carrying "an important petition demanding the interdiction of demonstrations and ceremonies which take place in Meknes as in Moulay Idriss on the occasion of the moussems of Sidi Ben Aïssa, Sidi Ali Dghoughi, and Sidi Ali Ben Hamdush" (*La Volonté du Peuple*, May 6, 1937, 6). The front page of the following edition (*La Volonté du Peuple*, May 20, 1937, 1) includes a photograph of the delegation. Seven men dressed in white: white jellabas with the hoods raised, white *balghas* (Moroccan slippers), against a black backdrop. Four men are seated in front, hands folded neatly or resting in their laps. Three men stand behind them forming symmetrical rows. All the men appear serious, unsmiling; one holds his head high and tilted slightly, a posture of formal dignity. They are conscious of themselves seen from beyond their own eyes and ears. This power is moreover connected to proper political power. The caption reads, "Our picture represents the delegation which presented to H.M. the Sultan, during his visit to Meknes, a petition of protest against the Aïssaoua and other groups of the same type whose annual demonstrations are contrary to Islam and to modern progress" (*La Volonté du Peuple*, May 20, 1937, 1).

19. Instructors in French lycées in the 1950s required their Moroccan students to tear out the king's portrait from the front cover of their textbook. While younger Moroccans often dismiss the vision, some attribute it to the circulation of a photographic negative of the king's face, further evidence of which I have not found. One nationalist resistance member has rather grandly taken credit for the mass vision, citing his group's circulation of the king's portrait framed in a heart (Rida 1994, 89). His popular history of the resistance and nationalist publishing includes a photograph of the king's face superimposed on the full moon, suggesting that this, indeed, is how the crowds saw his face.

20. As novelist Mohammed Berrada described the scenes of August 1953 first in Rabat, "an army of the youth launched the call to protest [*da'wat mudhaharat al-ihtijaj*]," and soon, with protests and bullets, the "demonstrations repeated, and the collective summoned itself and circulated its news across the multiple cities," enveloping multiple generations: "The word spread quickly from house to house. The rooftops filled at night with women and men and children searching the moon for the features of Mohammed V, whose face—so said the voices of *Radio Medina*—colonized the moon to remain, despite his exile, in contact with his people" (1992, 38).

## Chapter 3: Our Master's Call

1. For Clifford Geertz, the immense independence-era popularity of King Mohammed V, described at the end of the last chapter, signaled his embodiment of Moroccans' archetypal "marabout" or "warrior saint," the perfect Muslim leader fusing sacred and martial power (Geertz 1968, 8). Perceiving colonial-era reformism as a "scripturalist interlude," he viewed independence as a "revival of maraboutism" on a novel modern scale (Geertz 1968, 107; cf. Combs-Schilling 1989); Mohammed V was, Geertz wrote, "something no 'Alawite sultan, however powerful, had ever been before, an authentic popular hero" (1968, 80). In Abdellah Hammoudi's (1997) sophisticated extension of Geertz, too, the Moroccan monarchy deploys Sufi ritual mediation to enact divine power over national subjects.

2. There are provocative hints of technologized ritual in a number of important analyses of the Moroccan monarchy. For Hammoudi (1997) royal power rests on the communication of royal "blessing" to subjects (as material patronage, divine recognition, and even the gift of violence) through competing religious, genealogical, and socioeconomic elites. In his brief mention of television,

mass mediation extends the monarchy's person-to-person ritual stagings with elites ostensibly to everyone: "In ritual and ceremony [authoritarian power] takes the concrete form of prostration and hand kissing, which every notable must perform at regular intervals. Such images, enhanced by the court etiquette, enter every household through the media. The exercise of power, as a form of living energy, appears here in all the splendor of absolute and accepted submission" (Hammoudi 1997, 43). For Hammoudi, the effect is a distinctly modern political relationship—a putatively primordial and "direct relationship between the king and his people" (1997, 14). Other scholars too have emphasized Hassan II's successful use of mass media—television and radio in particular—to bolster the sacred legitimacy of his regime (see, especially, Moudden n.d.). Mohammed Tozy identifies the televised rituals of government officials' allegiance (*bay'a*) to the king as a way of helping the sovereign's sacrality to be "accepted [*intériorisé*] by the majority of the population" (1999, 81). I. William Zartman emphasizes the political force of mass-mediated connection itself under Hassan II: "Of all [political actors], only he does not stand for election. Instead he sits for television, using the media as a visible, incontestable channel to his people, the modernization of the direct link between king and countrymen" (1987, 11).

3. To be sure, the Moroccan monarchy has also retained power through violence and manipulation, through divide-and-rule patronage or outright liquidation of domestic rivals, even during periods of putative liberalization and "reconciliation" (Munson 1993; Slyomovics 2005; Waterbury 1970, 1978). Notably, Geertz's analysis of Morocco's "martial maraboutism" avoided discussion of Mohammed V's ruthless consolidation of control following independence, including his dispersal of the Liberation Army (*al-jaysh al-tahrir*) and disenfranchisement of those nationalist and salafi-minded leaders who imagined a more limited "symbolic" role for the monarchy (Lahbabi 1975). But the monarchy's religious power cannot be reduced to violence, just as it cannot be reduced to an older symbolic and ritualized relationship. Rather, the communicative force of the postcolonial monarchy incorporates technological forms of ritual mediation, technological forms of the call, constituting mass publics in general, and the Moroccan public in particular.

4. Extracts of Hassan II's October 16, 1975, address are posted online (http://www.youtube.com/watch?v=VViyPegH6Jk). I have drawn on these for visual descriptions, with additional passages translated from the complete Arabic text of the speech printed in the official organ of the Moroccan Ministry of Pious Endowments and Islamic Affairs, *Da'wat al-Haq* 17 (4): 12–18.

5. "In every jurisdiction volunteers for the march far outstripped the King's quotas, and marchers had to be chosen by lottery. For example, in Oujda 11,832 volunteered to meet a quota of 1,500; in Chaouen 4,423 for a quota of 500; in Rabat-Sale 20,018 for a quota of 10,000; and in Agadir 66,580 for a quota of 33,000" (Weiner 1979, 31).

6. Desjardins noted, "The [Moroccan] left's response is without doubt one of the most astonishing matters of the Western Sahara affair" (1977, 82). On the Moroccan Communist Party's enthusiastic participation in the Green March, see Yata and Paul (1977, 16–18).

7. John Waterbury suggests that the power of the Green March rested on Hassan II's traditionalism and his influence on "public opinion" rather than on patrimonial structures, but does not explore the structural or infrastructural (media) conditions for such a public to form (Waterbury 1978, 416).

8. See Lacouture and Lacouture 1958, on the ubiquity of the radio in post-Protectorate Morocco.

9. For Siegel, such passage occurred as crowds listened to President Sukarno and precisely by virtue of his address as a "performative act," or call that summoned them away from social origins and into a novel mode of belonging:

> No one is born a member of the people nor is it a sociological category. A farmer, for instance, is not a member of the people because of his profession, his place of birth, or the language he speaks. He becomes a member of the people by a performative act. In the Sukarno era he was one of those the president addressed either in the great stadium of the capital or over the

radio. When Sukarno, who styled himself "the extension of the tongue of the people," spoke in their name, those listening, even though hearing certain ideas for the first time, found that these ideas did indeed express what they thought. At that point they were members of "the people." (Siegel 2000c, 36)

10. Notably, the crier followed the original call—the presence of the live human voice rendered a supplement to the technological broadcast.

11. Mohamed Tozy, speaking at Democracy and the Media, a conference organized by the Center for Cross-Cultural Learning, Rabat, November 11, 2000.

12. The Green March points up the emotional stakes of Morocco's claims to the Western Sahara, a source of persistent Moroccan-Algerian and Moroccan-Sahrawi antagonisms (Mundy 2006; Zunes and Mundy 2010). Morocco's unresolved "reclamation" or "annexation" of the territory certainly included other critical material concerns: the wealth of the largest phosphate reserve in the world, mined there since 1963, the potential offshore oil reserves; Atlantic fishing grounds now in a serious state of depletion; 100,000 Sahrawi refugees in Tindouf, Algeria; Morocco's torture of Sahrawi peoples, and suppression of the Polisario, their rebel national liberation movement; the protracted and immensely expensive stationing of tens if not hundreds of thousands of Moroccan troops along its security walls, and not least, the repression of dissent on the Saharan topic within Moroccan domestic politics. For a geopolitical overview of the conflict, see Zunes and Mundy 2010.

13. Clips of these performances are posted on YouTube and, judging from the comments, enthusiastically received. See Ramy Ayach, "The Call of the Sahara" (*nida' al-sahara*), Mawazine Music Festival, Rabat, 2010 (http://www.youtube.com/watch?v=Vd2IeoXy734). Studio 2M, 2M Monde, "The Voice of Hassan Calls" (*sawt al-hassan yunadi*) (http://www.youtube.com /watch?v=hMPYenPF0V4).

## Chapter 4: Summoning in Secret

1. The tactic is similar to a 2008 AT&T advertisement series, in which an exasperated mother argues with her young daughter over her excessive texting charges. The daughter speaks in texteze, which the mother tries clumsily to reproduce. Any potentially disturbing parental rupture is quickly smoothed over by a grandmother entering the conversation cell phone in hand, and matching the daughter's text-eze, much to the mother's surprise and further exasperation. The advertisement announces an unlimited texting plan; the corporate solution uses the grandmother to ease any concerns that children and corporations rather than adults are running the household.

2. Regarding the logics of secrecy and exclusivity among *malams* northern Nigeria, Susan O'Brien writes, "Many local Sufi scholars still view the secrecy of prescriptions found in *kundi* (a *malam*'s bundle of loose papers containing his secret prayers and charms) to be critical to their efficacy. Moreover these same scholars view the close relationship between scholar and student as the only proper context for transmitting Islamic knowledge. For them, the impersonal nature of marketplace transactions render Islamic texts acquired in that way impotent; the secret knowledge transmitted from teacher to student is only effective if one has been granted permission (*izn*) to use it" (2001, 230).

3. In Ibn Juzayy's (1979) standard legal text at the Qarawiyyin mosque-university of Fez, it is non-Arabic inscription, rather than the writing of talismans and talismanic script itself, which is blameworthy. "It is permitted to hang amulets [*al-tama'im*], that is, the talisman [*al-'uda*] that is hung on the sick person and children upon which is written the Qur'an. . . . As for amulets [*al-huruz*] upon which are written seals [*khawatim*] in non-Arabic writing, this is not permitted for the sick or the healthy, because what it contains may be unbelieving or magical in nature [*dhalik aladhi fiha yahtamil an yakuna kufran aw sihran*]" (Ibn Juzayy 1979, 386–87, cf. chap. 20, sec. 5).

4. Vanessa Maher's study of village life in the Middle Atlas Mountains describes Aziz the fqih as drinking, playing cards, and married to a dancer: "Aziz is in some respects typical of many fuqaha', who have found it more convenient to 'be as other men are' and find a niche in the modern economy rather than seek to fulfill a faded religious vocation" (1974, 82).

5. Memorization of the Qur'an is not considered sufficient to being a fqih in Fez. There are specialists in the medina who recite the Qur'an; Fassis, however, hold the fqih to be a far rarer man, an expert. When, in conversation with the father of the household where I lived, Abdelqader, I referred to Qur'an reciters as fuqaha', he corrected me, saying that they were simply "talaba." Someone worthy of the title "fqih," he insisted, is a specialist in 'ilm al-ruhani.

6. If the skills of the fqih are therefore potentially general, their writings nonetheless spark people's imagination as old and secret, and thus unknown by ordinary people.

7. See Messick 1993, on spiral inscription in Islamic legal documents, later displaced by the straight lines of state-produced print forms. Though Messick's particular concern is Yemen, he first encountered spiral script in Morocco (personal communication with author).

8. The term is likewise used in the Sudan (Holý 1991, 30).

9. Fuqaha' refer to mluk al-jinn in the sense of royalty, specifically describing some mluk as Earthly Kings (*al-muluk al-ardiyya*), as opposed to angels, or Sky Kings (*al-muluk al-samawiyya*). Certain differences appear between the mluk of the fuqaha' and the mluk of the Gnawa, yet similarities in their names, personae, and tastes suggest an overlap. Patients of both the Gnawa and fuqaha', for example, assume that the mluk named Mimun and al-Buwab are the same whether identified by fuqaha' or Gnawa, a point Westermarck also makes (1968, I, 391).

## Chapter 5: Rites of Reception

1. This gendered distinction between men's knowing and women's unknowing is repeated across cultures of possession and mediumship. A classic work for grasping these distinctions in a Muslim society is Siegel 2000a. On gender politics and mediumship, see also Boddy 1989; Morris 2000; and Kendall 1985.

2. Hubert and Mauss's reading follows Durkheim in posing the sacred as irreducibly different and separate from the profane world, that which, always and everywhere, set apart. They propose that the sacrificial offering mediates between the two domains: that is, it serves as a means of communication between the two. "The thing consecrated serves as an intermediary between the sacrifier [the one to whom the benefits of the sacrifice accrue] and the divinity to whom the sacrifice is usually addressed" (Hubert and Mauss 1964, 11). Sacrifice is unique in their scheme, however; for the act of communication occurs only with the destruction of the offering, with its transformation into a victim. Thus the authors conclude, "Sacrifice consists in establishing a means of communication between the sacred and the profane worlds through the mediation of a victim, that is, of a thing that in the course of the ceremony is destroyed" (Hubert and Mauss 1964, 97).

3. 'Isawa had adopted the Gnawa's practices of exorcism (Brûnel 1926, 178).

4. Particular colonial observers viewed the Gnawa as corrupting the Sufi orders—certainly the "least Muslim" of the popular orders (El-Fasi and Dermenghem 1988 [1926], 21), or "not at all Muslim" (Michaux-Bellaire 1910, 426).

5. One thinks of discourses of secondhand smoke in the United States and Europe and the publicly funded campaigns and resources for quitting smoking. See James Siegel's discussion of addiction and possession in Barker and Rafael 2012.

## Chapter 6: Trance-Nationalism, or, the Call of Moroccan Islam

1. See, for example, the explicit wording of Morocco's tourism literature regarding the function of "festivals": "Morocco loves celebrating her arts and sharing her riches with her visitors. Voilà—even before summer, numerous festivals take place in all four corners of the country—cinema, music, dance, sports—to satisfy every taste! In Agadir, the tradition holds of celebrating tolerance throughout the world with a concert by the same name, on October 16. A plethora [*pléiade*] of international artists will work together to lift spirits in the name of tolerance, difference and acceptance" (Ministry of Tourism, http://www.visitmorocco.com/index.php/fre/Breves/Une-pleiade-d-evenements-au-Maroc).

2. I thank Hisham Aïdi for calling my attention to this clichéd formula.

3. Kapchan's (2007) distinction between Gnawa musicians in Morocco as "being possessed" and those abroad as "possessing culture" unfortunately reinforces the sense that only transnational Sufism is mass mediated.

## Chapter 7: "To Eliminate the Ghostly Element Between People"

1. This theme is evident in both older print and current online ruqya literature. One of many Internet sites dedicated to ruqya instruction (this one maintained by a thirty-three–year-old Algerian man, according to his profile) explains that the first rule of the cure is proper intention, followed by "emphasis on implanting doctrine [*tarsikh al-ʿaqida*] amongst the ill," "holding fast to the Qurʾan and Sunna," and "emphasis on daʿwa." ("Al-ruqya al-sharʿiyya and its rules and conditions" [al-ruqya al-sharʿiyya, al-qawaʿad wa-l-shurut] http://wahid2.maktoobblog.com.) For an exemplary Moroccan site for al-ruqya, with critiques of "Moroccan sorcery," see http://www.ra7mat.com. For other online instructions on al-ruqya in Arabic and English, see http://www.ruqya.net/; http://www.ruqyah.net/; http://www.alroqia.com/.

## Epilogue

1. See several articles and numerous reader comments on Yabiladi.com, for example, Ezzouak and Schmachtel 2011.

# References

Abu-Lughod, Janet L. 1980. *Rabat, urban apartheid in Morocco.* Princeton studies on the Near East. Princeton, NJ: Princeton University Press.

Abun-Nasr, Jamil. 2007. *Muslim communities of grace: The Sufi brotherhoods in Islamic religious life.* New York: Columbia University Press.

———. 1965. *The Tijaniyya: A Sufi order in the modern world.* London and New York: Oxford University Press.

———. 1963. The Salafiyya movement in Morocco: The religious bases of Moroccan nationalist movement. St. Anthony's papers XVI: 90–103.

Aherdan, Mahjoubi. 1976. *La masse . . . ira: ou, Le journal d'un marcheur.* Casablanca: Éditions G. Gauthey.

Akhchichine, Ahmed, and Jamal Eddine Naji. 1984. Le contact avec les médias au Maroc. PhD dissertation. Rabat, Morocco: Université Mohammed V.

Alaoui, Hassan. 2003. Culture, ouverture et modernité: À Essaouira, le Maroc dévoile son identité profonde. *Le Matin.* June 29.

Al-Fassi, Allal. 1954. *The independence movements of Arab North Africa.* Washington, DC: American Council of Learned Societies.

Al-Ghazali, Abu Hamid Muhammad. 1983. *Inner dimensions of Islamic worship.* Trans. Muhtar Holland. Leicestershire, UK: The Islamic Foundation.

Althusser, Louis. 1994. Ideology and ideological state apparatuses (notes towards an investigation). In *Mapping ideology,* ed. Slavoj Žižek, 100–39. London: Verso.

Anderson, Benedict. 2006. *Imagined communities: Reflections on the origins and spread of nationalism.* 3d ed. London: Verso.

———. 1998. *Spectre of comparisons.* London: Verso.

———. 1994. Exodus. *Critical Inquiry* 20 (2) (winter): 314–27.

Anderson, Jon W. 2005. Wiring up: The internet difference for Muslim networks. In *Muslim networks: From hajj to hip hop,* ed. Miriam Cooke and Bruce B. Lawrence, 252–63. Chapel Hill: University of North Carolina Press.

Anderson, Paul. 2011. "The piety of the gift": Selfhood and sociality in the Egyptian mosque movement. *Anthropological Theory* 11 (Mar.): 3–21.

Arif, Hakim. 2008. Super imams pour la sécurité spirituelle. *L'Observateur du Maroc.* Oct. 23, http://www.maghress.com/fr/lobservateur/1240.

Asad, Talal. 1993. *Genealogies of religion: Discipline and reasons of power in Christianity and Islam.* Baltimore, MD: Johns Hopkins University Press.

———. 1986. *The idea of an anthropology of Islam.* Washington, DC: Georgetown University Center for Contemporary Arab Studies, Occasional Papers series.

Aubin [Descos], Eugene. 1906. *Morocco of today.* London: J. M. Dent.

Baida, Jamaa. 2005. Mohamed al-Salih Missa. In *Ma'lamat al-maghrib: Qamus murattab 'ala huruf al-hija' yuhitu bi-l-ma'arif al-muta'alliqa bi-mukhtalif al-jawanib al-tarikhiyya wa-l-jughrafiyya wa-l-bashariyya wa-l-hadariyya li-l-maghrib al-aqsa,* ed. Jam'iyya al-Maghribiyya li-l-Ta'lif wa-l-Tarjamah wa-l-Nashr, vol. 21, 7343–44. Sala, Morocco: Mataba' Sala.

Barbari, Mouslim. 1931. *Tempête sur le Maroc; ou, les erreurs d'une "politique berbère."* Paris: Éditions Rieder.

Basbous, Antoine. 2002. *L'Arabie saoudite en question: Du wahhabisme à Bin Laden, aux origines de la tourmente.* Paris: Perrin.

Bazzaz, Sahar. 2010. *Forgotten saints: History, power, and politics in the making of modern Morocco.* Cambridge, MA: Harvard Center for Middle Eastern Studies.

Becker, Cynthia. 2002. "We are real slaves, real Ismkhan": Memories of the trans-Saharan slave trade in the Tafilalet of south-eastern Morocco. *The Journal of North African Studies* 7 (4) (winter): 97–121.

Behrend, Heike, Anja Dreschke, and Martin Zillinger, eds. 2013. *Trance mediums and new media: Spirit possession in the age of technical reproduction.* New York: Fordham University Press.

Bell, Catherine M. 1997. *Ritual: Perspectives and dimensions.* New York: Oxford University Press.

Benjamin, Walter. 2008. The work of art in the age of its technological reproducibility: 2d version. In *The work of art in the age of its technological reproducibility, and other writings on media,* ed. Michael W. Jennings, Brigid Doherty, and Thomas Y. Levin, 19–55. Cambridge, MA, and London: The Belknap Press of Harvard University.

Bernal, Victoria. 1994. Gender, culture, and capitalism: Women and the remaking of Islamic "tradition" in a Sudanese village. *Comparative Studies in Society and History* 36 (1) (Jan.): 36–67.

Bernichi, Loubna. 2003. Ambience et sécurité. *Maroc Hebdo International.* July 4–10.

Berque, Jacques. 1967. *French North Africa: The Maghrib between two world wars.* Trans. Jean Stewart. New York: Frederick A. Praeger.

———. 1957. Quelque problèmes de l'Islam maghrébin. *Archives des Sciences Sociales des Religions* 3 (3): 3–20.

———. 1955. *Structures sociales du Haut Atlas.* Paris: Presses Universitaires de France.

Berrada, Mohamed. 1992. *Lu'bat al-nisyan: Nuss riwa'i.* al-Rabat: Dar al-Aman.

Boddy, Janice. 1989. *Wombs and alien spirits: Women, men, and the zar cult in northern Sudan.* Madison: University of Wisconsin Press.

Boubia, Amina. 2012. Les festivals de musique au Maroc: Fusions artistiques, cultures globales et pratiques locales. In *Festivals, rave parties, free parties: histoire des rencontres musicales actuelles, en France et à l'étranger,* ed. Nicolas Bénard Dastarac, 361–85. Rosières-en-Haye, France: Camion Blanc.

Boum, Aomar. 2012. Youth, political activism, and the festivalization of hip-hop music in Morocco. In *Contemporary Morocco: State, politics and society under Mohammed VI,* ed. Bruce Maddy-Weitzman and Daniel Zisenwine, 161–77. London and New York: Routledge.

Boyle, Helen N. 2004. *Qur'anic schools: Agents of preservation and change.* Reference books in international education. New York: Routledge Falmer.

Brown, Kenneth. 1973. The impact of the dahir berbere in Salé. In *Arabs and Berbers,* ed. Gellner and Micaud, 201–15. London: Duckworth.

Brûnel, Rene. 1926. *Essai sur la confrérie religieuse des Aissaoua au Maroc.* Paris: Librarie Orientaliste Paul Geuthner.

Butler, Judith. 1997a. *The psychic life of power: Theories in subjection.* Stanford, CA: Stanford University Press.

———. 1997b. *Excitable speech: A politics of the performative.* New York: Routledge.

Chlyeh, Abdelhafid, ed. 1998. *Les Gnaoua du Maroc: Itinéraires initiatiques transe et posses-sion*. Casablanca: Éditions Le Fennec.

Claisse, Pierre-Alain. 2003. *Les Gnawa marocains de tradition loyaliste*. Histoire et perspec-tives méditerranéennes. Paris: Harmattan.

Clancy-Smith, Julia. 1994. *Rebel and saint: Muslim notables, populist protest, colonial encoun-ters: Algeria and Tunisia 1800–1904*. Berkeley: University of California Press.

———. 1990. In the eye of the beholder: Sufi and saint in North Africa and the colonial pro-duction of knowledge, 1830–1900. *Africana Journal* XV: 220–57.

Cohen, S. 2003. Alienation and globalization in Morocco: Addressing the social and political impact of market integration. *Comparative Studies in Society and History* 45 (1) (Jan.): 168–89.

Comaroff, Jean, and John L. Comaroff. 2003. Transparent fictions; or, the conspiracies of a liberal imagination: An afterword. In *Transparency and conspiracy*, ed. Harry G. West and Todd Sanders, 287–99. Durham, NC: Duke University Press.

———. 2000. Millennial capitalism: First thoughts on a second coming. *Public Culture* 12 (2): 291–343.

———. 1999. Occult economies and the violence of abstraction: Notes from the South African postcolony. *American Ethnologist* 26 (2): 279–303.

Comaroff, Jean, and John L. Comaroff, eds. 2001. *Millennial capitalism and the culture of neo-liberalism*. Millennial quartet book. Durham, NC: Duke University Press.

Combs-Schilling, M. Elaine. 1989. *Sacred performances: Islam, sexuality, and sacrifice*. New York: Columbia University Press.

Comité d'Action Marocaine. 1934. *Plan de réformes marocaines*. Paris: Imprimérie Labor.

Cornell, Vincent J. 1998. *Realm of the saint: Power and authority in Moroccan sufism*. Austin: University of Texas Press.

Crapanzano, Vincent. 1980. *Tuhami: Portrait of a Moroccan*. Chicago: University of Chicago Press.

———. 1977. Mohammed and Dawia: Possession in Morocco. In *Case studies in spirit posses-sion*, ed. Vincent Crapanzano and Vivian Garrison, 141–76. New York: John Wiley & Sons.

———. 1973. *The Hamadsha: A study in Moroccan ethnopsychiatry*. Berkeley: University of California Press.

Daoud, Muhammad ʿIsa. 1992. *Hiwar sahafi maʿ jinni muslim Mustafa Kangur* [Interview with Mustafa Kangur, Muslim jinn]. Jiddah, Saʿudiyya: Dar al-Bashir li-l-Nashar wa-l-Tawziʿ.

Daoud, Zakya. 2007. *Les années lamalif: 1958–1988, trente ans de journalisme au Maroc*. 1st ed. Casablanca; Mohammedia: Tarik; Senso Unico Éditions.

de Heusch, Luc. 1981. *Why marry her?: Society and symbolic structures*. Cambridge studies in social anthropology. Vol. 33. Cambridge and New York: Cambridge University Press.

de Vries, Hent, and Samuel Weber, eds. 2001. *Religion and media*. Cultural memory in the present. Stanford, CA: Stanford University Press.

Deeb, Lara. 2006. *An enchanted modern: Gender and public piety in Shiʿi Lebanon*. Princeton studies in Muslim politics. Princeton, NJ: Princeton University Press.

Derrida, Jacques. 1995. *The gift of death*. Trans. David Wills. Chicago: University of Chicago Press.

———. 1988. *Limited Inc*. Ed. Gerald Graff, trans. Geoffrey Mehlman and Samuel Weber. Evanston, IL: Northwestern University Press.

———. 1982. Différance. In *Margins of philosophy*, trans. Alan Bass, 1–27. Chicago: University of Chicago Press.

———. 1976. *Of grammatology*. Trans. Gayatri Chakravorty Spivak. Baltimore, MD: Johns Hopkins University Press.

Desjardins, Thierry. 1977. *Les rebelles d'aujourd'hui*. Paris: Presses de la Cité.

Dessaints, J. 1976. Chronique politique: Maroc. *Annuaire de l'Afrique du Nord* 14: 457–76.

Doutté, Edmond. 1908. *Magie et religion dans l'Afrique du Nord*. Algiers: Jourdan.

———. 1900. *Les Aïssâoua à Tlemcen*. Châlons-sur-Marne: Imprimérie Martin Frères.

Durkheim, Emile. 1995. *The elementary forms of religious life*. Trans. Karen E. Fields. New York: The Free Press.

Edwards, David B. 1993. Summoning Muslims: Print, politics, and religious ideology in Afghanistan. *Journal of Asian Studies* 52 (3) (Aug.): 609–28.

Eickelman, Dale F. 2003. Communication and control in the Middle East: Publication and its discontents. In *New media in the Muslim world: The emerging public sphere*, ed. Dale F. Eickelman and Jon W. Anderson, 2d ed., 29–40. Bloomington and Indianapolis: Indiana University Press.

———. 1985. *Knowledge and power in Morocco: The education of a twentieth-century notable*. Princeton, NJ: Princeton University Press.

———. 1976. *Moroccan Islam: Tradition and society in a pilgrimage center*. Austin: University of Texas Press.

Eickelman, Dale F., and Jon W. Anderson. 1997. Print, Islam, and the prospects for civic pluralism: New religious writings and their audiences. *Journal of Islamic Studies* 8 (1): 43–62.

Eickelman, Dale F., and James Piscatori. 2004. *Muslim politics*. Rev. ed. Princeton, NJ: Princeton University Press.

Eickelman, Dale F., and Armando Salvatore. 2004. Muslim publics. In *Public Islam and the common good*, ed. Dale F. Eickelman and Armando Salvatore, 3–27. Leiden and Boston: Brill.

———. 2002. The public sphere and Muslim identities. *European Journal of Sociology* 43 (1): 92–115.

El Fasi, Mohammed, and Emile Dermenghem. 1988 [1926]. *Contes fasis*. Rabat: C.C.C.N.A.

El Hamel, Chouki. 2013. *Black Morocco: A history of slavery, race, and Islam*. Cambridge: Cambridge University Press.

El Mansour, Mohamed. 1990. *Morocco in the reign of Mawlay Sulayman*. Wisbech, UK: Middle East & North African Studies Press.

El Meknassi [pseud.]. 1937. La Caméra dans nos murs. *L'Action du Peuple* (June 17): 1–2.

El-Tom, Abdullahi Osman. 1985. Drinking the Koran: The meaning of Koranic verses in Berti erasure. *Africa: Journal of the International African Institute* 55 (4; Popular Islam): 414–31.

Eneborg, Yusuf Muslim. 2012. Ruqya shariya: Observing the rise of a new faith healing tradition amongst Muslims in east London. *Mental Health, Religion, and Culture*.

Ennaji, Mohammed. 1999. *Serving the master: Slavery and society in nineteenth-century Morocco*. New York: St. Martin's Press.

Ezzouak, Mohamed, and Frederic Schmachtel. 2011. Les manifestations du 20 février au Maroc: La bulle Facebook? *Ya Biladi*. Feb. 8, http://www.yabiladi.com/articles /details/4507/manifestations-fevrier-maroc-bulle-facebook.html.

Foucault, Michel. 1979. *Discipline and punish: The birth of the modern prison*. Trans. Alan Sheridan. New York: Vintage Books.

———. 1978. *The history of sexuality, vol. 1: An introduction*. Trans. Robert Hurley. New York: Random House.

Furnivall, J. S. 1956. *Colonial policy and practice: A comparative study of Burma and Netherlands India*. New York: New York University Press.

Geertz, Clifford. 1979. Suq: The bazaar economy in Sefrou. In *Meaning and order in Moroccan society: Three essays in cultural analysis*. Cambridge: Cambridge University Press.

———. 1973. *The interpretation of cultures: Selected essays*. New York: Basic Books.

Gelvin, James L. 1998. *Divided loyalties: Nationalism and mass politics in Syria at the close of empire*. Berkeley: University of California Press.

Geschiere, Peter. 1997. *The modernity of witchcraft: Politics and the occult in postcolonial Africa*. Charlottesville and London: University of Virginia Press.

Ghoulaichi, Fatima. 2005. Of saints and sharifian kings in Morocco: Three examples of the politics of reimagining history through reinventing king/saint relationship. Master's thesis. College Park: University of Maryland.

Gonzalez-Quijano, Yves. 1998. *Les gens du livre: Champ intellectual et édition dans l'Egypte republicaine*. Paris: CNRS Editions.

Hafez, Sherine. 2011. *An Islam of her own: Reconsidering religion and secularism in women's Islamic movements*. New York and London: New York University Press.

Hajji, Said. 1934. Al-maghrib kama yarahu al-sharq al-'arabi [Morocco, as the Arab east sees it]. *Majallat al-Maghrib* (Oct): 4–8.

Halstead, John P. 1967. *Rebirth of a nation: The origins and rise of Moroccan nationalism, 1912–1944*. Cambridge, MA: Harvard University Press.

———. 1964. The changing character of Moroccan reformism 1921–1934. *Journal of African History* V (3): 435–47.

Hammoudi, Abdellah. 1997. *Master and disciple: The cultural foundations of Moroccan authoritarianism*. Chicago: University of Chicago Press.

Heidegger, Martin. 1996. *Being and time*. Trans. Joan Stambaugh. Albany: State University of New York Press.

Hirschkind, Charles. 2012. Experiments in devotion online: The YouTube khutba. *International Journal of Middle East Studies* 44 (1) (Feb.): 5–21.

———. 2006. *The ethical soundscape: Cassette sermons and Islamic counterpublics*. New York: Columbia University Press.

Hodgson, Marshall G. S. 1974. *The venture of Islam: Conscience and history in a world civilization*, 3 vols. Chicago: University of Chicago Press.

Holý, Ladislav. 1991. *Religion and custom in a Muslim society: The Berti of Sudan*. Cambridge studies in social and cultural anthropology. Vol. 78. Cambridge and New York: Cambridge University Press.

Hourani, Albert. 1977. Rashid Rida and the Sufi orders: A footnote to Laoust. *Bulletin d'Études Orientales* 29: 231–41.

Howe, John. 1978. Western Sahara: A war zone. *Review of African Political Economy* (11) (Jan.–Apr.): 84–92.

Hubert, Henri, and Marcel Mauss. 1964. *Sacrifice, its nature and function*. Chicago: University of Chicago Press.

Hughes, Stephen O. 2001. *Morocco under King Hassan*. 1st ed. Reading, UK: Ithaca.

Ibn Juzayy, Muhammad b. Ahmad. 1979. *Qawanin al-ahkam al-shar'iyya*. Rev. ed. Beirut: Dar al-'Ilm li-l-Milayin.

Ivy, Marilyn. 1995. *Discourses of the vanishing: Modernity, phantasm, Japan*. Chicago: University of Chicago Press.

Jaïdi, Moulay Driss. 2000. *Diffusion et audience des médias audiovisuels: Cinéma, radio, télévision, vidéo et publicité au Maroc*. Rabat: Al Majal.

Johansen, Baber. 1999. The city and its norms: The all-embracing town and its mosques (al-misr al-gami'). In *Contingency in a sacred law: Legal and ethical norms in the Muslim fiqh*, 77–106. Boston: Brill.

Kaitouni, Mohamed Idrissi. 2010. La sécurité spirituelle. *L'Opinion*. May 11. http://www.lopinion.ma/def.asp?codelangue=23&id_info=16993&date_ar=2010-11-12

Kapchan, Deborah. 2007. *Traveling spirit masters: Moroccan Gnawa trance and music in the global marketplace*. Middletown, CT: Wesleyan University Press.

———. 2000. La marché de la transe: Le cas des Gnaoua marocains. In *La transe*, ed. Abdelhafid Chlyeh, 157–68. Casablanca: Éditions Marsam.

Karam, Souhaïl, and Jean-Loup Fiévet. 2011. Le pouvoir marocain met en cause islamistes et gauchistes. *L'Express*. May 23, http://www.lexpress.fr/actualites/2/monde/le-pouvoir-marocain-met-en-cause-islamistes-et-gauchistes_995823.html.

Karam, Usama. 1990. *Haywar ma' al-jinn* [Interview with the jinns]. Cairo: Madbuli Press.

Kendall, Laurel. 1988. *The life and hard times of a Korean shaman: Of tales and the telling of tales*. Honolulu: University of Hawaii Press.

———. 1985. *Shamans, housewives, and other restless spirits: Women in Korean ritual life*. Studies of the East Asian Institute. Honolulu: University of Hawaii Press.

Khan, Naveeda. 2006. Of children and jinns: An inquiry into an unexpected friendship during uncertain times. *Cultural Anthropology* 21 (6) (May): 234–64.

Khan, Ruqayya Yasmine. 2008. *Self and secrecy in early Islam*. Studies in comparative religion. Columbia: University of South Carolina Press.

Kittler, Friedrich. 1999. *Gramophone, film, typewriter*. Trans. Geoffrey Withrop-Young and Michael Wutz. Stanford, CA: Stanford University Press.

———. 1990. *Discourse networks 1800/1900*. Trans. Michael Metteer, with Chris Cullens, foreword by David E. Wellbery. Stanford, CA: Stanford University Press.

Kruk, Remke. 2005. Harry Potter in the Gulf: Contemporary Islam and the occult. *British Journal of Middle Eastern Studies* 32 (1) (May): 47–73.

Kugle, Scott Alan. 2006. *Rebel between spirit and law: Ahmad Zarruq, sainthood, and authority in Islam*. Bloomington: Indiana University Press.

Lacouture, Jean, and Simonne Lacouture. 1958. *Le Maroc à l'épreuve*. Paris: Éditions du Seuil.

Ladreit de Lacharrière, J. 1934. Les événements de Fès. *L'Afrique Française: Bulletin du Comité de l'Afrique Française* 44 (5) (May): 266–71.

———. 1932. A l'aussaut du Maroc français. *L'Afrique Française: Bulletin du Comité de l'Afrique Française* 42 (9) (Sept.): 516–27.

Lahbabi, Mohamed. 1975 [1958]. *Le gouvernement marocain a l'aube du xxe siècle*. Casablanca: Éditions Maghrebines.

Lambek, Michael. 1993. *Knowledge and practice in Mayotte: Local discourses of Islam, sorcery and spirit possession*. Anthropological horizons. Toronto: University of Toronto Press.

Laoust, Emile. 1924. Le taleb et la mosquée en pays berbères. *Bulletin Économique et Politique du Maroc* (61) (Oct.): 3–18.

Laoust, Henri. 1932. Le réformisme orthodoxe des "salafiyya" et les caractères généraux de son orientation actuelle. *Révue des Études Islamiques* 6: 175–224.

Larkin, Brian. 2012. Techniques of inattention: Loudspeakers and urban space in Nigeria. Paper presented at the Annual Meeting of the American Anthropological Association. San Francisco, CA. November.

———. 2008. Ahmed Deedat and the form of Islamic evangelism. *Social Text* (96; Media and the Political Forms of Religion) (fall): 101–21.

Laroui, Abdallah. 1992. *Esquisses historiques.* Casablanca: Publications du Centre culturel arabe.

Le Tourneau, Roger. 1987 [1949]. *Fès avant le protectorat: Étude économique et sociale d'une ville de l'occident musulman.* 2d ed. Rabat: Société Marocaine de Librairie et d'Édition.

———. 1938. Molière à Fès. *Bulletin Économique et Politique du Maroc* (159) (Apr.–May): 261–67.

Lévi-Strauss, C. 1963a. The sorcerer and his magic. In *Structural anthropology.* Middlesex, UK: Basic Books.

———. 1963b. The effectiveness of symbols. In *Structural anthropology.* Middlesex, UK: Basic Books.

Levtzion, Nehemia, and Randall Lee Pouwels. 2000. *The history of Islam in Africa.* Athens: Ohio University Press.

Lewis, I. M. 2003. *Ecstatic religion: A study of shamanism and spirit possession.* 3d ed. London and New York: Routledge.

Maarouf, Mohammed. 2007. *Jinn eviction as a discourse of power: A multidisciplinary approach to Moroccan magical beliefs and practices.* Islam in Africa. Vol. 8. Leiden and Boston: Brill.

Mah, Harold. 2000. Phantasies of the public sphere: Rethinking the Habermas of historians. *The Journal of Modern History* 72 (1) (Mar.): 153–82.

Maher, Vanessa. 1974. *Women and property in Morocco: Their changing relation to the process of social stratification in the Middle Atlas.* London and New York: Cambridge University Press.

Mahmood, Saba. 2005. *Politics of piety: The Islamic revival and the feminist subject.* Princeton, NJ: Princeton University Press.

Masquelier, Adeline Marie. 2009. *Women and Islamic revival in a West African town.* Bloomington: Indiana University Press.

———. 2007. When spirits start veiling: The case of the veiled she-devil in a Muslim town of Niger. *Africa Today* 54 (30): 39–64.

———. 2001. *Prayer has spoiled everything: Possession, power, and identity in an Islamic town of Niger.* Durham, NC: Duke University Press.

Masud, Muhammad Khalid, ed. 2000. *Travellers in faith: Studies of the Tablighi Jama'at as a transnational Islamic movement for faith renewal.* Leiden and Boston: Brill.

Mattelart, Armand. 1996. *The invention of communication.* Trans. Susan Emanuel. Minneapolis: University of Minnesota Press.

Mazzarella, William. 2004. Culture, globalization, mediation. *Annual Review of Anthropology* 33 (1) (10/01): 345–67.

McLuhan, Marshall. 2001 [1964]. *Understanding media: The extensions of man.* Cambridge, MA: MIT Press.

Meeker, Michael E. 1979. *Literature and violence in north Arabia.* Cambridge studies in cultural systems. Cambridge and New York: Cambridge University Press.

Meneley, Anne. 2007. Fashions and fundamentalisms in fin-de-siecle Yemen: Chador Barbie and Islamic socks. *Cultural Anthropology* 22 (2) (May): 214–43.

Messick, Brinkley M. 1996. Media muftis: Radio fatwas in Yemen. In *Islamic legal interpretation: Muftis and their fatwas*, ed. Muhammad Khalid Masud, Brinkley Morris Messick, and David Stephan Powers, 310–20. Cambridge, MA: Harvard University Press.

———. 1993. *The calligraphic state: Textual domination and history in a Muslim society*. Berkeley: University of California Press.

Meyer, Birgit, and Annelies Moors, eds. 2006. *Religion, media, and the public sphere*. Bloomington: Indiana University Press.

Michaux-Bellaire, E. 1910. L'esclavage au Maroc. *Revue du Monde Musulman* 11 (6) (July–Aug.): 422–27.

Mitchell, Timothy. 1992. Orientalism and the exhibitionary order. In *Colonialism and culture*, ed. Nicholas B. Dirks, 289–317. Ann Arbor: University of Michigan Press.

———. 1988. *Colonising Egypt*. Cambridge: Cambridge University Press.

Mittermaier, Amira. 2011. *Dreams that matter: Egyptian landscapes of the imagination*. Berkeley: University of California Press.

Moaddel, Mansoor. 2005. *Islamic modernism, nationalism, and fundamentalism: Episode and discourse*. Chicago: University of Chicago Press.

Moors, Annalies. 2006. Representing family law debates in Palestine: Gender and the politics of presence. In *Religion, media, and the public sphere*, ed. Birgit Meyer and Annalies Moors, 115–31. Bloomington: Indiana University Press.

Morris, Rosalind C. 2000. *In the place of origins: Modernity and its mediums in northern Thailand*. Durham, NC: Duke University Press.

Moudden, Abdelhay. n.d. Mawakib al-khalidin: al-Watan wa-l-malik [Procession of the immortals: The nation and the king]. Unpublished paper.

Mundy, Jacob. 2006. How the US and Morocco seized the Spanish Sahara. *Le Monde Diplomatique-English Edition* (Jan.). http://mondediplo.com/2006/01/12asahara.

Munson, Henry. 1993. *Religion and power in Morocco*. New Haven, CT: Yale University Press.

Najmabadi, Afsaneh. 1993. Veiled discourse – unveiled bodies. *Feminist Studies* 19 (3; Who's East? Whose East?) (autumn): 487–518.

Newcomb, Rachel. 2009. *Women of Fes: Ambiguities of urban life in Morocco*. Philadelphia: University of Pennsylvania Press.

O'Brien, Susan. 2001. Spirit discipline: Gender, Islam, and hierarchies of treatment in postcolonial northern Nigeria. *Interventions: The International Journal of Post-Colonial Studies* 3: 222–41.

Ong, Aihwa. 1988. The production of possession: Spirits and the multinational corporation in Malaysia. *American Ethnologist* 15 (1) (Feb.): 28–42.

———. 1987. *Spirits of resistance and capitalist discipline: Factory women in Malaysia*. Albany: State University of New York Press.

Pandolfo, Stefania. 2008. The knot of the soul: Postcolonial conundrums, madness, and the imagination. In *Postcolonial disorders*, ed. Mary-Jo DelVecchio Good, Sandra Teresa Hyde, Sarah Pinto, Byron J. Good, 327–58. Berkeley: University of California Press.

———. 2000. The thin line of modernity: Some Moroccan debates on subjectivity. In *Questions of modernity*, ed. Timothy Mitchell, 115–47. Minneapolis and London: University of Minnesota Press.

———. 1997. Rapt de voix. *Awal: Revue d'Études Berbères* (15) (Apr.): 31–50.

Pâques, Viviana. 1991. *La religion des esclaves: Recherches sur la confrérie marocaine des Gnawa.* Bergamo, Italy: Moretti et Vitali Editori.

Pascon, Paul. 1980. Les rapports entre l'état et la paysannérie. In *Études Rurales.* Tanger: Ed. SMER.

Peletz, Michael G. 1996. Reason and passion: Representations of gender in a Malay society. Berkeley: University of California Press.

Pemberton, John. 1994. *On the subject of "Java."* Ithaca, NY: Cornell University Press.

Rabinow, Paul. 2007 [1977]. *Reflections on fieldwork in Morocco.* 30th anniv. ed. Berkeley: University of California Press.

———. 1989. *French modern: Norms and forms of the social environment.* Cambridge, MA: MIT Press.

Rachik, Hassan. 2003. *Symboliser la nation: Essai sur l'usage des identités collectives au Maroc.* Casablanca: Le Fennec & Fondation du Roi Abdul Aziz.

Racius, Egdunas. 2004. The multiple nature of the Islamic da'wa. PhD, Faculty of Arts, University of Helsinki.

Rafael, Vicente L., and Joshua Barker. 2012. The event of otherness: An interview with James T. Siegel. *Indonesia* 93 (Apr.): 33–52.

Rézette, Robert. 1955. *Les partis politiques marocains.* Paris: Presses de la Fondation nationale des Sciences politiques.

Rida, S. A. 1994. *'Amaliyyat matba'at al-atlas bi-l-dar al-bayda': Min tarikh al-muqawama al-sirriyya bi-l-maghrib* [The operations of the atlas print shop in Casablanca: From the history of the secret resistance in Morocco]. Rabat: Nashar al-mandubiyya al-samiyya li-qudama' al-muqawamin wa 'awda' jaysh al-tahrir.

Rivet, Daniel. 1988. *Lyautey et l'institution du protectorat français au Maroc, 1912–1925.* Collection histoire et perspectives méditerranéennes. Paris: L'Harmattan.

———. 1984. Exotisme et 'pénétration scientifique': L'effort de découverte du Maroc par les Francais au début du xx siècle. In *Connaissances du Maghreb: Sciences sociales et colonisation,* ed. Jean-Claude Vatin, 95–109. Paris: Éditions du CNRS.

Rollinde, M. 2003. La marche verte: Un nationalisme royal aux couleurs de l'Islam. *Le Mouvement Social* 1 (202): 133–51.

Ronell, Avital. 1989. *The telephone book: Technology—schizophrenia—electric speech.* Lincoln: University of Nebraska Press.

Salmon, Georges. 1905. Confréries et zaouyas de Tanger. *Archives Marocaines* 2: 100–14.

Santucci, Jean-Claude. 2005. Gros plan: Le pouvoir à l'épreuve du choc terroriste: Entre dérives autoritaires et tentation de l'arbitraire. *Annuaire de l'Afrique du Nord* 41: 243–48.

Schivelbusch, Wolfgang. 1986. *The railway journey: The industrialization of time and space in the 19th century.* Berkeley: University of California Press.

Shami, Seteney, and Nefissa Naguib. 2013. Occluding difference: Ethnic identity and shifting zones of theory on the Middle East and North Africa. In *Anthropology of the Middle East and North Africa: Into the new millennium,* ed. Sherine Hafez and Susan Slyomovics, 23–46. Bloomington: Indiana University Press.

Siegel, James T. 2006. *Naming the witch.* Stanford, CA: Stanford University Press.

———. 2003. The truth of sorcery. *Cultural Anthropology* 18 (2) (May): 135–55.

———. 2000a [1978]. Curing rites, dreams, and domestic politics in a Sumatran society. In *The rope of God,* rev. ed. Ann Arbor: University of Michigan Press.

———. 2000b [1969]. *The rope of God.* Rev. ed. Ann Arbor: University of Michigan Press.

———. 2000c. Kiblat and the mediatic Jew. *Indonesia* 69 (Apr.): 9–40.

———. 1997. *Fetish, recognition, revolution.* Princeton, NJ: Princeton.

———. 1979. *Shadow and sound: The historical thought of a Sumatran people.* Chicago: University of Chicago Press.

Simmel, Georg. 1950a. The stranger. In *The sociology of Georg Simmel,* ed. Kurt H. Wolff, 402–8. New York: Simon and Schuster.

———. 1950b. The metropolis and mental life. In *The sociology of Georg Simmel,* ed. Kurt H. Wolff, 409–24. New York: Simon and Schuster.

Skali, Faouzi. 2007. *Saints et sanctuaires de Fès.* Rabat: Marsam Editions.

Skovgaard-Petersen, Jakob. 1997. *Defining Islam for the Egyptian state.* Leiden: Brill.

Slyomovics, Susan. 2013. State of the state of the art studies: An introduction to the anthropology of the Middle East and North Africa. In *Anthropology of the Middle East and North Africa: Into the new millennium,* ed. Sherine Hafez and Susan Slyomovics, 3–22. Bloomington: Indiana University Press.

———. 2008. Financial reparations, blood money, and human rights witness testimony: Morocco and Algeria. In *Humanitarianism and suffering,* ed. Richard Wilson, 265–84. Cambridge University Press.

———. 2005. *The performance of human rights in Morocco.* Philadelphia: University of Pennsylvania Press.

Soares, Benjamin F. 2007. Saint and Sufi in contemporary Mali. In *Sufism and the "modern" in Islam,* ed. Martin van Bruinessen and Julia Day Howell, 76–91. London and New York: I. B. Tauris.

———. 2004. Muslim saints in the age of neoliberalism. In *Producing African futures: Ritual and reproduction in a neoliberal age,* ed. Brad Weiss, 79–105. Leiden and Boston: Brill.

Sontag, Susan. 2003. *Regarding the pain of others.* 1st ed. New York: Farrar Straus and Giroux.

Souriau-Hoebrechts, Christiane. 1975. *La presse maghrebine: Libye, Tunisie, Maroc, Algérie: Évolution historique, situation en 1965, organisation et problèmes actuels.* Paris: Éditions du CNRS.

Spadola, Emilio. 2004. Jinn, Islam, and media in Morocco. In *Yearbook of the sociology of Islam 5: On archaeology of sainthood and local spirituality in Islam,* ed. George Stauth, 142–72. Bielefeld, Germany: Transcript Verlag.

Spratt, Jennifer E., and Daniel A. Wagner. 1984. *The making of a fqih: The transformation of traditional Islamic teachers in modern times.* Cambridge, MA: Harvard University, Graduate School of Education.

Sreberny-Mohammadi, Annabelle, and Ali Mohammadi. 1994. *Small media, big revolution: Communication, culture, and the Iranian revolution.* Minneapolis: University of Minnesota Press.

Starrett, Gregory. 1995. The hexis of interpretation: Islam and the body in the Egyptian popular school. *American Ethnologist* 22 (4) (November): 953–69.

Stetkevych, Jaroslav. 1970. *The modern Arabic literary language; lexical and stylistic developments.* Publications of the Center for Middle Eastern Studies. Vol. 6. Chicago: University of Chicago Press.

Taussig, Michael T. 1986. *Shamanism, colonialism, and the wild man: A study in terror and healing.* Chicago: University of Chicago Press.

Thongchai, Winichakul. 1994. *Siam mapped: A history of the geo-body of a nation.* Honolulu: University of Hawaii Press.

Tozy, Mohamed. 1999. *Monarchie et Islam politique au Maroc.* Paris: Presses de la Fondation nationale des Sciences politiques.

Tremearne, Arthur J. N. 1914. *The ban of the Bori: Demons and demon-dancing in West and North Africa*. London: Heath, Cranton & Ouseley.

Vermeren, Pierre. 2002. Histoire du Maroc depuis l'indépendance. *Repères*. Vol. 346. Paris: La Découverte.

Warner, Michael. 2002. Publics and counter-publics. *Public Culture* 14 (1): 49–90.

Waterbury, John. 1978. La légitimation du pouvoir au Maghreb: Tradition, protestation et répression. *Annuaire de l'Afrique du Nord* 16: 411–22.

———. 1970. *Commander of the faithful: The Moroccan political elite—A study of segmented politics*. New York: Columbia University.

al-Wazzani, Mohammed Hassan. 1934a. Fès acclame les souverains marocains. *L'Action du Peuple* (May 12): 1–3.

———. 1934b. Le grand mystère du 10 mai. *L'Action du Peuple* (May 14): 1–3.

Weber, Samuel. 2001. The debts of deconstruction and other, related assumptions. In *Institution and interpretation*, rev. ed., 102–31. Stanford, CA: Stanford University Press.

———. 1996. Television: Set and screen. In *Mass mediauras: Form, technics, media*, ed. Alan Cholodenko, 108–28. Stanford, CA: Stanford University Press.

Weiner, Jerome B. 1979. The green march in historical perspective. *The Middle East Journal* 33 (1): 20–33.

West, Harry G., and Todd Sanders. 2003. *Transparency and conspiracy: Ethnographies of suspicion in the new world order*. Durham, NC: Duke University Press.

Westermarck, Edward. 1968 [1926]. *Ritual and belief in Morocco*. New Hyde Park, NY: University Books.

White, Jenny B. 2002. *Islamist mobilization in Turkey: A study in vernacular politics*. Seattle: University of Washington Press.

Wickham, Carrie Rosefsky. 2002. *Mobilizing Islam: Religion, activism, and political change in Egypt*. New York: Columbia University Press.

Wright, Gwendolyn. 1991. *The politics of design in French colonial urbanism*. Chicago: University of Chicago.

Yata, Ali, and Jim Paul. 1977. The Moroccan CP [communist party] and Sahara. *MERIP Reports* (56) (Apr.): 16–18.

Zahniser, A. H. Mathias. 2002. Invitation. In *Encyclopedia of the Qur'an*, ed. Jane Dammen McAuliffe, vol. 2, 557–58. Leiden and Boston: Brill.

Zartman, William. 1987. King Hassan's new Morocco. In *The political economy of Morocco*, ed. William Zartman. New York: Praeger.

Zeghal, Malika. 2008. *Islamism in Morocco: Religion, authoritarianism, and electoral politics*. Trans. George Holoch. Princeton, NJ: Markus Wiener Publishers.

Zerrouky, Hassan. 2007. Les islamistes à l'assaut de Casablanca. *L'Humanité* (Sept. 6). http://www.humanite.fr/2007-09-06_International_Les-islamistes-a-l-assaut-de-Casablanca.

Zillinger, Martin. 2010. Passionate choreographies mediatized: On camels, lions, and their domestication among the 'Isawa in Morocco. In *Animism*, ed. Anselm Franke, vol. 1, 214–27. Antwerp, Belgium: Extra City, M HKA, Kunsthalle Bern and Sternberg Press.

———. 2008. Rappen für gott, könig und vaterland: Über trance, folklore und macht in marokko und der marokkanischen migration. In *Wider den kulturenzwang. kulturalisierung und dekulturalisierung in literatur, kultur und migration* [Against the cultural current: Culturization and deculturization in literature, culture and migration], ed.

Özkan Ezli, Dorothee Kimmich, and Annette Werberger, 135–73. Bielefeld, Germany: Transcript, S.

Zunes, Stephen, and Jacob Mundy. 2010. *Western Sahara: War, nationalism, and conflict irresolution*. Syracuse studies on peace and conflict resolution. 1st ed. Syracuse, NY: Syracuse University Press.

# Index

EMILIO SPADOLA is Assistant Professor of Anthropology at Colgate University.

CPSIA information can be obtained
at www.ICGtesting.com
Printed in the USA
BVOW08s1224290317
479772BV00004B/270/P

9 780253 011374